The Milk Glass Book

Frank Chiarenza and James Slater

Schiffer Publishing Ltd

4880 Lower Valley Road, Atglen, PA 19310 USA

Dedication

To the memory of three Honorary Members
of the National Milk Glass Collectors Society

Regis Ferson
Mary Ferson
Rush Pinkston

who exemplified our society's purposes and goals
in the research, study, and love of
Milk Glass

Library of Congress Cataloging-in-Publication Data

Chiarenza, Frank.
  The milk glass book / Frank Chiarenza and James Slater.
    p. cm.
  Includes bibliographical references and index.
  ISBN 0-7643-0661-8 (hardcover)
  1. Milk glass--Collectors and collecting--United States.
I. Slater, James Alexander. II. Title.
NK5439.M54C55   1998
748.2'075--dc21   98-29623
                    CIP

Designed by Bonnie M. Hensley
Layout by Randy L. Hensley
Typeset in *Zapf Chancery Bd BT/Aldine 721 BT*

ISBN: 0-7643-0661-8
Printed in China
1 2 3 4

Published by Schiffer Publishing Ltd.
4880 Lower Valley Road
Atglen, PA 19310
Phone: (610) 593-1777; Fax: (610) 593-2002
E-mail: Schifferbk@aol.com
Please write for a free catalog.
This book may be purchased from the publisher.
Please include $3.95 for shipping.

In Europe, Schiffer books are distributed by
Bushwood Books
6 Marksbury Avenue
Kew Gardens
Surrey TW9 4JF England
Phone: 44 (0)181 392-8585; Fax: 44 (0)181 392-9876
E-mail: Bushwd@aol.com

Please try your bookstore first.

We are interested in hearing from authors
with book ideas on related subjects.

Contents

Acknowledgments

To the entire membership of the National Milk Glass Collectors Society we express our gratitude for their encouragement and support. Although it was not possible to include all the pictures of pieces which were sent to us, we wish to recognize and thank the following members who submitted photographs for our consideration.

Bachman, Harold and Jean
Barenchi, Norma
Baylor, Jack
Bettinghaus, Mr. & Mrs. E.
Bower, Audrey
Box, Thomas and Catherine
Brandenberg, Rebecca
Campbell, Donald and Julia
Chiarenza, Frank
Cimiano, Barbara A.
Cisler, Theresa
Costa, Bob and Pat
Cotton, Jim
Crider, Faye
Dahlquist, Nancy
Dennis, Chuck and Dee
Dequaine, Lester
Desmond, Bonnie
Eaton, Russell and Judy
Eaton, Virginia
Fabian, Caryl and Joe
Fix, John and Barbara
Friedrich, Robert

Fulcher, Robert
Gardner, Barton
Giddens, Betty L.
Glacy, Eva
Glaser, Pat
Grossarth, Wilma
Grubaugh, Joan and Beryl
Haas, Terry
Heal, Sharon
Hemm, Bill and Gretchen
Henning, Pauline
Hilgar, Gladys
Holowinski, Betty
Horsman, Margaret
Jones, Lowell
Klasen, Paul and Mary
Lawrence, Roberta
Lewis, Ray and Pat
Liveten, Norman and Helen
Lloyd, Judy and Andy
Manley, Dick and Noni
Martz, Jim and Jeannie
Morehous, Lilla

Rabin, Mollie
Reynolds, James and Judy
Saima, Don and Judy
Schmitt, Loretta and
    George
Scott, Barbara
Secrist, Ray
Sill, Walter A.
Simons, John
Simpson, Terry
Singler, Al and Dodie
Slater, James and Betty
Sohl, Stan and June
Storey, George and Helen
Sutton, Gail
Swihart, Gene and Jean
Tarbox, Lucy
Taylor, James
Ward, Harriet
Wills, Charles O.

We extend our special thanks to James Reynolds who was among the first to spearhead the project and who sent out the first call asking members to submit photographs.

From beginning to end, our enormous debt and thanks are due to Helen Liveten. She took on the colossal task of assembling the hundreds of photographs we received, cataloging them, and preparing our preliminary lists. When our resolve showed signs of weakening, as it did from time to time, Helen urged us (as well as the publisher) to persevere, and without her unflagging enthusiasm and determination this book might not have been completed.

To members of the staff at the Rakow Research Library of The Corning Museum of Glass, Gail Bardhan, Assistant Registrar Jill Thomas-Clark, and Head Librarian Patricia J. Rogers, our most sincere thanks for all their efforts to make possible the duplication of the 1908 Vallerysthal catalog and for securing permission to print these beautiful color page illustrations, surely one of the highlights of this book.

Finally, we express our appreciation to Peter Schiffer and his cooperative staff, especially Doug Congdon-Martin for taking many of the photographs, and Donna Baker, our mentor and guide throughout the process of preparing this book for publication.

Frank Chiarenza, Ph.D., English and Medieval Literature
James Slater, Ph.D., Biology

Introduction

Aims and Purposes

This book is the culmination of an ambitious undertaking in response to the desire of members of the National Milk Glass Collectors Society to produce a high quality, fully illustrated, photographic record of some of the finest pieces of opaque pressed glass, both domestic and foreign. All the items pictured in this book are drawn from the magnificent holdings in the private collections of the society's members. Many of these pieces are either not found in previous books on milk glass or appear in publications not readily accessible to most collectors.

In 1994, when the idea to publish such a book was first seriously considered, few could have foreseen what a difficult endeavor it would turn out to be or even imagined how long it would take to complete. The response to our initial appeal to members to submit photographs of pieces from their collections for possible inclusion in the book was overwhelming. It took months just to assemble and record hundreds upon hundreds of snapshots of varying quality, followed by sorting and weeding out the many duplicate submissions. The pieces we saw were dazzling and we wanted to include them all! It soon became evident, however, that such a book would be prohibitively expensive. Nor could we possibly handle the logistical problems, much less the expense, of arranging for professional photography of many collections from all over the country.

The only feasible and sane solution was to rely upon a half dozen or so large collections to serve as the main source for the majority of photographs. By so doing, we were able to reduce considerably the number of individual arrangements that had to be made to photograph pieces not available in these "core" collections. Because the photographs were taken at different times by different individuals — some professional and others not — you will find a good deal of variation in their quality. Often, a small piece may look huge alongside another item that is in fact much larger simply owing to the distance of the camera from the object in taking the shot. We tried to use the best pictures we could get, and in general we think they are remarkably good, especially considering the notorious difficulty of photographing opaque white glass.

The task of examining, researching, and writing up each item was left mainly to two members, both of whom have substantial academic credentials in their separate fields, but neither of whom pretends to be anything other than an enthusiastic collector like many others in the society. They made a serious effort to be as complete, reliable, and accurate in their descriptions and attributions of each piece, but limitations of time and resources did not always allow the in-depth research that they and you might wish. With more time to survey the field, many entries might have included a fuller account of variant forms and of other colors besides those we are aware of, although you will find a good deal of such information. And with more resources at their disposal, some of the many (unfortunately, too many!) "Maker Unknown" entries might have been properly identified. The rarity of so many of the pieces we illustrate only intensified the difficulty of making positive attributions. But in simple truth, too often the necessary documentation either has been lost or never existed. We have found ourselves sharing the same frustration often expressed by the British glass historian, the late Cyril Manley, in wondering why so many pieces as fine as these were not signed.

We believe this book will attract a wide audience, but we expect there will be some who may find it offers either too much or not enough. On the one hand, this is not a book that addresses the casual collector or the eager "investor" who is interested only in "pictures and prices." On the other hand, it may disappoint the really serious and committed specialists — those truly dedicated researchers, glass historians, and career professionals — whose study and knowledge of glass we stand in awe of.

What we have tried to present is hands-on examination, frequently detailed descriptions, and perhaps most of all, an enthusiastic appreciation of the beauty and artistry of the mould maker's designs and their wonderful creation through the glassmaker's skill. For some collectors, this kind of close scrutiny may appear overmuch, or even irksome, as they much prefer to look at pictures of items rather than to read about them. Yet we believe many collectors have often expressed frustration when confronted with pictures in books that have little or no accompanying commentary to help direct their attention to subtle details, to point out what is not clearly evident in the photograph, or to indicate what the piece looks like from behind or on the underside — in short, to instruct our eyes and to reveal what is not apparent especially when pictures are too small or indistinct.

Our aim throughout this book has been to encourage passive viewers of these wonderful pieces to become actively engaged in what their eyes are seeing. It is an instructive and rewarding task to set a favorite piece in front of you, especially one which is relatively intricate or which you think you know very well, and set about to write down what you see. Such an exercise will challenge and amaze you, for you will find wonderful details, qualities, and features you may otherwise never have noticed. If you study your pieces carefully, your enjoyment will be greatly enhanced.

How to Use this Book

Main Entries

The main body of the book is a collection of individual items, arranged according to categories of form or function, with accompanying commentary. Each entry has been treated in a common format, pretty much strictly adhered to, that includes the following components in the following order. This will greatly facilitate your knowing exactly where to look to find what you want to know about the item illustrated:

(1) Description

Each entry begins with a commentary in which we describe in some detail the piece illustrated. These descriptions include what may be fairly evident in the photographs, but also features and qualities that cannot be observed in the photograph alone. We have not hesitated to call attention to particular aspects of the piece which we find compelling — and in a few instances even repelling. We have allowed ourselves to "read" or interpret objects that are representational, especially the covered dishes and ornamental items, and have not curbed our enthusiasm over beautiful and intricate designs.

(2) Attribution and Reference Citations

In many ways, this is perhaps the most important part of each entry, and the one in which we have tried as much as possible to be accurate. We have avoided making any statements that we could not document, preferring to err on the side of omission than to perpetuate errors by repeating unfounded or incorrect information from other sources, either in print or by hearsay. As stated previously, we regret so many of the items, especially those rarities of which this book has many, must be attributed to "Maker Unknown." In other instances,

we have cited previously published books and articles where additional information may be found concerning the item. Obviously, such references are not exhaustive, and we are certain we have overlooked a good many that we would have cited were we aware of them.

The works cited in our text are listed in the bibliography, "Selected Readings," printed at the back of this book. Most citations are simply by the author's name and a page reference, as "Lattimore, p. 45," for example. But to avoid needless repetition of works frequently cited, we have also adopted abbreviations which you will find in the bibliography, arranged alphabetically. For example, SW is for the magazine *Spinning Wheel;* PC is for the 1933 Portieux Catalog; L-VG is for the book by Ruth Webb Lee, *Victorian Glass,* and so forth. Often the references are highly condensed, as when we cite items in our book that are also illustrated elsewhere. For example, "F-4" refers to plate No. 4 in the book by Ferson listed in the bibliography. Once you become familiar with these handy abbreviations, you should not find them puzzling or irksome.

(3) Colors

This, too, is a very perilous matter where documentation either does not exist or is hard to come by. For that reason, we have studiously restricted ourselves to naming only those colors which we ourselves have actually seen. To underscore that restriction, we have methodically stated "Known to us only ...." or words to that effect in each and every entry. Following that, we have cited other sources in whom we can place a measure of trust that they are accurate in reporting colors.

(4) Measurements

With some exceptions, the measurements that are given were taken directly from the items we held in our hands. When that was not possible, we have relied on the society's members who submitted the photographs to supply us with accurate measurements.

(5) Availability

This is the part of the entry about which we were most wary, and for obvious reasons. So many of the items in this book are extremely rare, we were tempted simply to avoid trying to determine the degree of rarity. On the other hand, collectors expected this determination because in many ways it is more helpful than estimating dollar values, and we felt obliged to comply. The judgments were based on how frequently a given item appears in the collections of our members, and from reports given us by avid milk glass hunters as to how often the piece turns up at antique shows, malls, and flea markets. Some of our members are major dealers in milk glass and their assistance has been invaluable in trying to assess availability. From most common to least, we have adopted the terms: Available, Hard to Find, Scarce, Rare, and Extremely Rare. These categories are of course somewhat arbitrary and the degree of availability does vary in different parts of the country.

Famous Pieces in Rare Colors

One of the criteria we established for including or excluding items from this book was the extent to which they were already well known and adequately represented in previous books devoted to milk glass. As a result, we have reluctantly omitted many wonderful pieces because it would be redundant to show them again. We have departed from that restriction occasionally, however, if we felt a piece previously shown was not treated adequately, was poorly illustrated, or was incorrectly attributed. In addition, mindful of our book's visual appeal, we have devoted this small section to illustrating extremely beautiful and highly sought after pieces in colors so rarely seen as to be deemed out of the reach of most collectors. The Atterbury Boar's Head, for example, though rare enough in milk white glass, is so extremely rare in opaque blue that a photograph of it seemed to us worthy of inclusion in this book.

Special Feature Articles

This is really only an extension of the Main Entries section of the book, where we devote more space to an item, or group of items, because they require fuller treatment. We regard these as "mini-articles," dealing with objects that have been especially troublesome to collectors, owing to many variants, extensive reproductions, or identical patterns and designs used to make many different types of objects, such as candlesticks, covered dishes, extended tableware, and the like.

As stated at the start, our main purpose in creating this book is to present some truly exceptional milk glass pieces, most of which have gone previously unrecorded in the standard literature, thus affording an expanded reference base for collectors. We regard it as a "work in progress" with the hope that readers who can identify items we were unable to attribute will share their knowledge with us so that we can update and revise a future reprinting. In fact, we earnestly invite and will greatly appreciate your corrections and comments of whatever kind. Please address them to the National Milk Glass Collectors Society, in care of Frank Chiarenza, 80 Crestview, Newington, CT 06111-2405.

A Brief Chronicle of the National Milk Glass Collectors Society

Laying the Cornerstone...

Although officially organized in Nashville, Tennessee on April 18, 1987, the genesis of the National Milk Glass Collectors Society took place some years earlier.

The impetus for the creation of the society came from two sources. First was the tremendous surge in interest in Milk Glass following the publication of *Yesterday's Milk Glass Today* by Regis and Mary Ferson in 1981. This book sparked the interest of Walter Sill, a Nashville collector and entrepreneur. Sill conceived the idea of holding a convention of milk glass collectors to come together to talk about and learn about this opaque glassware. He made early contact with the Fersons who gave him great encouragement, even to the extent of opening their files to him and writing letters recommending the convention to their many correspondents and book purchasers. Walter Sill was the ideal man for the time. He was not only collecting enthusiastically — as evidenced by his correspondence with the Fersons asking whether they knew where he could obtain some scarce pieces — but perhaps more importantly Walter was a natural organizer.

Once he had persuaded the Fersons to come to a convention as "bait," he was off and running a campaign of national advertising, local publicity, and total dedication that surely is the primary reason that a thriving society exists today.

By late 1983, Walter Sill was eager to pursue his idea to have a convention. He was in contact with the Fersons that October, and by November 1, 1983, he had definitely resolved to go ahead with his plans. Walter moved fast! By November 23rd he had placed ads for the convention in the *Antique Trader*, and soon after in a number of other trade journals.

Conventions

The First Convention...

The first convention was scheduled to be held at the Sheraton Downtown in Nashville, Tennessee, with Terry Hudson as the auctioneer. After his extensive advertising and the Fersons' letters to their many collector friends, Walter Sill sat back and hoped that someone would come. By February 20th, he had reservations from ten states and by March 11th he reported to the Fersons that he had fifty paid reservations and expected to have between seventy and one hundred attendees.

The agenda adopted at this first convention in large measure established the format that is substantially the same as the one the society still uses. It included a Dealer's setup, exhibits of rare pieces — a complete set of signed McKee animal covered dishes by Margaret Horsman — a trading area, an auction of three hundred pieces, and a business meeting that, interestingly, included a discussion of a possible National Milk Glass Museum. The meeting was all that Walter Sill had hoped for. Enthusiasm ran high. There was general agreement that the group should meet again the following year.

Convention 1985...

Plans for the second convention presented some problems. Walter felt strongly that the meeting should again be in Nashville, citing concerns about the transport of glass, advertising, and other logistical questions. But the Fersons prevailed and the meeting was held in Pittsburgh, Pennsylvania on April 13, 1985 at the Parkway Center Inn.

At this meeting a "Panel Discussion" was organized by the Fersons with Faye Crider, Mary Ferson, Helen Storey, and James Slater as discussants. This convention also saw the first formal suggestion of a newsletter. Once again, Walter Sill was indefatigable in organization and publicity, and the Fersons were charming hosts. Pieces of milk glass at the 1985 auction have some relevance to what the society has done to the prices of milk glass. The high bid that year was $650 for a perfect "Here's Happy Days" plaque nicely mounted, followed by a chocolate Greentown rabbit at $375, and a blue Atterbury rabbit at $300. How times change! One may easily triple those figures in the current market.

Convention 1986...

Once again, Walter Sill invited the group back to Nashville where the convention was held on April 5, 1986 at the Ramada Inn South, with a night before party featuring a magician for entertainment. The format was similar to the previous meetings, with a panel discussion that included Helen Storey, Rush Pinkston, and James Slater.

Convention 1987...

This fourth gathering of the group marked a banner year. As usual, Walter Sill used all of his organizational skills and once again scheduled the convention in Nashville on April 17, 1987 in the Ramada Inn. This meeting was memorable as it marked the formal organization of the National Milk Glass Collectors Society. Officers were elected, terms of office established, and an executive board organized. The following were elected to office: President, James Slater; Vice President, George Storey; Secretary, Judy Reynolds; Treasurer, Kathy Mroz. The executive board members were Helen Storey, Terry Baker (Simpson), Margaret Horsman, Stan Sohl, and James Reynolds serving as its Chairman.

The society was formally underway with Mary Ferson, Regis Ferson, and Walter Sill voted to be Honorary Presidents (later modified to Honorary Members). The name of the society was selected. Charter Membership was to be open from the end of the business meeting on April 18, 1987 to the opening of the convention in the following year.

Convention 1988...

The year 1988 marked the first meeting of the "group" as a formal society. We were incorporated as a nonprofit organization in the State of Minnesota as of June 16, 1987. The convention was held on April 29-30 at the Airport Days Inn in Bloomington Minnesota, and hosted by Basil and Kathy Mroz. At this meeting Rush Pinkston gave a scholarly address on Vallerysthal and Portieux glass. *Opaque News* became the official publication of the new society, a constitution and set of bylaws were adopted, and our first commemorative piece, a domed rabbit in green slag, was made for the society by the Summit Art Glass Company of Ravenna, Ohio. Each member received a Charter Membership certificate. The original charter members numbered 214, of which 86 were still members as of December 1997.

While the idea of a newsletter had been considered as far back as the 1985 convention, it was actually the initiative of Kathy and Basil Mroz that started *Opaque News* independently. They produced the first issue in December, 1985, giving it the name it still has together with the logo of the Atterbury 9" rabbit in the upper left corner. It was a modest publication of four pages (8 1/2" x 7") with "Whatsit," "News," and "Haves and Wants" sections.

Kathy and Basil continued to produce the newsletter independently and with enthusiasm and dedicated work for three and a half years. When the National Milk Glass Collectors Society became a formal organization, they generously allowed their "child" to become the official publication outlet. Beginning with the September 1989 issue, Frank and Claudia Schultz became the editors.

It must indeed be a source of pleasure for the Mrozes to see their initiative grow and expand until now it is a high quality product usually of nineteen to twenty pages. Technical articles as well as entertaining notices are contributed by members, and the issues are replete with pictures, old catalog reprints, sketches, and more recently even a glossy page of color photographs. No society ever began with such a head start publication and, together with the annual conventions, much of the success of the society can be attributed to having an in-hand house organ to keep it in touch with its ever growing number of members.

Convention 1989...

Hosted by Judy and James Reynolds, the 1989 convention was held on March 31-April 1 at the Sheraton Inn, in Springfield, Illinois. Mary and Regis Ferson rejoined us after being sorely missed for three years. Mary Ferson gave the major address on milk glass table pieces at the evening meeting. Other speakers included Jim Reynolds on photographing milk glass; Basil Mroz on Atterbury glass; and Walter Sill on modern cups and mugs. The auction was moved from a late night to a morning session. Faye Crider was elected an Honorary Member.

Convention 1990...

Returning to Pittsburgh, Pennsylvania, the convention was once again hosted by Mary and Regis Ferson. It was held at the Sheraton Hills Hotel on April 13-14, 1990. An "Experts Panel" was initiated with Faye Crider, Rush Pinkston, Mary Ferson, and Helen Storey successfully wrestling with the origin, scarcity, and variability of a bewildering assortment of unusual pieces. Rod Dockery gave the evening lecture on Easter milk glass; Dr. James Measell spoke from his extensive knowledge of Northwood glass; and Jim Phillips showed slides of a wonderful variety of rare milk glass bottles.

Convention 1991...

The 1991 convention was held on March 30-31, at the Marriott Hotel in South Bend, Indiana, with Catherine and Thomas Box as our hosts. Faye Crider, filling in for a scheduled speaker who was indisposed, gave a delightful extemporaneous talk, recollecting her long experience as a collector and student of milk glass. James Slater spoke on the variety and differentiating features of milk glass hen covered dishes. The panel of

Faye Crider, Rush Pinkston, and Helen Storey once again brought their expertise to help members identify "mystery" pieces. The Boyd Crystal Art Glass Company began making the commemorative covered dishes for the society. Rod Dockery was elected to succeed James Slater as president.

Convention 1992...

By 1992, the society had grown by leaps and bounds and ventured into the southwest with the meeting, hosted by Arlene Johnson, held on April 10-11 in Arlington, Texas, at the La Quinta Inn. Our speakers were Frank Chiarenza on "The Victorian Double Hands Dish;" Myrna and Bob Garrison on Imperial milk glass; and John Grey on Sowerby glass. Once again, Faye Crider and Helen Storey served on the experts panel joined for the first time by Stan Sohl.

Convention 1993...

This year saw the convention's return to the Midwest. On March 27-28, 1993, we gathered at the Stouffer Dublin Hotel, in Dublin, Ohio, with Pat and Bob Lewis as our hosts. Dr. James Measell returned to speak about Greentown opaque glass; John Boyd discussed glass making and hand pressing at his company's plant; and Robert Lucas surveyed the glass of the Challinor, Taylor Company. Frank Chiarenza joined the experts panel. The auction returned to its original evening time period at this convention.

Convention 1994...

In 1994 the society met on April 16-17 in Wichita, Kansas, at the Wichita East Hotel, hosted by June and Stan Sohl. Lorraine Kovar was the banquet speaker on Westmoreland glass. Stan Sohl spoke on early candy containers; Norman Miller on legal aspects of financing, gifting, and tax procedures; and Robert Puckett on the milk glass collection at the Wichita Historical Museum. Many members visited the museum collection where the milk glass was very attractively displayed. Succeeding Rod Dockery, Helen Liveten was elected president.

Convention 1995...

On March 31-April 1, the 1995 convention was held in Hershey, Pennsylvania at the Hilton Hotel, hosted by Helen and George Storey. The evening talk on Gillinder Glass was by Gay LeCleire Taylor, curator of the American Museum of Glass at Wheaton Village. Charles West Wilson spoke on Westmoreland glass; and Russell Eaton on milk glass pieces commemorating the Spanish-American war. Many members traveled by bus to the famed Renninger Antique Market. The experts panel of Frank Chiarenza, Mary Ferson, Stan Sohl, and James Slater did its usual struggle with the unusual pieces brought by members to test their knowledge.

Convention 1996...

The society returned to Kansas for its 1996 convention. It was held in Overland Park, Kansas, on April 19-20, at the Marriott Hotel, hosted by Wilma Grossarth, Jean Swihart, and Jane Gardner. A movie of a skit produced by members of the Westmoreland Glass Collectors Society was shown to the great amusement of the audience. Lee Garmon spoke on Fostoria's "Jenny Lind" milk glass, and Eason Eige gave the banquet address on the beauty and variety of notable pieces of milk glass. The experts panel was the same as in 1995.

Convention 1997...

The 1997 convention convened near the Ford Museum in Dearborn, Michigan, on April 18-19, with Jim and Bob Culver as hosts. By this time, the number of attendees had grown to 180, and the highest bid for a piece at auction was a record setting $4,500. The speakers were Basil Mroz on Atterbury glass; Bob Culver on miniature milk glass oil lamps; and Dr. James Measell on some distinguished glass makers and their products. Betty Newbound and George Storey were the newcomers to the experts panel. This meeting also elected Frank Chiarenza as president, to succeed Helen Liveten.

Convention 1998...

With a return to Nashville, Tennessee, the 1998 convention held on April 16-19 at the Howard Johnson Airport Plaza Hotel brought the society full circle to where it all began. Our hosts were Basil and Kathy Mroz, with Walter Sill — the man who started it all — once again in the limelight. Nashville was hit with a tornado the day before the opening of the convention, but it did not dampen the high spirits of the record breaking 197 members who attended. John Weishar of the Island Mould and Machine Co., Wheeling, West Virginia, gave a slide presentation on the history of the company and a fascinating film showing the complete process of creating the plunger for our Atterbury-type rabbit covered dish which was made for us in blue milk glass by Boyd as this year's commemorative. Our other speaker was Lorraine Kovar whose slide presentation offered an interesting survey of some early Westmoreland Specialty Company pieces. Members were disappointed that an experts panel was not scheduled and asked that it be reinstated as a regular feature at next year's convention. The auction was lively as usual, and once again the prices realized on many pieces exceeded all expectations. Following the Saturday evening buffet dinner, Walt Sill introduced his friend Mr. Kevin King, renowned magician and illusionist who entertained the members with his wit and wizardry.

Some Afterthoughts...

One of the ever popular features of all of the conventions, and one of the society's great attractions, has been the annual auction, usually of three hundred pieces of milk glass. These have consistently ranged from relatively inexpensive items to those of great rarity. The society has been blessed with the presence of Ed Kuhlman as its auctioneer every year of its formal existence from its meeting in Minnesota. Over the years he has become something of an expert on milk glass, has attained the title of "Colonel," and can recite "white waffle open fish pickle dish" faster than the eye can blink.

The success of the National Milk Glass Collectors Society has not been achieved without the dedicated efforts of a great many of its members. People who do the hard work of manning booths, registration, planning of space and time are the core of the society.

The following officers represent only a few of the many members who have contributed to conventions, to the *Opaque News* articles, and in countless other ways.

President:
1987-1990 James Slater
1991-1993 Rod Dockery
1994-1996 Helen Liveten

1997-1999 Frank Chiarenza

Vice President:
1987-1988 George Storey
1989-1990 Helen Storey
1991-1993 Helen Liveten
1994-1996 Frank Chiarenza
1997-1999 Pat Lewis

Secretary:
1987-1990 Judy Reynolds
1991-1993 Judy Saima
1994-1995 Cay Bettinghaus
1996-1997 Judy Lloyd
1998-1999 Arlene Johnson

Treasurer:
1987-1989 Kathy Mroz
1990-1996 Arlene Johnson
1997- Delores Sacherich

The following members have served on the society's Board of Directors:

Rod Dockery, Helen Liveten, Judy Saima, Julie Campbell, Frank Chiarenza, Nancy Dahlquist, Roberta Lawrence, James Keenan, Arlene Johnson, Cay Bettinghaus, Thomas Box, Pat Lewis, Jim Reynolds, June Sohl, Judy Lloyd, Charles McNair, Claudia Schultz, Barton Gardner, Basil Mroz, Delores Sacherich, Virginia Eaton, and John Vosevich.

NMGCS Annual Commemoratives

Beginning in 1988 at its first formal convention, the society has commissioned a different animal covered dish each year to be produced in limited numbers specifically for its members. All, except for the full-figured Rabbit issued in 1998, are set on a split rib base to commemorate the McKee Bros. Glass Co. of Pittsburgh, Pennsylvania, who originated that design. Many, but not all, of the covered dishes have McKee type animal covers as well. It was established from the start that the commemoratives would be made in various colors, alternating, however, with one in milk white glass every other year.

For the first three years, 1988-1990, the commemoratives were made by Summit Art Glass Co., in Ravenna, Ohio, from moulds owned by Mr. Russ Vogelsong who is the head of that company. The first is a reproduction of the domed rabbit originated by the Greentown Indiana Tumbler and Goblet Co. The second is a horse or pony reproducing a McKee original and the third is a Bird with Berry, again a reproduction of Greentown.

In the following years, the commemoratives were produced by Boyd's Crystal Art Glass Co. of Cambridge, Ohio from moulds whose tops were graciously provided by the L.G. Wright Glass Company of New Martinsville, West Virginia. Except for the hen, the turtle, and the lamb (which faces right instead of left) all the other animal covers are reproductions of McKee originals.

Each of the commemoratives is impressed with the society's logo, a crouching rabbit on a block bearing the initials NMGCS. The year and location of the convention is also impressed. For example, "88 MN" marks the year 1988 and the location Minnesota.

A departure was inaugurated in 1998 when the society's commemorative was a reproduction of an Atterbury-type 6" Rabbit in a light blue milk glass. In subsequent years, the Rabbit will be issued every other year, but never in the same color twice.

The full series is illustrated here and documented in the following table.

Date	Location	Animal	Color	Mould Top	Mould Base	Maker
1988	Minnesota	Rabbit	Green Slag	Summit	Summit	Summit
1989	Illinois	Horse or Pony	White	Summit	Summit	Summit
1990	Pennsylvania	Bird w/ Berry	Blue Slag	Summit	Summit	Summit
1991	Indiana	Lamb	White	Boyd	Boyd	Boyd
1992	Texas	Hen	Black	Boyd	Boyd	Boyd
1993	Ohio	Turkey	White	Wright	Boyd	Boyd
1994	Kansas	Frog	Light Green	Wright	Boyd	Boyd
1995	Pennsylvania	Rooster	White	Wright	Boyd	Boyd
1996	Kansas	Turtle	Chocolate	Wright	Boyd	Boyd
1997	Michigan	Swan	White	Wright	Boyd	Boyd
1998	Tennessee	Atterbury-type Rabbit	Light blue	Wright	Wright	Boyd

1988 Rabbit

1989 Horse

1990 Bird

1991 Lamb

1992 Hen

1993 Turkey

1994 Frog

1995 Rooster

1996 Turtle

1997 Swan

1998 Rabbit

Defining "Milk Glass"

Glass consists primarily of sand (silica) which can represent as much as 50 percent or more of the glass formula. Other essentials are solvents, an "alkali" or "flux," usually soda lime or potash and — depending on the specific type of glass to be produced — small amounts of lead oxide ("litharge"), saltpeter (to increase oxidizing), manganese and other ingredients may be added. Mixed together, the components create what is called the "batch" or "frit," and when melted or fused together it is called "metal."

To produce milk glass, the additional ingredients required differ considerably in products made in earlier periods compared to those of more recent times. Bone ash (calcium phosphate) and arsenic, for example, produce a slightly off-white color typical of older glass and also a distinctive feature of the early products made by the Vallerysthal company. When one compares products made by different manufacturers of milk glass, it is obvious that the types and amounts of ingredients used in their specific glass formulations vary greatly. Many of the late nineteenth-century English pieces in milk glass, sometimes called vitro-porcelain, were clearly formulated to achieve a close approximation of and an inexpensive substitute for fine porcelain.

To render glass opaque requires the addition of whitening agents or "opacifiers." These include bone ash, fluor, and feldspar, and until it was exhausted in 1963, cryolite (a fluoride of sodium and aluminum) from Greenland. Other colors besides white are achieved by the addition of metallic ingredients — oxide of cobalt or copper scales for different shades of blue, iron scales for green, for example. An engaging account of Westmoreland's glass formulas found in a notebook of Sam'l Brainard West is given in an article by his nephew Charles West Wilson (*Opaque News*, VIII: 4, Sept. 1993, p. 847). Among them are 16 formulations for making "opal" wares, the term for milk glass used most often by nineteenth-century glass makers in America.

But collectors of milk glass must wonder what it is they have been collecting all these years when they hear Ruth Webb Lee — as far back as the 1930s — declare: **"there is no such thing and there never was"** (L-EA, p. 598). Although unhappy about the use of the term "milk glass," Lee admits it is too entrenched in popular usage ever to be discarded. And she then proceeds to devote an entire chapter to it.

The word "milk" to describe a certain type of glass may have been used initially as a way to distinguish "opaque white" from transparent glass, which was often called "clear white glass." Originally, the description was more fully spelled out as "milk-white glass" or "milky white glass," but over time the phrase was abbreviated simply to "milk glass." Whatever the appropriateness of the term may have been when it was first used, Ruth Webb Lee is correct in calling it a misnomer, because "milk glass" today is considered neither necessarily white nor entirely opaque. Odd as it may be, we speak of blue, yellow, pink, green, and even black "milk glass." Collectors also include opaque glass with various mixtures of colors called slag, marbled, mosaic, malachite, or — another misnomer — "end-of-day."

One thing seems certain, when Belknap titled his book *Milk Glass* and Millard titled his *Opaque Glass*, they had the same type of glass in mind. In current usage, we find that milk glass has simply become a blanket term for non-transparent glass of virtually any kind and of whatever color, excluding only the most highly specialized Art Glass creations such as "Peachblow," "Burmese," and other such distinctive types.

In referring to the white varieties specifically, Lee proposed the following categories to differentiate among various shades or degrees of opaqueness:

Milk-white - that through which the light does not show at all.
Opaque - which is not dead white but partly translucent
Opal - milk-white that shows "fire" when held against the light.
Opalescent - which is much more opalinely translucent than Opal.

These distinctions are helpful, and we often find ourselves resorting to one or another of them to describe the varieties of opaque white which can range from a dense "chalky white" to luminous "clambroth" or "skim milk" as seen in many pieces of Boston and Sandwich and other older glass. Milk glass also varies greatly in thickness and weight, and when tapped lightly, it usually produces a dull thud sound, although many early pieces having some lead content will ring like a bell.

In regard to colored milk glass, the different shades are not easily categorized. Some particular colors, such as "chocolate glass" and "custard glass," are specialized types, collectible in their own right, but nonetheless considered milk glass simply because they are opaque. Opalescent glass in all colors is also accepted as "milk glass" by most collectors today. Indeed, pushed to the furthest extreme, even objects which have but a modicum of opaqueness somewhere in the glass, such as Fenton's "Diamond Lace," Imperial's "Dewdrop Opalescent," or the English "Patent Blue Pearline" of George Davidson, barely sneak into the "milk glass" category. Cased glass pieces, too, which combine milk white with overlays of various colors, are often considered by some people as allowable within the expanded definition of milk glass collectibles.

Thus, we may conclude that "milk glass," from its original meaning of opaque white, has come, over time, to be a term applied much more broadly to include varying degrees of "opaqueness," as well as virtually any colors and color mixtures or overlays.

Main Entries

Bottles

1 - ALLIGATOR BOTTLE

A striking bottle, reminiscent of the famed Atterbury Duck bottle, this open-mouthed creature also appears to be swallowing a cylinder. The reptile sits placidly on its curled scaly tail with its front feet folded over its chest and stomach in a beatific attitude (if you can conceive of alligators in that manner!). The back has eight rows of armored scales. The bottom is deeply concave. It is faintly embossed on the side of the base "Depo[?]rt".

Known to us only in white. Height 10"; base diameter 3 1/4". Rare.

2 - SHAGGY BEAR BOTTLE

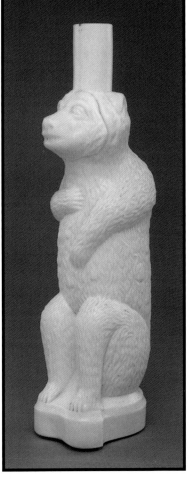

A handsome fellow, indeed, who may superficially look like the familiar white or black bear bottles shown in F-432 and B-242, but he is quite different. The fur on this bear is much coarser and more detailed. Most striking is the face, which appears to be applied separately as though "pushed" into the head making the surrounding area look like a hood! Whether intentional or not, the glass of this applied face, with large teeth and a broad grin, is not as white as the rest of the bottle.

Maker unknown. Known to us in white and black milk glass. Height to top of head 9 1/2" with a 1 3/4" bottle neck above the head. Maximum length of base 3"; width 2 5/8". Rare.

Note: Compared to the more familiar bear bottles mentioned above, this one has better detail and may be the prototype from which the more common, mass-produced bottles were modeled. The teeth, ears, and claws are sharply defined, and the face is alive with expression. By comparison, the bear bottle shown in F-432 seems a crude imitation.

The Fersons note that "black" bottles are actually made in green glass so dark as to appear black. Less often seen are "black" bottles that are really dark amethyst. We have examined one of these amethyst bottles with its original contents intact and bearing an oval paper label attached to the bear's stomach with a narrow band running around the body. The paper label reads "Allasch Kummel auf Russische Art Non-alcoholic Made by Carl Mampe A.G. Berlin S.W. 11 Germany" and the band bears the number 6026.

White bottles of the F-432 type are scarce; "black" ones hard to find especially in amethyst.

A cautionary note for beginning collectors: You may encounter these bear bottles made in clear glass but painted either white or black all over, making them appear to be opaque glass. They are easily recognized by the embossed words on the shoulders of the back: "Federal Law forbids sale or re-use of this bottle."

4 - BABY HEAD BOTTLE

Well formed and well proportioned, this baby head bottle is very appealing. It is made in a two-part mould, with minimal but nicely detailed features, particularly the ears. There is a slight Oriental appearance in the baby's eyes, perhaps suggesting the bottle's origin in Japan or China.

Maker unknown. Known to us only in white. Height 2 3/8". More than scarce.

3 - MONKEY BOTTLE

A droll bottle formed as a crouching, large-toothed monkey, humorously sporting a hat, his paws resting on his knees. His tail wraps around, also coming to rest on his knees. Emerging from the top of his hat, the spout is embossed at the back with the words "Trade Mark." The underside of the bottle has a mark that looks like a pair of attached letters "T."

Maker unknown. Known to us only in white. Height 4 1/2"; width 1 5/16". Rare.

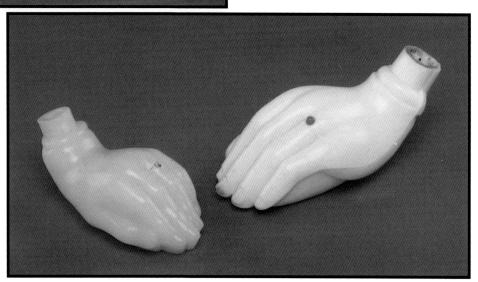

5 - HAND BOTTLES

Hands and feet appear to have been favorite anatomical features for bottle designs. These are ladies' hands, in two sizes, positioned slightly closed and appearing to be holding a small box. Details include a finger ring moulded with a flat socket for affixing a colored glass stone, and well shaped fingers and nails.

Maker unknown. We know these only in white. Large: 5 1/2" long; Small: 4 1/2" long. More than hard to find.

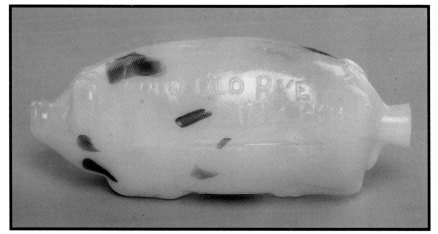

6 - PIG BOTTLE

Lying serenely, feet resting under its body, this pig is an anatomically correct male. The spout is at the tail end, and to be certain no one mistakes it for anything other than a lowlife swine, embossed on the side are the words "Good old Rye in a Hog's ..." (we leave it to the reader to finish the verse).

Maker unknown. For additional references and a fuller discussion of this bottle and its several variants, see O.N., X:4, Sept. 1995, pp. 8-9.

Known to us only in white, but with colored flecks of red, green, blue, and black scattered through it, sometimes called "spatter glass." Length 8 3/8" overall; height 3 1/4". Very rare, but be on guard for reproductions of this piece.

7 - WHISKY KEG BOTTLE

A charming little bottle, and given its small size, possibly intended for perfume. Cryptically embossed S . I . / COMP, it is a traditional keg with two staves near each end, and a vertical spout on top. The flat bottom keeps it from rolling.

Maker unknown. Known to us only in white. Length 2 3/8"; height 2 1/4". Availability unknown.

9 - OUR LADY OF FATIMA BOTTLE

The well-known and beloved Lady of Fatima is splendidly rendered in this bottle with its soft satin finish and, of course, the distinctive blue girdle or cincture that dominates the figure. As an attribute of the Virgin, it represents chastity, and is especially celebrated in the legend that tells of her lowering her girdle from the sky to prove to a doubting St. Thomas that she was indeed ascended to heaven. The beautifully detailed head serves as the closure for this bottle.

Maker unknown. Embossed "DEPOSE," on the bottom, it is most likely French. We know it only in white. Height 16 1/2". Rare.

8 - GRAND-FATHER'S CLOCK BOTTLE

A stately and ornate figural bottle in the form of a grandfather's clock, it is of good quality glass and quite heavy. The clock face, whose Roman numerals mark 23 minutes after twelve, is set within a scrolled frame and rests on large ribbed pillars. The pattern on the back of the bottle is identical in all respects except that a blank circle replaces the clock face. A mammoth pendulum embossed with a star is painted gold in this example, as were the clock numerals at one time. The stopper, which repeats the ribs of the lower portion of the clock's base and adds a double row of beads, is hollow.

Maker unknown. Shown, without the stopper, in N-6. It is marked DEPOSE on the underside, suggesting a French origin.

Known to us only in white. Height 12 1/2" (with stopper, 14 1/4"); the base measures 4 1/4" by 2 3/4". Scarce.

10 - WASHINGTON BUST BOTTLE

Made of a thin, highly opalescent glass with a slight bluish-gray cast, this blown-in-the-mould early bottle is truly exquisite. The finely detailed stopper is modeled as a bust of George Washington in military uniform overlaid with Roman toga drapery in true classical fashion. The four-part moulded base is a traditional pedestal, adorned with garland swags and a border of laurel leaves around the bottom. The early date of this elegant creation is evidenced by a three-quarter inch pontil mark and the less than perfectly round base.

Maker unknown. Purchased in California by its current owner who reports that the dealer stated it came from Challar Mansion, Virginia City, Nevada, and dates from the 1840s. Known to us only in white. Height 7"; base diameter 3". Extremely rare.

11 - COLUMBUS BOTTLES

A stately, columnar bottle with a figure of Christopher Columbus standing atop a large ball, his right arm outstretched. Oddly, the ball which would seem to represent the globe has a row of beads running around the base, another vertically over the top, and a fleur-de-lis at its base. Just below the column is an ornate recessed rectangular panel above which is an octagonal band and two rings. The bottle separates at the top of the column. It has indistinct lettering, reading in part "Maresa atori[?]s," suggesting an Italian origin.

Maker unknown. Known to us only in white. The larger one is 17 1/4" high, base diameter 4 5/8". We do not have the dimensions of the smaller bottle. Both are rare.

12 - CZAR AND CZARINE BOTTLES

Regal in his garb and sporting his medals, the bearded Czar Nicholas II is indeed an imposing figure. But it is the Czarine who captures one's attention. With hair nicely coifed, and an elegant string of pearls, she is the essence of aristocratic refinement. And yet, this imperial lady has sad, haunting eyes, or is it just our imagination? These bottles should not be confused with similar ones shown in Ferson (F- 422 and 424), which are all of one piece and fitted with metal closures at the base. The ones pictured here are much rarer because the separate head closures that slip over the necks of the bottles are easily damaged through use and are often missing altogether. The bottles have pontil marks and are embossed "CZARINE" and "CZAR" on the front of the base.

Maker unknown. Known to us only in white. Height 10 1/2". Both are rare.

13 - LADY BUST BOTTLE

A nicely designed bottle of a handsome girl with a stately bearing and prominent bust shielded by a draped scarf held in place by a pin on the right side.

Maker unknown. Known to us only in white. Height 5"; base diameter 1 3/4". Probably scarce.

14 - ROMAN WARRIOR PERFUME BOTTLE

This toilet water or oversized perfume bottle is a Roman bust, complete with helmet and raised visor. The warrior-statesman wears an ample toga fastened at his right shoulder, where blocks denoting his body armor may be seen, then drapes in sweeping folds across his body and over his back. His aquiline nose and proud bearing suggest a person of high status.

Maker unknown. Illustrated in N-2, but difficult to see the fine detail. Undoubtedly a modern piece, but of good quality glass and excellent mould work.

Known to us only in white. Height to top of head 5"; width across shoulders 4". Apparently more than hard to find.

15 - SPANISH LADY WITH FAN BOTTLES

This bottle is found in two sizes, both exactly alike. Wearing a pearl choker and holding a large fan demurely held over her breast, the lovely Señora is dressed in a floor length gown raised slightly in a great swirl to reveal her pointed slipper. Her mantle is tied with a bow behind her, the ends of the ribbon curling gracefully down her back. The head, serving as the bottle's stopper, is delicately featured with hair tied in a bun and held in place by a tall arching comb, the kind used to hold a mantilla. The glass is heavy and of good quality.

Maker unknown. Embossed in large letters around the base at the back are the words "M. QUILES-BENETUSER (VALENCIA)," suggesting a Spanish origin, perhaps for the distiller, if not the glassmaker.

Known to us only in white. Large version is 14" high and 4 3/4" in diameter at the base. Smaller version is 11" high and 3" in diameter at the base. Both are more than hard to find, the larger one scarce perhaps.

16 - MATADORS AND SPANISH LADIES BOTTLES

This is an attractive group of four Spanish figural bottles which may have been issued as male and female pairs, although the shape of the base of the Señora at the far right is slightly different from the others. The first matador, wearing a tall hat and holding his cape relaxed in his left hand, would appear, in size at least, to be paired with the lady wearing the elaborate mantilla. The two figures in the center are most likely a pair. He has the traditional red cape draped over his right arm, and is dressed with formal vest, coat, and tie. The label on this bottle identifies its contents as "Cacao." His lady, wearing a red shawl and floor length pleated dress, may be a Spanish dancer as she carries a tambourine tucked under her left arm.

Maker unknown. Known to us only in white and almost invariably painted. They range in height from about 12 1/4" to 13 1/2". Hard to find.

17 - ELEPHANT BOTTLE [Small]

The detail of this little bottle is not very good. The elephant's bent head almost fuses with the un-differentiated front legs and its trunk is barely discernible. The spout at the center of the animal's back extends upward from a saddle held by a strap around its stomach. The lobed ears are small and the tail, curving to the left, is a mere wisp. It is certainly not a piece of which a mould maker should be proud.

Maker unknown. Known to us only in white. Length 3 1/4"; width 2"; height excluding the spout 2". Scarce.

18 - ELEPHANT BOTTLE [Large]

A spectacular piece of heavy, high quality milk glass, with the elephant's large head serving as the stopper. Its huge trunk curls back into the mouth and a tusk converges on each side. The large ears suggest it is an African not an Asian elephant. A solid mass of elephant grass fills the area between its legs. The body, cleverly moulded to simulate hide, gives the surface a surprisingly realistic feeling.

Maker unknown. Known to us only in white. Length 10"; height to top of head 7". Very rare.

19 - FROG BOTTLE

Resting on a grassy mound, this nicely detailed frog seems to have swallowed a bottle, because the cylindrical object protruding from its mouth is in fact the bottle neck.

Maker unknown. We know it only in white. Height 4 1/2"; width 4 1/2". Rare.

20 - SPANISH PARROTS BOTTLES

The two front toes of these imposing, big beaked parrots cling to a horizontal log. Directly below, we see a crown-like emblem and a smooth slab where a paper label might be affixed. The head and bill are nicely detailed, but the body and wings are less well moulded. The removable head fits over a two tiered cylinder which must also have once held a cork.

Maker unknown. Embossed in large letters on the base are the words "DESTILERIAS EL LORITO" and in smaller letters "Beretuser (Valencia)" indicating a Spanish origin perhaps.

We know these aristocratic parrot bottles only in white. The large parrot is 10" high with a 3" diameter base. The smaller one is 8" high with a 2 1/2" diameter base. Both are hard to find.

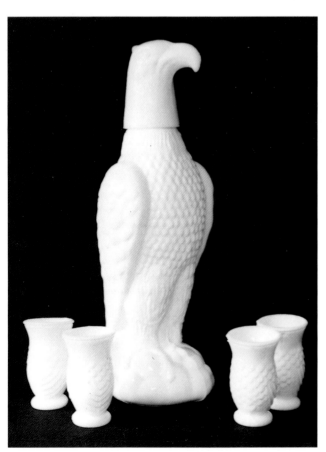

21 - EAGLE BOTTLE AND CORDIALS SET

You may be surprised, as we were, to come upon this All-American set, featuring our popular national emblem, only to discover it flew in from foreign shores. The glass, while not of outstanding quality, is nonetheless quite acceptable, fairly heavy and with a high gloss. The mould work, too, is respectable, but somewhat weak, especially the Eagle's head with very faint feathering and a somewhat disproportionate beak. The four mould lines running down the middle, front and back, and down each side, are prominent and sharp enough to cut your fingers on. The little cordials are modeled as the lower portion of an eagle's body, its two well-detailed claws in front and tail feathers in back. An attractive set, when viewed from a distance.

The bottle is boldly marked "MADE IN TAIWAN" on the underside, as are each of the cordials, though somewhat more faintly.

Known to us only in opaque white. The bottle is about 11" tall; the 1 oz. cordials measure 2 3/4". Available, but perhaps not easily found as a complete set.

22- THREE BUSTS BOTTLE

Imperial in all respects, this highly collectible long-necked bottle commemorates three Italian nobles whose busts appear above a tall wide-ribbed pedestal bearing a coat of arms at the front. They are believed to represent King Humbert I (1844-1900), his cousin Margherita of Savoy whom he married in 1868, and his son Victor Emmanuel who succeeded him. The features are not too sharp, but the over-all appearance is quite impos-ing and the cased white glass very attractive.

Maker unknown. Known to us only in white. Height 13 1/4"; diameter at the base 4 1/4". Scarce.

23 - BOY AND GIRL CLIMB-ING TREE BOTTLE

This "figures-in-action" bottle depicts a girl standing by the trunk of a tree helping a young lad to climb up it. It is made in cased glass of good quality with three mould seams fairly promi-nent. The children have wonder-fully expressive faces, and they are positioned in a manner that cap-tures the strenuous effort of get-ting up the tree.

Maker unknown. Listed in Umberger, No. 117, who says the missing stopper was a bird's nest, as we might have expected. He attributes it to France with later copies made in Italy, and states that rare variants occur that have a group of children around the tree trunk.

We know it only in white cased glass, but Umberger lists clear, and clear with frosted fig-ures as well. Height 14 1/4"; base diameter 4 1/4". Scarce.

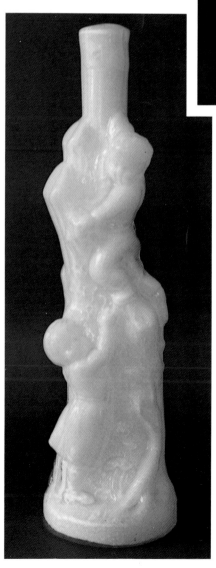

24 - SOMERS, CONNECTICUT, COMMEMORA-TIVE FLASK

Although traditional in its elliptical shape and short round opening, this is a modern flask of fine quality milk glass. On the front is a long-necked demijohn, with the words "Somers, Conn. Bottle Club" embossed around it, the letters "EST." to the left of it and the date "1971" to the right, all framed within a circle. On the reverse is a raised torso, truncated at the waistline, of a man dressed in coat and tie. Embossed in script below the torso is the signature *Charlie / Gardner* slanting upward. Above the torso is a flaring banner with embossing that is difficult to read: "ANTIQUE / CONN S[?]OIAN OF / BOTTLES." Near the bottom of the flask is the date "1973."

Maker unknown, but Pairpoint has been considered a possibility. This bottle does not appear to be one of the series of Wheaton reproduction flasks as it has a rough pontil scar on the underside. Moreover, the glass, though new (1973), is not the heavy stark white typical of most modern milk glass.

Known to us only in white. Two slightly different sizes have been found. One is 6 1/4" high and the other slightly under 7" high. The width also differs by 1/2" — 4" as against 4 1/2". Availability unknown.

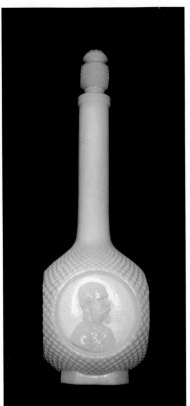

27 - FRANZ JOSEPH COMMEMORA-TIVE BOTTLE

A stately bottle with an extremely long neck and a square body bearing different portraits on each side. The main figure is of Franz Joseph I (1830-1916), emperor of Austria and king of Hungary, whose annexation of Bosnia-Herzegovina in 1908 made all of Europe uneasy, and whose attack on Serbia in 1914 precipitated the first World War. On the opposite side of the bottle is his wife, Elizabeth of Bavaria, who was assassinated by an anarchist in 1898. The other two figures are assumed to be his daughter-in-law and his son Rudolf who committed suicide in 1889.

Maker unknown, possibly dating from early 1880s. Known to us only in white. Height with stopper 11 3/8"; base 2 1/4" square. Rare.

25 - CONFEDERATE FLASK

Apparently a modern flask with the embossed profile of Robert E. Lee on one side and Jefferson Davis on the other. A band of stars and bars forms the wide side margins. The names of the profiles are poorly defined below the figures. The opening is irregularly scalloped.

Maker unknown, but appears to be either a reproduction, perhaps by Wheaton, of an early flask of the Civil War period, or a commemorative bottle possibly of the Civil War Centennial.

Known to us only in white. Height 7 1/2"; width 5 1/4". Availability uncertain.

26 - PERFUME BOTTLE

If the "whisky keg" shown in plate 7 seemed suitable for perfume, this "perfume" bottle is large enough to hold a fifth of Bourbon. It is, of course, a cologne bottle bearing the name "Robinson's Standard Perfumes" in black letters around an attractive large blossom. The bold commercial advertisement suggests it may not have been intended for home use but for the trade in beauty salons. The solid, ground stopper is of good weight as is the bottle itself. Number "22" is marked in gold on the surface of the polished pontil.

Maker unknown. We have seen it only in this lovely opaque lavender, a relatively uncommon color for milk glass, with the notable exception of a few Atterbury products. This bottle is almost certainly of foreign origin, however, and not too recent. Height 8" (with stopper, 10"); width 3 1/4". Availability unknown, but at least hard to find.

28 - GERMAN IMPERIAL FLASK

Very opaque, high quality milk glass is well protected by the splendid metal casing that covers this regal flask or bottle. Only 3" wide at most, the bottle narrows to a long neck constricted at its base to receive a tightly fitted metal ring and tapered at its open end. The ornate metal casing is dominated by a pair of Imperial German Eagles from which rays spread out, each ornamented with faces. More eagles and faces — some benign, others fiercely gargoyle-like — continue along the sides. The closure is a spreading-wing Eagle from which a chain extends to the middle. The flask stands on four metal legs.

Origin unknown, but one cannot doubt that it has all the earmarks of a Prusso-German officer's equipage dating to the Bismarck period.

Known to us only in white. Height of bottle 8", length of neck 3 1/2". Rare.

29 - DIAMOND PATTERN PERFUME BOTTLE

This impressive hexagonal bottle is well documented and highly prized by collectors. Made of very heavy glass, it features a fine diamond pattern on each side, and an imposing stopper. Designed and patented by Henry Whitney, July 2, 1868, it appears in an 1868 New England Glass Co. catalog, reprinted in Kenneth Wilson (*New England Glass*, Fig. 292, p. 338) and Watkins (Plate 45, p. 107); also illustrated in Revi (p. 255) and Spillman (Plate No. 1085).

Known to us in white and blue but reported by Revi in other colors as well. Just under 5" high. Scarce, possibly rare.

30 - ELONGATED LOOP COLOGNE BOTTLE

This attractive hexagonal cologne bottle has long ovals in each of the side panels and a flaring dilation around the bottom, extending out about 1/2" and slightly elevated above the base itself. The bottle's design combines formal lines with a graceful petal-like "skirt" and the glass is top-notch. There is a pontil mark on the underside.

The maker may be determined by a process of elimination, using information derived from Barlow and Kaiser. They illustrate bottles made at Sandwich with the same design (Volume 3, Nos. 3108 and 3109), but they also identify other companies that made almost identical bottles — the New England Glass Company; Cristalleries de Baccarat in France; and reproductions by various perfume houses in 1985. Barlow and Kaiser further state, "The Sandwich and Baccarat colognes have polished pontil marks. The New England Glass Company cologne and the reproductions do not." From this, we surmise the one shown here with a pontil scar is either Sandwich or Baccarat. Because the stopper of this example is not consistent with the Sandwich ones illustrated by Barlow and Kaiser, we conclude it may be Sandwich with a replacement stopper, or Baccarat with the correct stopper.

Known to us only in white. Height without stopper 3 3/4"; with stopper 4 7/8". At least scarce.

31 - DANCING INDIANS COLOGNE BOTTLE

Most unusual, this bottle is shaped as a rhombus, but although it actually is four sided, the oblique angles are so wide that when viewed straight ahead the bottle appears to have only two sides, a "front" and a "back." The two front panels each have what appears to be a dancing Indian, with feathered headdress, holding a triangle high overhead in one hand and a long pipe or baton in the other. The back panels have deep set, framed ovals, perhaps for paper labels, with floral elements above and below. The short neck has a swirl design and a laid on ring opening. The underside shows a deep set, unpolished pontil scar. The glass is fiery opalescent through and through and unquestionably of very early vintage.

Maker unknown, but American circa 1830-1850, according to McKearin, *American Bottles and Flasks* (1978), p. 394, No. 10. In his *American Glass*, he also pictures an example in transparent light green glass (plate 244, No. 5), noting that this bottle was "blown in a full-size piece mould." See also H. E. Keyes, "Glass: Ancient and Antique," *American Glass*, Vol. I (circa 1924), Fig. 2, p. 71, and Umberger, *Top Bottles*, pp. 51-52.

We know it in white opalescent and in clear light green. Height 5"; maximum width 2 7/8". Extremely rare in milk glass.

32 - FAMILY GROUP BOTTLES

This set of highly stylized bottles is remarkable for its representation of a Family Group in the simplest, most artless way imaginable to denote their identities. The Father's bow tie, lapel coat, and creased trousers are augmented only by a breast pocket detailed by a handkerchief sticking out of it. The Mother is signified merely by her pleated dress and a single string of pearls. The Child's gender is totally obscure because it wears only a baby's bib. The glass stoppers, however, one square and the other two round (one of which is slightly smaller than the other), are not interchangeable as they bear cartoon-like embossed faces of a male with mustache, a female with full lips and arched eyebrows, and a wide-eyed child. The absolute composure of the adults is expressed through their hands clasped serenely in front of them, while the child's hands remain apart, perhaps open to whatever the future holds. The glossy milk white glass is of very fine quality and the seams from the two-part moulds are barely visible.

A silver paper sticker printed "LOBECO/Handcrafted in Italy" marks the country of origin. Known to us only in milk white. The transparent stoppers are found in either amber or blue. Without the stoppers, height of Father 6 1/4"; Mother 6 1/2"; Child 5". Although not old, individual ones are hard to find and the complete set is very scarce indeed.

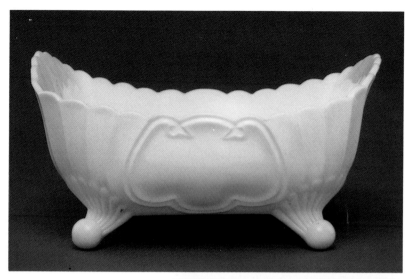

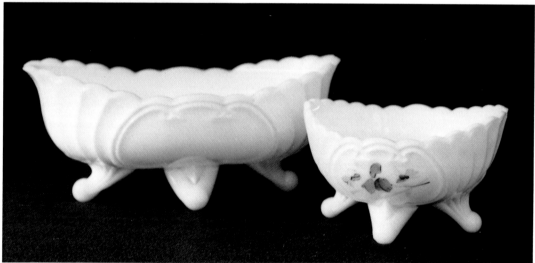

33 - SHELL FOOTED RECTANGULAR BOWL

In a well-known pattern, this unusual rectangular bowl with scalloped edge features a large central panel enlarged at the bottom and surrounded by wide, vertical stripes. A cluster of smaller stripes at each end of the bowl gradually taper, spread outward and end in large round balls that serve as feet. The glass is much like Atterbury's, a pure opaque white.

Apparently previously unattributed, the pattern is found in a variety of pieces. Belknap shows an oblong 10" bowl (132b) and a tall water pitcher (95a). Millard shows a blue creamer (210) and a four piece set — sugar, elongate creamer, mug, and waste bowl (216). Notice, too, the similarity to a large "grape tureen" (M-90a), said to be a rare piece. Warman notes a milk pitcher (41-C) and a sugar (53-B). Barlow and Kaiser illustrate an oblong bowl (No 1252), 10" by 5 3/4" and 4 1/4" high, found in white and blue, and note four smaller ones, one of which is given as 5" long, 3" wide, and 3 1/4" high

Despite the variety of pieces already documented in the basic milk glass literature, we have not found a positive attribution for this handsome pattern. Barlow & Kaiser assign it to late Sandwich (1895-1908) based upon fragments dug at the Sandwich site. It seems probable that the pattern was also produced by other companies. Among them, Challinor, Taylor has been mentioned because the painted decoration on some pieces is quite similar to that found on other products known to be Challinor's. We have examined pieces in both flint and non-flint glass.

The examples illustrated here are known to us only in white, but as noted above pieces of this pattern also occur in blue. Length of the large bowl across the top 8", width 6"; height to flared ends 4 1/8"; height to center 3 1/4". The smaller decorated one is nearly round measuring 4 5/8" by 4 1/4" and but 2 5/8" high. The four legs are equally spaced to form a star-shaped pattern when viewed from below.

This pattern is a challenge to the serious collector to understand and to obtain a complete set. Illustrated pieces scarce, others range from hard to find to scarce.

34 - LOOP BASKET WEAVE OVAL BOWL

This large, impressive bowl is modeled as a wicker basket whose ribbed strands crisscross in great loops, creating an openwork border of interlocking arches. Two single cords of rope, one near the top and another at the "waist," circle around the sides to bind the woven loops together. The bowl rises from a concave base whose pattern is an extension of the woven loops. On the recessed oval underside is a basket weave pattern of linked single strands running horizontally.

We have been unable to determine the maker of this bowl, or even its country of origin, but because of the peculiarity of the glass, it would appear to be either English or French. More than translucent "clambroth," it is nearly clear glass with wisps of milky opal running through it. Lattimore cites an English tradesman who, in the late 19th century, described this type of glass as coming from "a cow with the iron tail." Lattimore explains this odd description as a reference to "the habit of certain milkmen of watering down their wares at the village pump" (p. 51). The name given to this distinctive glass by Sowerby, who introduced it in May 1880, was *blanc de lait*, but it is curious that a French phrase was adopted to describe it. In any case, other pieces of similar appearance are known with certainty to be products made in both England and France, but which was the originator of this type of glass is a matter of debate.

Besides the one shown here, an identical bowl has been found in a dense opaque white, more typical of English milk glass than French, and this may suggest the former as the likely country of origin. Length 9 3/8"; width 7 1/2", height 4". Very scarce.

35 - PATENT BLUE PEARLINE COMPOTE

Set on a plated silver tripod with dolphin motif, this stunning compote, created through a glass process of color turning to opaque white, was the invention of George Davidson in 1889. This is but one example of many popular tableware and novelty items produced in this type of opalescent glass.

The imitation cut diamond design of the compote illustrated here was registered by Davidson on September 6, 1893 (No. 217752). See T-1, p. 17.

Also made in Primrose (yellow) and brown, as well as the blue shown here. Height 8" overall; diameter 9 1/4" across the top of the bowl. Perhaps rare, as shown.

36 - VINE AND GRAPES COMPOTE

This English compote was created by cementing a shallow plate to a tripod base, for the company also issued the plate separately as part of a desert service. The design on the face of the plate is of grape leaves and vines with four grape clusters, all in bold relief. The openwork border of linked arches is one used by this company in other plates, and a number of variants of this pattern can be found in pieces made in America as well. The base appears to have been especially fashioned for this plate, as it repeats the open arch design. The splayed feet, however, are not clusters of grapes, as might appear in the

Photograph, but lions' paws, complete with small, sharp claws. This is truly an example of pressed glass design at its best, made in a dazzling opaque blue that glistens when held to the light.

Made by Greener, it does not have a trademark but the tripod base as well as the plate carry the design lozenge for July 29, 1876 (incorrectly printed as "23 July 1876" in Lattimore, p. 83). See Thompson's accurate listing of the Henry Greener design registrations (T-1, p. 14).

Known to us in blue and in white. Murray lists it in "turquoise slag," and compares it to a similar open latticed edge basket weave compote by Sowerby (p. 74). Diameter 8 3/4"; height 5". Murray, cited above, states. "There are far fewer Greener plates available than Sowerby plates. Neither are found easily but the Greener plate is almost a rarity." This compote assuredly is.

Boxes

37 - CHILD PORTRAIT UNDER GLASS EGG BOX

This large, two-part egg is most unusual as it is fitted with a picture of a young child within a beaded oval frame and protected by an overlay of clear glass. Painted floral decorations are applied in typical fashion.

Unmarked, the maker is unknown. Known to us only in white. Length 5 7/8"; width 4". Scarce.

38 - PORTRAIT DRESSER BOX

Among the many ultra-Victorian items for "Milady's Dressing Table," this glove box holds its own with the most elegant of them. Except for a border of leafy scrolls at the lower edge of the base, the sides and much of the cover are virtually covered by small rose buds. A rose in full bloom is placed at each end of the lid and at the midpoint of the sides of the base. Often the profile of a gentlewoman is embossed in an oval beaded medallion in the center of the cover. In the example shown here, a picture under glass is affixed instead to the recessed oval, adding to the appeal.

Variously called Unidentified Woman, Actress Head, Lady Bust, and even Jenny Lind, this so-called "Roses and Poppies" pattern was used for many years by Fostoria in an extensive line of dresser pieces, as well as a large pitcher dating back to 1904. See F- 514; N-38; and Weatherman, *Fostoria - Its First Fifty Years*, p. 11.

Known to us only in white, but other pieces in this pattern are found in opaque blue as well as pink. Height 2 1/2"; width 3 3/4"; length 10". Hard to find.

39 - HORSESHOE DRESSER BOX

Beautifully designed and executed, the cover of this box is shaped like a horseshoe and bears the profile, in high relief, of a great stallion, mouth open, mane blown back, and obviously eager to run like the wind. The head is framed by a large realistic horseshoe. An ornate floral design superimposed upon a long riding whip and a military bugle decorate the sides of the base. A pair of interlocked horseshoes is embossed on the front.

A Sandwich piece shown in Barlow & Kaiser (No. 3237), who believe it was made to hold collar buttons on a man's chest of drawers. They show a souvenir piece made for the Alton Manufacturing Co. and comment that this verifies the Sandwich origin as the lettering is typical of the fine work of this famous company.

Known to us only in white. Barlow & Kaiser give the dimensions as: Height 1 3/4"; length 3 1/2"; width 3 1/2". Scarce.

40 - "KNEELING CHILD WITH BALL" COVERED BOX

This delightful piece made in a milky, extremely heavy opalescent glass, fairly bursts into flame when held up to the light. For those familiar with Sabino products, the glass is quite similar. The solid figure of a naked child, kneeling on a geometrically patterned carpet, and holding a ball resting on its knees, is in the grand tradition of Art Deco designs. Beautifully moulded, the features of the child's face and hair are finely delineated, as are his hands and fingers. The cover slips over a raised inner lip of the base for a precise and secure fit.

The underside of the base is embossed "ETLING FRANCE" followed by the number "274." The Kovals describe the glass as "very similar in design to Lalique and Phoenix glass" and identify it as "made in France for Etling, a retail shop, dating from the 1920s and 1930s" (see *Kovals' Antiques & Collectibles*, 20th ed., 1988, p. 215).

We are not aware of its being made in colors other than milky white opalescent, as shown. The box is 3 1/2" square, and about 4 1/4" high. Scarce.

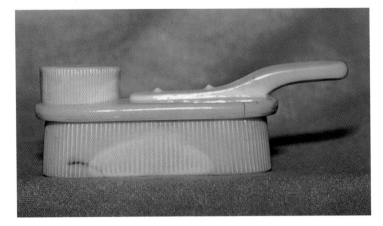

41 - SHOE BRUSH DRESSER BOX

Taking realism to the extreme, this shoe brush is something of a marvel. The bristles of the two brushes are proportioned to their intended use, the ones on the top finer than the large buffing brush below. The blue opaque glass has a whitish portion and a bit of black embedded, not uncommon in many of the early products. The underside of the base has an embossed 36-point star design which fills the entire surface.

A Challinor, Taylor novelty item, continued by U.S. Glass (see catalog reprint in Lucas, p. 57). We know it only in opaque white and blue. Length 4 5/8"; height 1 5/8". Very scarce.

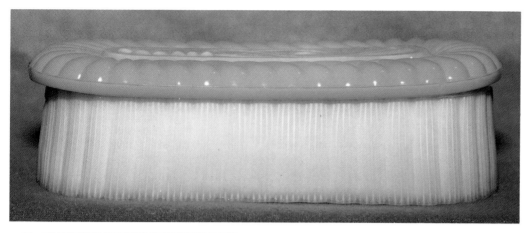

42 - CLOTHES BRUSH DRESSER BOX

The details of this brush are well delineated, as each of the large tufts is a gathering of five bristles. The contrasting blue lid has a swirl design around the edge while a pattern of symmetrically opposed loops and swirled fans fills the central area. On the underside of the base we find an embossed 42-point star that covers most of the surface, with a plain 1/4" border all around.

A Challinor, Taylor novelty item, continued by U.S. Glass (see catalog reprint in Lucas, p. 57). We know it only in the white and blue combination, as shown here, but may have been made in all white and all blue. Length 6 3/8"; height 1 7/8". Scarce.

43 - HAIR BRUSH DRESSER BOX

An obvious companion to the shoe and clothes brushes, the details of the bristles and the design around the edge of the lid are very similar. The pattern on the top of the lid, however, is somewhat different, having concentric swirls in the center and a herringbone design running down the handle. On the underside of the base an embossed 40-point star covers most of the surface, with a plain 1/4" border all around.

A Challinor, Taylor novelty item, continued by U.S. Glass (see catalog reprint in Lucas, p. 57). We know it only in white. Length 6 1/2"; height 1 5/8". Possibly rare.

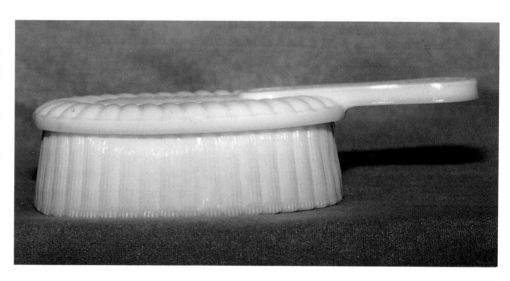

44 - MUSHROOM HINGED BOX

A plump, umbrella-shaped fungus whose variety appears to be wholly stylized and probably unidentifiable in botanical terms, though it is somewhat similar to a type of mushroom known as "reddish agaric," deadly poisonous. The milk glass is a light custard color, and the fleshy pileus is painted red with enameled white dots overall. The fat stalk is splashed with green paint at the base. Hinged metal bands with a clasp connect the top and bottom. A most attractive novelty, and one wonders what might have been the inspiration for or the intended use of such an unusual piece. On display, it makes a good conversation piece.

Maker unknown, but a European origin is most likely. We know it only in custard, as shown. Height 4 3/4"; diameter of the umbrella top 4 1/4"; base diameter 3 3/8". At least scarce.

33

46 - LILY COVERED BOX

Compact and intricate in design, this piece features what appear to be lilies or daffodils. The flowers, embossed on a stippled ground, are separated by a complex play of ribbons that defies description. The ribbed elements at each corner emerge on the cover to frame a large oval and expand slightly at the bottom of the base to form feet. The conical finial appears, appropriately enough, to be an unopened bud.

Not illustrated in any Vallerysthal catalogue available to us, but embossed "Vallerysthal" inside the bottom of the base. Previously shown in N-49 where it is called "flower square covered box."

Known to us only in white. The base is 3" high, 3 1/2" wide at the top, and 3" wide at the bottom. Overall height 5 1/2". Scarce.

45 - SUEDOIS POWDER BOX

This jar, named for a country (Sweden) — as are many of the Portieux designs — is part of an eighteen piece "service de toilette." Items featuring this pattern decorated in blue, red, or gold fill three full color pages in PC (p. 296-298).

The following pieces, all with the same alternating scroll and angled bar design, are illustrated (p. 145, Nos. 2020-2047):

Cologne (or toilet water) bottle; perfume (or vaporizer) long brush tray; powder box without finial; rectangular soap box; water jug; open ring or collar tray; and sponge tray.

In addition to the above items are five sizes of toilet water bottles; four sizes of powder boxes with finials; tumbler (for rinsing mouth) and a plate to place the tumbler on, making a total of eighteen pieces in the complete set.

Our illustrated example is in the rich blue of Portieux, but it also occurs in white judging by the catalog's colored plates. It is embossed on the base "Portieux / France." Height about 5 1/2" with a diameter opening of 3 1/8". More than hard to find.

47 - DOG ON DIAMOND BASE COVERED BOX

An outstanding item, well-designed and beautifully proportioned. The dog which serves as the finial appears to be a shepherd and measures scarcely 1 1/2" long. For so small a piece, its long ears and shaggy coat are remarkably well detailed. Diamonds constitute the overall pattern, bordered by a rim of beads on the cover and repeated around the bottom of the base. The pseudo-cut diamonds on the outside surface of the base, however, are pressed instead on the *inside* of the cover, so from the outside they would be visible only in clear glass. On one side of the base the diamonds are replaced by an octagonal plain surface, suggesting perhaps that the box or jar was intended to carry a paper label identifying the contents.

Maker unknown, but probably English. Known to us in opaque white and in clear crystal. The base is 2 1/2" across, 2" wide, and 2 1/4" deep; with cover, the piece measures 4" high. Rare.

48 - WOODEN CRATE

As a representational piece, this box is the essence of simplicity. It makes no attempt to be anything more than it is — *just a wooden crate*. For that reason, compared with so many imaginative, indeed spectacular French designs for covered dishes, this one succeeds by having almost the same shock value as Andy Warhol's famous Campbell soup can painting. Created long before the rise of Pop Art, the whole point of this piece may be summed in the expression "Artless Realism." The cover is almost wafer thin, with an inner lip that fits inside the base for a seamless union. Top, sides, and even the underside are horizontal simulated wooden slats, exactly four in number, all bound by vertical ones, two at each of the short ends and two about equidistant on the long sides, across the top and across the bottom. At each intersection, a single nail head marks their juncture, and rope handles are set at both ends. If you turn the box upside down, it looks exactly like it does right side up. So simple, and so extraordinary.

Unsigned, it is a Vallerysthal product shown in SW whose editors call it a "Strong Box" (p. 8, third item in next to the bottom row). It also appears in both VC (1907), p. 240, and VCC, p. 310 (in color); apparently discontinued thereafter and absent from the 1933 Portieux catalog.

We know it only in white. Length 4"; width 3 1/2"; height 2 3/8". At least scarce, and possibly rare.

49 - DRUM POMADE

A military snare drum, highly opalescent, whose cover is a flat disk with crossed drumsticks serving as the finial, but only barely because they are so slightly elevated and difficult to grasp. The sides of the drum have ten vertical cords at the top which gather at the center and spread out to the bottom where they join a horizontal stripe circling near the base.

Made by Sandwich and illustrated in B-K (No. 3259) in a somewhat larger size (3 1/4" x 2 1/2").

Known to us only in blue. Barlow and Kaiser mention a similar drum in amethyst. Height 2 1/2" and 2" in diameter. Very rare.

Busts/Statuettes

50 - BALLROOM DANCERS FIGURALS

A pair of delicately fashioned and engaging figures, they were intended perhaps to serve as tops for perfume or cologne bottles. The lean faced male has an aristocratic air, confirmed by his elegant attire. Holding a dashing hat in one hand and his long tailcoat in the other, he is resplendent in his fancy tie and waistcoat. His equally charming lady, holding a basket of flowers, is ravishing in her voluminous ball gown daringly low cut. Coifed with every strand of hair in place, she seems ready to join him in the Blue Danube Waltz.

Maker unknown, perhaps of relatively recent vintage. Known to us only in white. Height of male 5 3/8"; female 5 1/8". Somewhat hard to find.

52 - YOUNG VICTORIA STATUETTE

We tend to think of Queen Victoria as dignified, matronly, and somewhat aloof, and indeed even censorious. But here we see the comely young woman who won the heart of her beloved Albert. She is dressed in sweeping garments that resemble a Roman toga. Her head is held proudly erect with shoulders bare, hair pulled back into a bun. Her right breast and leg are visible through the diaphanous drapery folding over her left shoulder, curving around her waist, and ending in a long series of folds draped over her left arm. She has a wreath in one hand and a scroll in the other. On the rim of the base, just above a series of vertical bars, the name "Victoria" is embossed in large letters. The semi-translucent glass is almost clambroth. An ornament to any collection.

Maker unknown to us, but presumably English in origin. Known to us only in white. Height 9"; diameter of base 4 1/2". Rare.

53 - ROYAL BUST FIGURAL

A bearded monarch, whose identity we do not know, is seen wearing a magnificent crown ornamented with pearls. It is difficult to determine whether this hollow blown figural may have been intended as a bottle or a vase. The opening at the top has a metal cap, but it is not secure enough to prevent the flow of liquid and may not be original. The quality of the glass and the mould detail is superb, a prize for any collection.

It is marked "MUSTER / GE-SCHÜTZT" on the underside, the same as found on the magnificent Hen and Covered Chick Egg Cup Breakfast Set (No. 122 in this book). No doubt, of course, of its German origin.

Known to us only in white. Height 3 3/4". Rare.

51 - F. D. R. BUST

Although it has been shown before as a frontispiece in Warman (W-1A), we include this splendid Franklin Delano Roosevelt bust because Warman's book is not readily available to most collectors. The bust is blown in a three part mould, the seams almost invisible, with special care taken to avoid having any mould line marring the face. His eyes are very expressive, the sagging bags giving evidence of worry and ill health. The pupils are formed as small depressions in the manner of ancient marble statuary. Almost life size, the likeness is extraordinary, down to the detail of the mole on his right cheek. The glass is of top quality, with a high gloss that catches light and shadows beautifully.

Maker unknown. On the back, one is just barely able to make out a faint embossing which reads: "M. Altwater/ 33." We have been unable to trace the identity of Altwater, who we suppose was the designer, if not the actual maker. As to when it was made, Warman suggested the 1940s, but perhaps the number "33" is a clue, as it was 1933 when Roosevelt announced his "New Deal" program for a national recovery from the economic crises.

Known to us only in white. Height 12"; maximum width at the base 6 1/4". Extremely rare.

54 - QUEEN VICTORIA BUST PAPERWEIGHT

Much admired, even revered, England's Queen Victoria throughout her sixty-four year reign (1837-1901) inspired the creation of a vast number of commemorative pieces in china, pottery, metal, paper, glass — indeed, practically any medium one can imagine. This hollow, opaque black bust, produced for the Queen's Diamond Jubilee of 1897, is skillfully moulded and makes no attempt to beautify her countenance. Her round, pudgy face is somber, and the puffy eyelids and deep folds under her eyes bespeak a weary monarch whose death, at age eighty-two, was not far off. The glass is of good quality, and the facial features finely detailed. On each side, the seams of the two-part mould are barely evident only at the base below the shoulders. "QUEEN / VICTORIA" is embossed in front.

Lattimore appears to have been the first to publish an ad, reproduced here, from the *Pottery Gazette* of June 1, 1897, showing this bust and other "Penny Glassware" made by the firm Thos. Kidd & Co., Holt Town Glassworks, Manchester. This small manufacturer, whose main products were household and utilitarian items, was founded about 1892 and closed near the turn of the century, according to Lattimore (p. 114).

Known to us only in black, it is reported by Slack to be found also in "translucent brown, blue and clear" (p. 127). A very attractive one in blue is illustrated by Brenda and James Measell in "Queen Victoria Commemorative Glass" (GCD, 1:5, Oct/Nov 1987, p. 45).

Height 3 1/2"; oval base 3 3/4" by 2 7/8". It is rare, one in opaque black having sold at auction in England on Sept. 20, 1989 for £170, about $280.

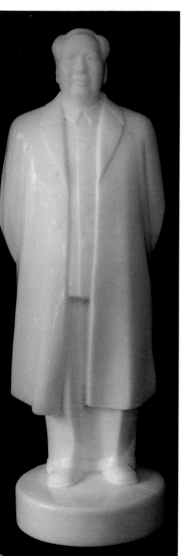

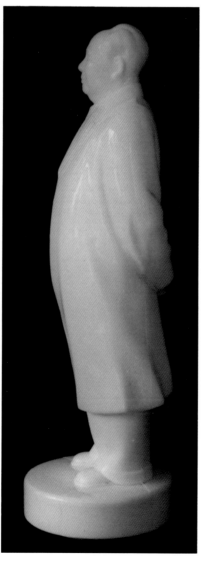

Advertisement in the *Pottery Gazette* (June 1, 1897) for Diamond Jubilee items made by Thomas Kidd & Co., Manchester, England.

55 - MAO TSE-TUNG STATUE

When first seen from a distance at an antique show in Farmington, Connecticut, this looked like Chinese porcelain as it was placed among other Oriental artifacts. On examination, it proved to be milk glass. The full length statue of Chairman Mao Tse-tung is hollow, perhaps intended to be a light globe. The likeness is excellent, and the pose, with hands clenched behind his back, is wholly characteristic. It appears to have been blown in a four-part mould whose fire polished seams are only faintly discernible. The glass is of superior quality, with a high gloss and of substantial weight.

Maker unknown, but we assume it was made in China and probably dates from the early 1950s when Mao established the People's Republic or perhaps the mid-1960s with the start of the Cultural Revolution when he was in high favor. By the early 1970s, at the time of Nixon's visit, he was already falling into disfavor, so it is doubtful that a commemorative such as this would have been made to mark his death in 1976. The dealer who sold this piece was unable or unwilling to say how it found its way to New England.

Known to us only in white. Height 15". Extremely rare.

56 - UNIDENTIFIED STATUETTE

Although we have not been able to determine who this handsome gentleman is, the bust is no doubt not generic but intended to represent and memorialize some historical person. This surmise is based on the curious appearance of nineteenth century muttonchops on the face of a man who paradoxically appears to be dressed in a Roman toga! Honoring contemporary notables by equating them with classical models is frequent in both painting and sculpture. On busts, we usually find laurel wreaths adorning the head of the honoree.

Maker unknown. It is embossed "COPYRIGHT SECURED" on the back, wording which may suggest an English origin. White milk glass with satin finish. Height 4 1/4". Rare.

Candlesticks

57 - NEW ENGLAND GLASS CANDLESTICK

Kenneth Wilson, who shows a similar stick (*American Glass*, No. 1394), states that the Toledo Museum example probably dates from 1920-1925, and adds rather indecisively that the origin is "probably United States, possibly Europe." His conclusion seems to be based on the glass surface, the lack of significant wear on the underside of the base and elsewhere. He cites, however, an 1869 New England Glass Co. Catalogue (Plate 125 No. 1340) which shows a candlestick identical to his No. 1394 except that there are two small steps on the hexagonal plinth instead of one and he cites a vaseline example that has the upper edge of the octagonal base beveled rather than rounded.

Using Wilson's approach we conclude that the example shown here dates from the nineteenth century. The upper edge of the octagonal base is beveled; there are two small steps on the hexagonal plinth; and there is evidence of wear not only on the underside of the base but also around the socket. It appears to be identical to Watkins sketch (Plate 45) of the 1869 candlestick, shown in two sizes, in the catalogue of the Cambridge New England Glass Co.

Known to us only in opaque white. Height 8"; base 3 7/8". Scarce.

58 - NEW ENGLAND TYPE CANDLESTICK (#1)

This is a handsome, wafer joined, pure white candlestick. It is shown in Archer (No. 11, Plate 2), dated circa 1850-1860, unattributed but thought to be from the "New England area." The Archers suggest it was made by Jarvis & Cormerais of South Boston (later Mt. Washington Glass Co.).

Known to us only in white opaque. Height 7 1/2"; base diameter 4". Scarce.

59 - NEW ENGLAND TYPE CANDLESTICK (#2)

Many similar candlesticks were produced in New England from about 1840 to 1870. This is a handsome piece with an elongated stem. All these early candlesticks are desirable and of high quality glass. This one closely resembles a candlestick illustrated in Wilson (*American Glass*, plate 674), but is taller (20.2 mm.).

Known to us only in opaque white. Height 8 1/2"; base 3 3/4". Scarce.

61 - SACRE-CŒUR (MARIA) CANDLESTICK

This is a lovely candlestick, representing the Virgin Mary with her hands at her breast supporting the radiant heart of devotion which is the focal point of the figure. With its large, flaring socket and massive base, it is truly imposing. Each of the four raised corners bears the face of a winged angel.

It is marked Portieux on the underside. We have found this candlestick in an early 1903 catalog (folio 214A, No. 4119) illustrated alongside a matching one of the Sacred Heart of Jesus (No. 4118). Both candlesticks are also continued in the 1933 Portieux catalog (p. 128, Nos. 1813 and 1814).

Known to us only in white. Height 11 1/2". Rare.

60 - COLONNE ORDINAIRE CANDLESTICK

Similar to early American candlestick designs produced by the New England and Sandwich companies, the base of this French one is slightly more splayed, but otherwise beautifully proportioned.

Embossed "Portieux" on the underside, and shown in PC (p. 129, No. 1817). Known to us only in a stark white rather unusual for a French piece. Height 8". Scarce.

62 - WINGED LADY CANDLESTICK

On both sides of this charming piece are busts of a buxom lady. Two strings of pearls adorn her ample bosom, and long pleated tresses flow down both sides of her head. An angelic or mythological association is suggested by the tapering wings that rise up behind. The deeply recessed candle socket is elaborate, expanded and surmounted by a series of sixteen large notches. Below the bust the stem consists of three horizontal bands followed by paired vertical stripes interspersed by rows of five large beads.

Although unsigned and not illustrated in catalogues available to us, this is almost certainly a French stick probably by Vallerysthal.

Known to us in opaque blue, white, and dark amber. It is a tall piece, 10 1/4" high with a strongly flared, scalloped base 5 1/2" in diameter. Scarce.

63 - LADY HOLDING URN CANDLESTICK

Contrasting with her hair tied in a prim bun, this lady is somewhat daringly clothed in a gossamer gown that flows down below her feet to form the base of the candlestick. Her upraised arms support the candle socket modeled as an urn embossed with petals at the bottom and ribbed sides above. The glass has a grayish tint.

Maker unknown. Known to us only in opaque white. Height 8 1/4", base diameter 4 1/2". Scarce.

65 - SWIRLING CANDLE-STICK

A wildly swirling designed French candlestick. The stem bears three floral fronds and what may be a flower (or abstract face?) on the swollen lower portion of the stem. Both the base and the socket are moulded with massive swirling interwoven floral designs.

Some examples are embossed "Vallerysthal."

Known to us only in white. Height 8 5/8"; diameter of the base 5"; diameter of the socket 3" and designed on the inner surface like an open flower. Scarce.

64 - MOUSQUETAIRE, MAN AND WOMAN, CANDLESTICKS

A finely crafted pair of candlesticks with each figure extending an arm to support the unusually large candle socket. Their features and costumes, apparently representing French Royal Bodyguards (from 1622 to 1786), are beautifully moulded. The base bears three abstract reptilian heads with a floral design emerging from behind.

Illustrated in PC (Nos. 1845 and 1846, p. 121).

Known to us in white and in crystal with the figures and "dragon" heads frosted. Each is 10 3/4" high. Scarce.

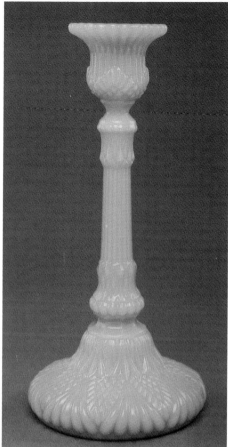

68 - ARTESIAN CANDLESTICK

Here is a very austere candlestick which commands attention as much for its stately size as for the closely meshed elements of the ornate design that covers every inch of the surface. The main stem is finely ribbed, as is the upper portion of the candle socket. The rest of the design employs a complex arrangement of beads and shell-like clusters leaving no part of the surface untouched.

Illustrated in PC ("Artesien," No. 1856, p. 132), the name given derives from the French town Artois.

We know it only in blue, but doubtless made in white and perhaps other colors. Height 9". Scarce.

66 - CHIMERES CANDLESTICK

This dazzling candlestick is well named "fantastical" or "imaginative!" Embossed on the bulbous portion of the stem is a mythical bird, rather Archeopteryx-like (except for the head) with a long curling reptilian tail and sweeping wings that taper, almost touching the coils of the tail on the opposite side. The surface of the stem and the ornate base is pebbled. The socket is formed as eight flower petals. Illustrated in PC (p. 132, No. 1865) and also in color (p. 323, No. 6440).

Known to us in white and blue. Height 8"; 2 1/2" across the top; 4 1/2" in diameter at the base. Hard to find.

Note: For other items made in the "Chimeres" design, see the listing in "Special Feature Articles."

69 - BAMBOUS ORDINAIRE a BOBECHE CANDLESTICK

Impressive and well-proportioned, this candlestick is very ornate with a bulbous elongated paneled stem and flaring socket.

Illustrated in PC (p.129, No. 1827), also shown with four similar sticks each with variations in socket or in circled details.

Known to us in opaque blue, crystal, and amber. It is a large stick 10 1/2" high with the socket 5" in diameter. Scarce.

67 - RICHLIEU CANDLESTICK

This is a handsome elaborate stick with a particularly appealing spiraling stem and flaring feet. The three slender stripes that taper from top to bottom simulate dripping wax.

Illustrated in PC (p. 131, No. 1843) and again as a lamp with ball font to hold lamp oil (p. 137, No. 1948).

Known to us in white and blue. Height 9 1/4". Scarce.

70 - TORTOISE CANDLEHOLDER

Riding on the back of a large turtle is a fearsome animal with a beak-like face, silky-coat upper body, and a scaly serpent's tail that curls and fans out at the end to form the handle. The large, scalloped candle socket resting on its head is also patterned as a mass of scales. Unlike this fanciful creature, the turtle itself is realistic, more or less, and closely resembles in conception the large "Turtle with Snail Finial" covered dish (No. 151 in this book).

Made by Portieux, it appears as "Tortue" in PC (p. 133, No. 1885). We know it in opaque white and blue. Length 5 1/2", height 4 1/2". Very scarce.

72 - BELL-GLASS CANDLEHOLDERS

One needs a spacious salon to display these majestic "flambeaux verrines" to their best advantage. They consist of two parts. The candlestick proper, pressed from a four part mould, is extremely heavy, with an intricate pattern combining moulded beads, oval medallions, and flame-like elements, all in high relief. The removable hurricane shade, actually a bit taller than the stick itself, has a 1 1/4" wide metal casing cemented at the bottom to assure a snug and secure fit in the large socket. Handling these pieces is not for the faint hearted.

Illustrated in VC 1907, No. 5032, p. 306. Known to us only in blue. Overall height 21 1/4". Candlestick: height 9 3/4"; base diameter 5 1/4". Bell shade: height 11 1/2"; top diameter 6 1/4". More than scarce.

71 - DOLPHIN CANDLESTICKS

Three dolphins' heads set above a vertical ribbed border form the triangular plinth of these candlesticks, shown here in a deep, almost black, purple marbled glass. The dolphin's features are highly stylized, grotesquely anthropoid in appearance with large nostrils and a mouth which spreads across the full width of the face. The octagonal stem is capped by a vertically ribbed and deeply recessed candle socket.

Unmarked, the design appears in an undated Davidson catalog, circa 1885, made from moulds which Davidson purchased from W. H. Heppell, according to Slack, p. 76.

Also found in white, jet black, and possibly other colors. Height 7". Scarce.

Bell-Glass Candleholder illustrated in the 1907 Vallerysthal catalog, item 5032, p. 306.

5032
(265 et 240 ™m)

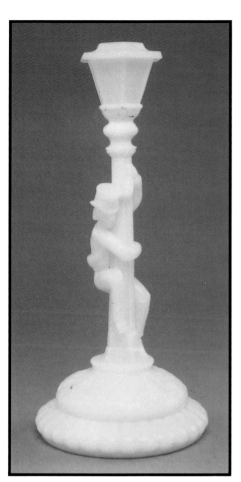

73 - THE DRUNKARD ("Pochard") CANDLESTICK

Imagine the waggish delight the mould maker of this candlestick must have enjoyed when he first saw his creation actually pressed in glass! The figure is no lowlife drunkard. Having had one too many, the dapper, well-dressed fellow hugs the post, whose large hexagonal top simulates a lamp globe. The plinth is two-stepped, the upper having a ring of beads surmounting — quite appropriately — large clusters of grapes and leaves, while the lower step is formed more traditionally as a series of rounded ribs

Illustrated in PC (p.131, No. 1849). The same figure is shown in PC (p. 137, No. 1946) with a flat plate and round ball to hold lamp oil in place of the "lamp globe" socket.

Known to us only in white. Height overall 10"; height of lamp post alone 8". The hexagonal top is 2" across with a 3/4" opening for the candle. The diameter at the base is 4 1/2". Rare.

75 - "MADONNA AND CHILD" CANDLESTICK

A beautifully designed and executed religious candlestick. The stem incorporates an expanded, detailed representation of a Madonna and Child cameo in high relief with a sunburst border. The socket is an opening flower surrounding a rayed round projection to receive the candle. There is a wafer below the figure. The base is three stepped and hexagonal. At the back, between the top and bottom wafers, is a very thick median bar that arises from three short basal "petals." Embossed on the back of the cameo is "Patented Oct 19, 1875." The glass is of superior quality.

Maker unknown. Known to us only in white. It is a large stick, 11" tall with a basal diameter of 3 3/4" and a socket opening of 1 1/8". Scarce.

74 - POPE LEO XIII CANDLESTICK

Wearing traditional vestments of the papacy, the man who is honored in this candlestick was crowned Pope in 1878, indicating perhaps an approximate time when it was made [see Heacock, referenced below]. The figure is skillfully designed and the glass of high quality. Robed in all the requisite vestments of his office, his position as head of the Roman Catholic Church is signaled by his pectoral cross, and the mitre which is the head-dress worn only by the Pope. In his hands, crossed in front of him, he holds a scroll bearing his name. Perhaps the only jarring feature is what appears to us to be a disproportionately large mitre, perhaps necessary to form the candlestick's socket. The large, round and scalloped plinth seems most fitting to convey the steadfastness of the head of the church.

Made by Geo. Duncan and Sons, and apparently unlisted prior to Heacock's discovery (*The Glass Collector*, Winter 1982, pp. 4-5). See also O.N. X:3 June 1995, pp. 5, 12.

Known to us only in white. Height 9 1/2"; base diameter 4". Rare.

76 - CARRE CANDLESTICK

Although austerely "square," this is nonetheless an elegant and graceful candlestick whose pattern reflects baroque elements around the socket and the stem. The design in high relief on the base is difficult to make out and may be either a ram's head or a very stylized version of Mephistopheles.

Illustrated as a Vallerysthal piece in SW (p. 7, middle row, third from the left). The Portieux example shown here (8" size) differs from those illustrated in PC (p. 132, No. 1854 and also in color, p. 323, No. 6424) in having a notched or "tooth" pattern around the socket, whereas the catalog sketches appear to have a pattern of widely spaced beads.

Known to us in white, blue, and green. Made in three sizes (7", 8", and 10"). Hard to find in white or blue, scarce in green.

77 - BEADED CIRCLE OR BEADED ELLIPSE CANDLESTICK

This handsome stick appears to be part of the "Beaded Circle" pattern of which the Fersons show the Creamer and Spooner (F-321, 322). The candlestick is heavy, of excellent quality glass with the vertical beads on the stem beautifully moulded. A lovely piece worthy of a place in any collection.

The Fersons tentatively assign the pattern to Sandwich. Known to us only in white. It is 9 1/2" tall, 2" across the socket, and 4 3/4" in diameter across the base. Scarce to rare.

Note: This beaded circle or beaded ellipse pattern may well have been reproduced as we have seen this design on a large compote, a banana boat, and a sugar of relatively inferior quality milk glass.

78 - HUNTER CANDLESTICK

A nicely proportioned figural candlestick representing a classical hunter in the Grecian or Roman style. His apparel is modeled as a toga of sorts, which begins at his left shoulder, sweeps under his right arm, and drapes down to his left mid-thigh and right lower calf. The hunter's trophy hanging at his left side is a furry creature that appears to be a small fox. Flat against his right side he holds his bow, while his left arm, in anticipation of the next quarry, is raised to reach an arrow in the quiver on his back. Three lion heads are moulded equidistantly and in high relief around the ribbed and beaded plinth. An impressive piece both in workmanship and in the quality of the milk glass.

Unmarked, the maker has not been identified, but it is most likely European. Known to us only in white. Height 10 5/8"; diameter of socket 2 1/2"; diameter at the base 4 5/8". Very scarce.

79 - SIRENE CANDLESTICK

This fascinating candlestick is formed as a comely mermaid with a fish-like scaly tail that curves upward expanding at the end into a fan that frames the head and upper torso. From the middle of the tail a series of long, spectral toes cling tightly to the convex elevated, ridged base. Another example of the amazing originality and technical ability of the French mould makers.

Illustrated in color in PC (p.323, No. 6444) and in black and white (p. 131, No. 1852). The colored figure is bronzed, with the base and socket painted blue. The same piece is shown as a lamp in PC (p. 137, No. 1947) fitted with a round ball, instead of a socket, to hold lamp oil.

Known to us only in white and pale creamy French opaline, but probably made in other colors as well. Height 9 1/2". Scarce.

81 - SCROLL AND CROSS CANDLESTICK

This massive, leaded milk glass candlestick weighs fully three pounds. Pressed in a three part mould, the upper and lower parts are joined by a wafer. The octagonal top is formed as vertical panels and horizontal bands below which are acanthus-like triangles. The ornate base, with thick scrolls set above three blocky feet, has as its central feature a cross surrounded by flowers and cased within a circular frame. The glass is opalescent of a clambroth quality.

The maker is uncertain but thought to be a Gillinder product.

Known to us only in white. Height 10 7/8". More than scarce.

80 - CANDLE HOLDER LANTERNS

Two examples of a type of candle holder modeled as a lantern, which serves as a reflecting globe as well as protection against gusts of wind. The one in pink milk glass is a round house with brick walls and a shingle roof. The windows on the sides are moulded in the glass, while those on the roof are knocked out to allow greater illumination and flow of air. The white one is formed as a beehive with bees swarming around it. Both are fitted with looped brass hangers.

Makers unknown. The pink lantern is marked "DEPOSE PANATIN REG 120760," and the one in white "SCHUTZ 7968." Height (pink) 8" and (white) 7 1/4". Scarce.

82 - THE GUNNER ("Artilleur") CANDLESTICK

This austere French artilleryman, probably of the Franco-Prussian War, bears a flag draped over his right shoulder, the staff fitted into a holder at the bottom of his short tunic. He stands at attention with a sword by his left hand and cannon balls at his feet. The socket, also embossed with cannon balls, is almost square, and has a knob protruding from the center of each margin. The base is very elegant, strongly expanded with crossed cannons, floral designs and an enigmatic egg-like object as a central element. The base is rectangular with rounded and expanded corners.

Embossed "Portieux" on the underside, it is illustrated in PC (p. 131, No. 1847). The same figure is also shown in PC (p. 137, No. 1943) with the candle socket replaced by a plate and a round ball for holding lamp oil.

Known to us only in white. Height overall 10"; height of figure 4 1/2"; width of base 4 1/4". Rare.

83 - ENGLISH CONDIMENT SET

A trim and formal design, combining geometrical symmetry and classic lines. The tray, with squared scoop handles, has shallow hexagonal indentations for the proper placement of the four condiment containers — salt, pepper, cruet, and a sugar or mustard jar with a slotted metal lid. The gleaming thin brass screw tops harmonize with the gilt on the stopper of the cruet and the trim on the edge of the tray. Blue, red, green, and yellow floral decoration lends a feminine touch to the otherwise austere look of this elegant set. Stark white, the milk glass is of fine quality.

Maker unknown, but the sugar spoon is marked "Made in England," suggesting the country of origin, as if the design of the set alone were not enough of a clue!

Known to us only in white. Tray 7" by 4 1/16"; Height with closures: cruet 4 1/2"; salt and pepper 3 3/16"; sugar 2 11/16. Availability unknown, but assumed to be at least hard to find.

85 - EGG-SHAPED CONDIMENT SET

Condiments in many shapes and sizes appear to have been very popular sellers in earlier times. This is among the more unusual having a milk glass base consisting of three cavities resembling half eggs. A metal handle, passing through a hole in the center, is affixed by a screw underneath. When the salt, pepper, and mustard containers are inserted into the cavities, the set appears to be a trio of eggs standing on their ends. The hand painted decoration is of trees and shrubs, with a split rail fence in the foreground and mountains behind, all done in warm sepia colors.

Maker unknown, but the painting may give a clue to the decorator of these sets which were probably sold as blanks. Previously listed in Lechner's *The World of Salt Shakers* (earlier 1976 edition, plate XXXXXI), it was given the name "Violet Sprig Condiment" because of the floral decoration of the example shown. Lechner calls attention especially to the impractical design of this set, making "the survival factor obviously very poor" (p. 110).

Known to us only in opaque white. The salt, pepper, and mustard containers individually measure 2 1/4" high. Very scarce, according to Lechner.

84 - ROUND FOOTED CONDIMENT SET

We have pictured this set to show you its separate elements unassembled. The raised platform, typical of many similar ones, is pressed with deep (1") sockets to receive the containers and hold them secure. When in place, the narrowed bottoms of the salt, pepper, sugar shaker, and mustard jar are hidden, so they appear to be ordinary table pieces set on a flat top tray. The example shown here is somewhat unusual as each of the pieces has a different decoration and the closures, too, are not matched. This may suggest later replacements of damaged or missing parts. The triangular handle, painted gold, is fixed by a thumb screw.

Maker unknown, but either Dithridge or Eagle are likely possibilities. Known to us only in white. Tray 8" in diameter; Height with closures: salt and pepper 5 5/16"; sugar 5"; mustard 4 7/16". Somewhat hard to find.

86 - CAROUSEL TRIPLE SALT OR CONDIMENT (#1)

A two-part set consisting of a central tall shaft which serves to support a removable revolving tray of three small cupped salt or condiment containers. The overall design is a pattern of graceful swirls, those surrounding the cups fusing at the bottom into a large bead.

Embossed with the letters S V on the underside. Known to us in a creamy caramel and in fiery white opal. 7" high; 3 3/8" diameter of base. Scarce

87 - CAROUSEL TRIPLE SALT OR CONDIMENT (#2)

Like the preceding, this two-part item has a removable revolving tray of three salt or condiment cups supported by a center column. Its pattern, too, is a swirl design, but more austere, with the main shaft perfectly straight, and capped by a blunt, knob-like top. Examples have been found in which one of the trays is fitted with a notched lid.

Unmarked, but possibly Portieux-Vallerysthal, as in conception it is similar to various "Menageries Moulees" items illustrated in their catalogs. Known to us in white and blue milk glass. Height 6 1/2"; diameter of base 3 3/8". Hard to find.

Covered Dishes

Animals

88 - SITTING CAT COVERED SALT

One of the many small milk glass animal covered salts being produced in the United States during the past few years. This long-haired cat, with its head uplifted and turned to the right, and its large fluffy tail commanding attention, is haughty indeed. The base has a flat, flared and scalloped edge, plain on the upper surface but with a double braid on the underside. The sides have a pattern of very thin vertical stripes, while the design under the base is a complex weave of crossing strands, a design used extensively by Vallerysthal many years ago. The mould work is somewhat muddled, especially the fur, but the cat's arresting posture, plus the "old fashioned" appearance of the base, give the entire piece a certain charm.

Made by Mosser Glass, Inc., and embossed on the inside of the base with an "M" with a line below it.

Known to us only in white, but we assume it may be made in colors as well. Cat cover 2" long and 1 5/8" wide; Base (across the top) 2 3/4" long, 2 3/8" wide. Overall height about 2 1/2". Readily available.

89 - RECLINING COW COVERED DISH

Of extraordinary appeal, this cow, resting on a mound of grass, rivals comparison with other representations of her kind in glass. The head is magnificent, with short, sharp horns and wide spread ears. An air of mighty tension is achieved as she strains to lick her haunch — the powerful, sculpted neck muscles contrasting sharply with the relaxed, splayed out legs. The base is no less remarkable. The underside of the plain wide scalloped rim is embossed with a pattern of twelve six-petaled flowers framed in circles which alternate and connect with a diamond figure. The three large panels on the sides of the base each portray a pair of cows in various postures. Between the panels three raised stripes converge to the bottom of the base where they meet to form three large realistic hooves. The base underside surface is pebbled, with a smooth raised circle at the center. Much of the exquisite design is not visible, of course, in opaque glass, suggesting that it was probably made in clear and in transparent colors as well.

Illustrated in VCC (p.308, No. 3820). See also R.W. Lee, "Antiques Journal," July 1951, p. 19, plate II. It is listed in the 1957 Abraham and May catalogue of the Frances Cross collection as No. 19 and offered for about one fifth more than the equally rare Vallerysthal Alligator.

Known to us in opaque white and blue. Height overall 5". The top is 4 1/4" in diameter. The width across the flanged base is 6 1/4". Rare.

90 - COW ON RECTANGULAR BASE COVERED DISH

The entire conception of this magnificent covered dish is most unusual. The large recumbent cow looks like an Asian or African animal, rather than one of our familiar domestic breeds. Although it is quite realistic in most respects, there is an exotic chiseled quality about it, reminiscent of primitive sculptures. This quality is further augmented by the enormous rectangular slab on which it rests, and whose design of grass and flowers also conveys a studied intent to appear "sculpted" rather than naturalistic. The glass is of very fine quality and highly opalescent.

Maker unknown. Known to us only in white. Length 5 1/2"; height 5 1/2". Rare.

91 - COW COVERED BUTTER DISH

No collector can fail to admire this English milk glass oval covered dish. From its distinctive horizontal horns to its tail resting over its hind leg, the full-figured recumbent cow is well proportioned with fine anatomical features. It lies on a knoll of grass and flowers atop a three-tier platform, the central one consisting of a series of vertical blocks. But it is the intricate design of the base which makes this piece so outstanding. The outer edge of the flared upper rim is embellished by a series of beads, separated each from the other by two parallel bars. Four large beads are moulded on the inner margin of the rim, two in front and two behind, placed so as to hold the cover securely in place. The sides of the base are moulded with an elaborate leaf and shell motif in high relief. The underside of the base has a rayed oval pattern surrounded by 16 knobbed feet.

Made by Henry Greener, circa 1876-85, it carries the earlier Greener trademark inside the cover and the base. See Slack, Plate XXVI. Found in white and marbled glass in three different colors — purple, blue, and a very unusual brown. The cover, measured across its bottom, is 5 3/4" by 4"; the base, across the top, measures 7 3/4" by 6 1/4".

A prize for any collection, it was offered for sale in purple marble by Maud Feld in 1962 (see O.N., VII:1, Dec. 1991, p. 718). One in brown marble was sold at a London auction in 1989 for £1,100 (about $1,700). Rare in white, more so in marbled colors.

92 - STARTLED DOE COVERED DISH

This outstanding piece has a thin cover bearing the figure of a resting doe, but her head turned sharply to the right and her small ears erect imply she is alert to danger. The large elliptical base is embossed with two fighting stags, heads lowered and antlers interlocked. The doe is wise to be alert.

Maker unknown. Known to us only in opaque white. Height overall 8 5/8". Base measures 4" by 2 3/4". Very rare.

93 - DOG ON BIRD PANELED BASE COVERED DISH

For such a relatively diminutive piece, this has a great deal of intricate detail. The dog looks much like others that adorn the lids of covered dishes — Vallerysthal's dog on a flowered base, for example. The embellishments on the base of this piece, however, give it a most distinctive appeal. Framed within a row of ovals that edge the lid and the bottom of the base, the panels of the four sides are embossed with birds in various poses. On the long front panel we see two birds facing each other, and on the back panel a mother bird with babies. On the short sides, a bird in a nest fills one panel and birds in flight appear on the other. The inside of the base has raised slats for use, perhaps, as a soap dish. The glass is of top quality, almost translucent in some portions.

Marked "S V," this is yet another of the pieces shown often in this book bearing the same letters which we have not been able to track down. Known to us only in white. Length 4 1/2"; width 2 7/8". Rare.

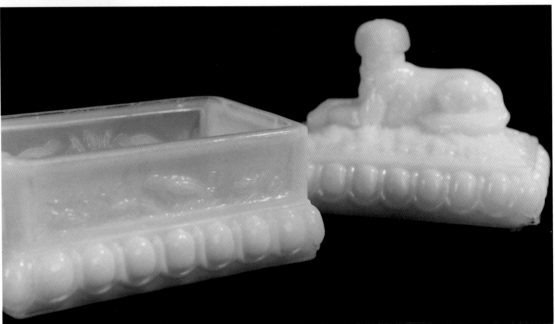

94 - DOG-ON-CUSHION ON WICKER BASKET COVERED DISH

The finial for this box-shaped covered dish is an alert little dog resting on a cushion. The remainder of the cover and the entire base is a tightly woven wicker design, austerely plain, except for small handles moulded on each end. A very attractive piece, although the proportions of the dog in relation to the basket are somewhat equivocal.

Signed Vallerysthal, it is shown in SW (p. 8, next to bottom row). It bears only a very slight resemblance to the better known Dog-on-Rug on Flower base (shown in N-126).

Known to us in white and caramel. Length 4 1/4"; width 3". Very scarce.

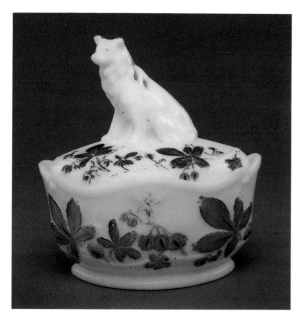

95 - WOLF-DOG COVERED DISH

Somewhat bulging in the middle, this oddly shaped oval dish has a large, alert dog or wolf on the cover. Resting on its hind legs, and looking intently at something in the distance, he appears ready for action. Strawberries and leaves are embossed on the surface in front of the animal, but the back portion is smooth. In like manner, the base has a pattern of vegetation in front and no design on the back. The bottom of the base is perfectly elliptical with a deep marginal rim. The glass varies from pure milk white to translucent opalescence.

Maker unknown. The peculiar design and mould work suggest it is probably fairly recent. Known to us only in white and opalescent. Length 4"; width 2 7/8". Scarce.

96 - SPANIEL DOG COVERED DISH

This attractive, nicely designed spaniel, extending the full length of the cover, has its head turned to face us. The great ears lie flat beside its head and extend well below its muzzle. The dog rests on a surface that appears to be a mass of straw or heavily textured fabric. The base has the scalloped top and basket weave pattern commonly used by L.G. Wright for its animal covered dishes.

This piece is an enigma. Many of Wright's animal covered dishes, recognized as reproductions, can be traced back to their originals, but the origin of this spaniel is unknown. It is illustrated in clear green glass in Cook's "L. G. Wright Covered Animal Dishes" (GCD, Oct/Nov 1991, p.32), with the comment "the dog is unique as far as I can determine." Measell and Roettels list it as Wright's No. 80-4, noting that it was first introduced in January 1991 in black glass — "the first time this color was offered by Wright" (p. 48) — but they do not illustrate it nor do they shed any light on its origin.

In opaque glass, it is known to us in clear green and black. Length 5 1/2". If it isn't already, it soon will be quite hard to find.

97 - SETTER DOG COVERED DISH

This engaging piece manages to capture the hunter's faithful companion in a moment of rest but with head erect, alert to the coming chase. The rectangular shape is greatly softened by the many projecting leaves and flowers exquisitely moulded on both the cover and the sides of the base. Four square projections, one at each corner, elevate the base slightly. The dog is especially well detailed and meticulously rendered even to having the paw of its hidden right hind leg protrude from beneath its body. On the leafy mound of the cover, the setter's left paw rests on the barrel of a long rifle, and the hunter's meshed game pouch lies nearby. Deservedly, a covered dish much admired and sought after.

Shown in an excellent full page picture by Belknap (plate 159), but incorrectly attributed to Flaccus. Made by Vallerysthal, sometimes signed or faintly etched "Made in France" inside the base. Illustrated in SW, p. 4; VC (1907) p. 234; and VC (1908) p.304 where it appears with a group of other sugar containers.

Known in opaque white and blue , as well as amber and a light amethyst. About 6" long, 4" wide, and 5 3/4" high overall. Scarce.

98 - DUCK ON OVOID BASKET WEAVE BASE

Unlike many of the animal covered dishes whose bases are perfectly oval or round, this duck sits on a base that tapers like an egg at one end to conform with the shape of the duck's body. The basket weave pattern is traditional, with three vertical strands interlaced by two horizontal ones, although the braided scalloped rim is unusually large and prominent. The duck is well proportioned — head erect and straight ahead, bill realistically formed, and feathers nicely detailed. Among the many other duck covered dishes, this one is quite distinctive.

Embossed S V inside the cover. We have found it only in white milk glass. Length 5"; height 4 1/2". Very scarce.

Reproduction note: An obvious copy of the duck on ovoid base is the "Duck on Basket" shown, alongside the original, in black with a white head. The copy resembles the original remarkably well, with good mould definition. The main difference is the configuration of the duck's head, which appears to be deformed. The bill sags down and the elongated head has a deep depression on both sides, just behind the eyes. Although these imperfections might appear to be the result of poor pressing or an annealing problem with just this particular specimen, we see exactly the same deformity in the duck which is illustrated in the company's own catalog.

Marked "M" inside the base, it is shown as #187 "Duck on Basket" in a 1985 catalog of Mosser Glass, Inc., Cambridge, Ohio.

Known to us in black (amethyst) with white head, crystal, clear blue, custard, blue milk glass, and green slag. Length 5"; height 4 3/8". Somewhat hard to find.

99 - DUCK ON MARINE BASE COVERED DISH

With its well-formed head pointing straight ahead and its tail turned up, this duck floats along blissfully. The ends of the wings join together to form a dapper little peak just above the tail. Particular care appears to have been taken in matching the top to the base, as the fine ribs circling the edge of the cover correspond to identical ribbing around the top edge of the base. The base itself is unique in creating a nautical motif. Water lilies and rushes cover the sides, while the underside is virtually a pond teaming with life — a large fish, frog, and crayfish all swimming in water moulded to simulate bubbles.

Made by the Central Glass Co., it appears as "Etched Duck No. 727" in a late 1800s catalog page, reprinted in Revi (p. 115). Shown in F-79 in opaque blue as "Duck on Cattail Base" (though there are no cattails in it) and said to occur only in blue. It has been found, however, in opaque white as well, and most commonly in clear frosted. Length of top, tip of bill to tip of tail, 7 1/4"; width 4 3/4". Length of base 7 1/8"; width 5 3/8". Rare in opaque blue and white, somewhat hard to find in clear frosted.

Note: There is a somewhat smaller variant, possibly the precursor of the Central Glass version, with fine detail and known only in blue. The top measures 6 1/2" long and 3 7/8" wide; the base is 6" long and 4 1/4" wide. It is rare.

100 - DUCK ON SINGLE STRAND BASKET WEAVE OVAL BASE

Appearing sedate and contented, this cute mother duck is nonetheless wide-eyed as she guards four large eggs placed symmetrically, two on each side. Extraordinary attention has been paid to the feathering, which is artfully configured by intricate curves and swirls, not at all like the feathers of any real ducks we've ever seen. A wide rim on the underside of the cover rests on the narrow ledge of the oval base, and none too securely we should add. The broad scalloped flange has a two-strand braid design underneath. The sides consist of closely placed horizontal single strands crossed by widely spaced vertical ones. The underside of the base has the same basket weave in a concentric pattern, and a central oval filled with four strands running lengthwise.

Maker unknown, but presumed not to be of American origin. Known to us in opaque white and blue. Length 4"; height about 2 3/4". Very scarce.

101 - DUCK SAUCE BOAT WITH LADLE

A truly exceptional creation, this sauce boat does not merely provide a notched lid for the insertion of a spoon or ladle but instead has a completely open end. How a piece such as this avoids being broken is a marvel because the cover simply rests on the base with nothing to keep it from sliding off. The glass, bearing traces of green paint on the feathers and gilt on the beak, is of fine quality and the bird's features well delineated.

Maker unknown. Known to us only in white. Height 5"; length from tip of tail to beak 5 1/4"; overall length 5 7/8". Rare.

102 - SEA GULL COVERED DISH

With its head snugly resting against its body, this plump sea gull looks as contented as it can be. The body is well proportioned and the feather detail is exceptional. The slightly scalloped flange on the base is plain on the upper surface but the underside is ridged with wavy lines. Above the flange, the sides of the base have a brick work design surmounted by a plain wide band.

Maker unknown, but believed to be European. Most collectors will see some resemblance to L. G. Wright's 5" Duck (#80-5) whose mould we are told was made by Botson in 1961 (see M-R, p. 75). Despite the slight similarity, there are too many significant differences between them for the one pictured here to be considered the prototype for the Wright duck.

Known to us only in white. Length from tail to beak 6 3/4"; base alone 5 1/4". Very scarce.

103 - SWIMMING DUCK COVERED DISH (Large and Small)

Most collectors who are aware of Vallerysthal's 5" "swimming duck" believe that it was also made in a larger size. In fact, there is indeed a slightly larger version, but it is a very different canard. The difference, readily seen in the photo, is in the position of the small duck's head which, unlike the larger one, tilts upward markedly, and in the bill of the larger duck, which is very broad and flat. While both ducks have excellent feather detail, the feet of the larger one are more distinct.

Sometimes found embossed "Vallerysthal" inside the base, the large one is shown in SW (p. 2 in three different decorations), and VC (1907, p. 236, No. 3802). The smaller one, in four decorations, is shown in VCC (p. 305, No. 3771). See also, F-17; N-127, 131.

We know the larger size only in white; the smaller is found in many opaque and transparent colors as well.

Large Duck: maximum length from tip of bill to tip of tail is 6 3/8"; width of top 3 3/8"; length of base opening 5".

Small Duck: maximum length from tip of bill to tip of tail is 5 1/2"; width of top 2 3/4"; length of base opening 4 1/2".

The large duck is much harder to find than the small one, which appears to have been made over a longer period of time. A notable example of the newer issues, some bearing an "OPALE VERITABLE," gold paper sticker is shown in N-127.

104 - FOX ON LOGS

While it may be just as appropriate to regard this animal as an alert little dog, we prefer to view it as a wary Red Fox, preparing to flee from his refuge atop a log house structure if discovered before he invades the coop. The whole piece conveys an intriguing light tension counterpoised by an intelligent self-confidence. .

Maker unknown. Known to us only in white. Length 6"; width at bottom of base 3 3/4"; width at top of base 2 3/4"; height overall 6". Very rare.

105 - SANDWICH HEN COVERED DISH

Among the many hen covered dishes, this one is incomparable, especially for the hen's unusually long neck and distinct differentiation of the upper and lower parts of the beak. Equally striking is the configuration of the cover. The hen itself sits on a straw-lined surface whose irregularly flanged edge extends out and over the base, a dramatic departure from the more usual placement of a flange on the base element. The hen's tail, rising straight up and rounded on top, has five asymmetrical ridges at the back. The base too, is exceptional. Much like the pattern of the Heart and Scale Creamer (No. 332 in this book), the side of the base consists of thirty panels, each having five draped loops separated by double grooved vertical stripes. The pattern on the underside of the base is twelve rows of square raised blocks, eight blocks across at the widest point.

This is yet another example of the extraordinary beauty and exceptional designs of many Sandwich glass pieces. The hen is illustrated on the dust cover of *Victorian Glass* by Ruth Webb Lee who notes that fragments have been excavated at the Sandwich site, attesting to its having been made in jade green, a translucent white, yellow, translucent blue, clear, clear blue, and translucent green. Barlow & Kaiser (fig. 3253) date the hen between 1850-1870 and say it was made in opaque white, clambroth, clear, canary, green, and several shades of blue.

Dimensions (as given by Barlow and Kaisers) are: Top: 4" high, 8" long, 5 1/4" wide. Base: 1 7/8" high, 7 3/4" long, 5 1/4" wide.

Extremely rare in any color. The price guide for this hen in Barlow & Kaiser ranges from $750 (in clambroth) to $2,800 (in green). One in yellow sold at auction in 1997 for $5,000.

106 - VALLERYSTHAL 3 1/2" HEN COVERED DISH

This little hen is about one inch larger than the more familiar, ubiquitous small "hen salts" made by many different companies. There are no eggs along the hen's body, and the solid tail, rounded at the top, looks like the dorsal fin of a fish! The head, turned very slightly to the left, has a very small wattle in contrast to its prominent comb that rises straight up and is pinpoint sharp at the top. The base has a single-braid scalloped rim and a pattern of interlaced single horizontal and vertical strands around the sides. The underside of the base is a basket weave design with five long strands at the center. A slight variant is found in which the base is separated into two sections by a glass divider. In all other respects, however, they are identical.

Made by Vallerysthal, this hen is often signed, and sometimes also found impressed or lightly etched "Made in France." It should be noted that the hen illustrated in F-225 and identified as a Westmoreland product appears to us to be this 3 1/2" French hen. Westmoreland's version is totally different, having a much thicker neck, a head turned sharply to the right, a huge wattle, and a divided, very pointed tail. There is no danger of a "marriage" because these hen tops do not fit well on each other's bases.

Known to us in white, blue, and green milk glass. We have also examined a lavender piece embossed "Vallerysthal" on the inside of the base.

Top: 3" by 2", and 2" high to top of comb, 1 3/4" to top of tail. Base: 3 1/2" by 2 1/2" and 1 1/4" deep. Hard to find in white or blue, more so in green.

107 - "S V" LARGE HEN COVERED DISHES

When painted, these are certainly among the most beautiful of the hen covered dishes and can easily be mistaken for Staffordshire pieces. The surface inside the sharply cocked divided tail is completely covered with long irregular grooves; the finely moulded tail feathers come to a smooth, slightly convex end at the top; and the customary eggs are large and shiny with the slightly smaller ones up front. A band of heavy double braids, just below the scalloped rim, protrudes slightly around the top of the base whose basket weave is two horizontal strands interlaced by three vertical ones.

Embossed "S V" inside the top. Three examples are shown here, two of which, with different coloring, resemble Staffordshire hen decoration. One also bears an imprinted red mark indicating a dealer in "Marseille" France. The third example in black milk glass differs only in having an embossed number "1" below the letters "S V" inside the cover, and two cleat-like bars intersecting the central stripes on the underside of the base instead of only a single bar. For a full description of this hen, comparing it with the Vallerysthal hen of the same size, see Lloyd, O.N., X:3, June 1995, pp. 10-11.

Known to us in plain white, white painted as shown, and black. Top: 7 1/2" by 5 3/4" and 4 3/4" high to top of head, 5 1/8" to top of tail. Base: 8" by 6 3/8" and 2 3/4" high. All are rare.

Note: We have examined a smaller (7") hen which is identical to the larger ones described above, but bearing a number "2" embossed below the letters "S V" inside the lid. This hen cover, incidentally, will not fit on the base of any signed Vallerysthal 7" hens.

108 - QUAIL PIE COVERED DISH

A choice item for any collection, the name given to this covered dish may relate to the pie it was meant to contain rather than the bird on the cover. It appears to be a hen, though an uncommon one. It lacks a wattle, has a short stubby tail, and its body feathers look like the chained links of a coat-of-mail. Set on a domed lid lightly incised with flowers and leaves, the hen's outstretched wings protect nine little chicks huddled all around her body. The design of the 3" high base is quite elaborate, combining a variety of different basket weave patterns. Starting at the top is a 1/2" row of looped arches; next is a discrete 1/2" braided band; then comes the main portion, a 1 1/2" band of single interwoven strands; finally, around the bottom 1/2" are four rope-like cords. The underside of the base is more typical, consisting of multiple rings of double interwoven strands with twelve vertical bands at the center. We try to use the word sparingly, but this item is nothing less than magnificent.

Previously unlisted and unidentified, it has only recently been discovered in an early undated

(circa 1880s) catalog page, reprinted by C. W. Gorham, *Riverside Glass Works* (1995), plate l, p. 5. A discussion of the probable earthenware origin for the design of this dish may be found in O.N., XI:3, June 1996, p. 17.

Known to us in white and camphor (clear frosted) glass. Base diameter 7 1/8"; height overall 6 3/4". Rare.

109 - HEN ON FISH SCALE BASE COVERED DISH

The way the lid and base of this hen dish come together is most unusual. The top has a broad edge matching a similar one on the upper rim of the base, so the two pieces fit together by flanges sliding between one another inside the wide margins. The pattern on the sides of the base looks like fish scales pointing upward and arranged in seven horizontal rows. Rectangular panels, one at the front of the base and one in back, bear a long stemmed rose, three leaves, and two rosebuds. On the underside, twenty-four pointed rays extend from the center to the outer rim

Maker unknown. Known to us only in opaque white and the blue shown here. Length overall 5 3/4"; width 4 1/2"; height 5 3/8". Rare.

110 - HEN ON A WHEAT BASE COVERED DISH

Previously unlisted, this hen is as striking as any you may encounter. The gawking head turns left and is remarkable in having almost human eyes, bulging cheeks, faint ear lobes, gangly wattles, and a comb that looks like a malignant outgrowth. The hackle is finely detailed and quite attractive, as are the main tail feathers. When viewed from behind, the divided tail is ovoid, much like peering through a Gothic cathedral archway. The cover, made from a three-part mould, is also unusual in having only one egg on each side up front, rather than the customary two, and one on each side at the tail end. The base has four mould marks, one on each side and one at both ends. Topped by a roped border, the sides of the base are embossed with spikes of wheat set within five panels separated by vertical rope-like lines. A pattern of converging rays is found on the underside.

The maker of this remarkable hen is unknown, but it appears to be European, dating from the late 1800s. Known to us only in opaque white. It measures 5 1/4" long, 4" wide, 2" deep, and 4 1/8" high to the top of the comb. Very rare.

111 - TWIN HEN SALT COVERED DISH

This twin hen salt is much less common than the many single hen versions made by a great number of companies over many years. Most of them are quite similar, with differences occurring mainly in the designs of the bases, a variety of basket weaves being the most prevalent type. The pattern on the sides of this base is of a series of fine vertical ribs. The underside has been found with either a perfectly plain surface or an overall basket weave design. The double base is joined by a handle moulded as a plume, both on the upper and lower surface.

This twin hen salt, together with the Lizard on Strawberry (No. 128 in this book), was advertised in 1903 by the German firm "Gebrüder von Streit, Moulded Glass Works, Berlin S.W. Alexandrinen-Strasse 22" who featured "Always Novelties" for "Home Trade and Export." For a full discussion of this and related hens on ribbed bases, see O.N., XII:4, Sept. 1997, pp. 14-17.

We know it in all blue, all white, and in white tops with a blue base. Length 3 3/8", width 4 1/4". Rare.

112 - HENS ON BULGING RIM BASE COVERED DISHES

These hens are named for the distinctive rim of the base which has a smooth top and bulging double braids around the sides. The hens have elliptical, moulded eyes, short thick bills, and a smooth area on the back of the neck. The feather detail is good. The lower half of the divided tail has distinct coarse lines. The basket weave pattern is of two horizontal and three vertical strands.

Maker unknown. Various students have assigned these hens either to Atterbury or Challinor, Taylor, but to our knowledge a positive attribution has not been made. Shown by Belknap in black milk glass (B-149a).

They are found in a surprising variety of color combinations. Besides all white and all black, these hens are known to us in white with a black head, black with a white head (shown here), white with both head and tail in black, and white with a cased blue head. The hens measure 5 1/4" long. None is easy to find and some colors are rare.

Note on variant forms: Virtually identical hens, one of which is shown here in milk white, have affixed glass eyes (usually red) instead of eyes moulded directly in the glass. In addition to white, we have seen them in green slag. The rim around the cover of these glass-eyed hens is convex rather than flat. Another variation occurs in which the bulging rim of the base is scalloped. This variant is known to us in white with an amber cased head and white with a blue cased head.

113 - HEN COVERED DISH

A relatively recent barnyard occupant, this hen on a diamond basket weave base is included because it has had little if any mention in the standard milk glass literature and is sometimes mistaken for the similar and much more familiar Westmoreland version. Moreover, it seems to us this hen, with only very minor modifications, resembles the one made by Kemple most of whose moulds were sold to Wheaton and perhaps to other companies after John Kemple's death in 1970. Some elements of the cover, such as the size of the eggs, the configuration of the tail, head, and beak, for example, may seem to differ somewhat from Kemple's, but these differences are due largely to an excessive amount of glass poured into the mould (this hen weighs at least three pounds!) and consequent weak pressing. A large, prominently rimmed circle, sometimes with a K in the center, found on the underside of the Kemple base may still be discerned on this piece, a mere vestige of the large circle but enough to give a clue to its probable Kemple origin.

Made by Kanawha Glass Company of Dunbar, West Virginia, number 905 in their catalogs of the 1970s, followed by either the letters M (for milk glass) or ED (for End of Day).

As noted, made in milk white and in variegated color combinations of green, orange, blue, and yellow. Across the base it measures 7 1/4". Although fairly recent, somewhat hard to find.

114 - HEN ON FLARED BASE WITH ARCHES COVERED DISH

The unusual base for this hen has a scalloped rim, flaring out almost a full inch, with a pattern on both the top and underside consisting of overlapping half circles that look like a series of McDonald's arches. The basket weave base consists of single, horizontal "bubble strands" crossed by two short, narrow vertical ones. The mould work of the hen itself is crisp, with good detail. The feathers are well defined; its large bill is almost like a parrot's; and its eyes are moulded as an ellipse. On each side we find the customary two eggs forward and one behind, but all the eggs are somewhat larger than usual. The inside of the tail has a crisscross triangular design near the bottom, while most of the upper part is a long "V."

Maker unknown. Possibly French, but we have no proof. A slight variant of this hen is found in a more opalescent, almost clambroth glass. For a full discussion, see Morin, "Hens With No Names." O.N., XI:2, March 1996, pp. 5-8.

Known to us only in white. It is about 6 3/4" long. Very scarce.

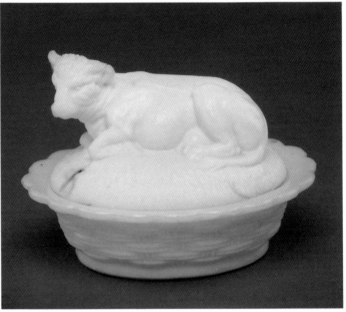

115 - HEN ON FLARED BASE COVERED DISH

This hen resembles the 6" Vallerysthal hen but is set on a base whose rim is scalloped and flares out, with a smooth upper surface and a conventional double strand braid underneath. The basket weave sides consist of two horizontal and three vertical strands. The hen has fairly good feather detail. The area inside the divided tail is coarsely and irregularly striate in a basal triangle, and the rest of the area is an acute "V".

Maker unknown. This hen appears to be part of a series, all on the same base, and includes a cow (shown here), a pigeon, a duck, and a horse. The hen looks a bit like the smaller hen shown by Wills, p. 15. An English attribution is often given for this hen, but we have no positive confirmation.

Known to us only in white. It is 6" long. Hard to find.

Reproduction note: The cow on the tub base has been reproduced, probably in Taiwan, in several opaque colors, including blue and purple slag, as well as in clear and transparent colors. A.A. Import Co., in Catalogue #56 (item PG1641), offers it in "pink depression" glass.

116 - HEN COVERED DISH

This small hen covered dish, made from a three-part mould, has the characteristic basket weave base, two horizontal strands interlacing three vertical ones, and a braided scalloped top. The underside of the base carries through the basket weaving in the typical fashion. Resting on a straw lined ground, the hen turns its head very slightly to the right. The large comb, sharp beak, and oval eyes are accented in the painted example shown here. Four eggs, one in front and one at the tail end on each side, are perfectly round and quite prominent. Except for the neck area, which is only faintly feathered, the feathers of the body and the divided tail are well detailed.

Embossed "S V" both inside the cover and the base. Known to us only in white, but may occur in other colors. Length 3 5/8"; height 3 1/2". Very scarce.

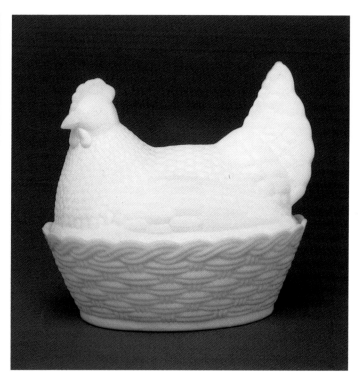

117 - LARGE HEN AND ROOSTER COVERED DISHES

These two covered dishes are among the largest to be found. They are readily recognizable by several distinctive features.

The Hen: With two wide braids crossing below the tail feathers, the tail itself is sharply upturned and divided to form a large triangular area filled with a mass of irregular grooves. The beak is extremely small, extending 3/8" at most beyond the lower wattle. The second anterior egg is very large, much larger than the first egg or the one near the base of the tail. The feather detail is excellent and the glass of good quality. The base is unusually deep with a shallow scalloped top and an indistinct double braid around the rim. Known to us in white, clear crystal and amber. Base 8 1/2" by 6 1/2" and about 3" deep. Top 7 5/8" by 6". Height to top of tail 5 3/4", to top of head 5".

The Rooster: Presumed to be the companion to the large hen, this rooster (or partridge?) has a much shorter and narrower tail than its mate, but with the same coarsely striated surface between the tail feathers and two large braids across the base of the tail. The almost perfectly round, bulging head is quite different, however, having a larger, pointed beak and prominent elliptical eyes not very well delineated. A single wavy crest runs along the top of the head. There are no eggs on this cover. Known to us in white and transparent blue, but presumably occurs in other colors. Base 8 1/2" by 6 1/2" and about 3" deep. Top 7 5/8" by 6". Height to top of tail 5", to top of head 4 5/8".

The maker of both is unknown. The hen has been dubbed "the Polish hen" by some collectors who believe it is of eastern European origin. Both are somewhat hard to find.

118 - HEN ON "PLUMED WARRIOR" BASE COVERED DISH

An especially handsome piece, this hen cover rests on a base having a wide, scalloped flange that is smooth on the flaring upper surface but strongly double-braided on the underside. The weave on the sides differs from most others whose design usually employs two or more horizontal strands. This base has single elongated "bubble" strands running lengthwise, intersected by depressed thin ones vertically. The bottom of the base has two parallel rows of eight "bubble" strands much like the ones on the sides but larger. The hen is nicely proportioned, with a cocked tail, rather narrow bill, and well defined feathering. The entire area inside the divided tail is coarsely grooved. A crisscross pattern is moulded around the outermost edge of the cover.

Maker unknown. Many examples do not have any markings, but some are found with a puzzling embossed logotype centered inside the base. As seen in the accompanying sketch, the mark resembles a plumed warrior brandishing a great mace, occasionally somewhat indistinct. We have not been able to identify this trademark which has also been found sometimes in one of the various bases for the Love Birds covered dish (see No. 124 in this book).

This hen is identical to the one illustrated by Belknap (B-145) who dubbed it the "Straight Head Hen," because he says the "hen looks straight ahead rather than at the usual angle," adding further that the hen should be fitted with glass eyes. Both these statements are incorrect, as the head is looking to the left and the eyes are moulded directly in the glass. Many collectors have searched in vain for this "straight ahead hen" which in fact does not exist. For a very detailed discussion of this and other "mystery hens" see "Hens With No Names," by Morin (O.N. XI:2, March 1996, p. 5 ff.)

Known to use in white and blue. Length 6 7/8"; width 5 7/8". Scarce.

Sketch of the unidentified "Plumed Warrior" trademark.

119 - ROOSTER ON OCTAGONAL FLOWERED BASE COVERED DISH

There is a wonderful incongruity, it seems, between the large, somewhat ungainly rooster on the lid and the elegant pattern on the rest of this covered dish which is the essence of femininity. Perhaps the contrast was intentional, giving it a special charm. The rooster's cocked head with short, fat beak, large comb and wattle are in perfect harmony with its enormous tail. The eight panels on the high domed lid are matched with those of the base, each separation emphasized by the arching top edges and by vertical rows of beads between each panel. To complete the contrast, each of the panels is embossed with delicate sprays of flowers.

Maker unknown, but most likely Continental. Known to us only in white. Height 4 1/2"; diameter 4 7/8". Rare.

120 - STANDING ROOSTER COVERED DISHES

These four popular standing roosters are included mainly because when unmarked they may pose identification problems, especially for beginning collectors. Pictured, from left, are the Westmoreland, Portieux, L.E. Smith, and Kanawha roosters.

The Portieux version is the prototype, extremely well reproduced by Westmoreland and very difficult to tell apart if not signed. The top of the Portieux rooster, however, is too large for a "marriage" with a Westmoreland base, although the Westmoreland top will fit — but loosely — on a Portieux base.

Unlike these two look-alike versions which have their left foot placed forward, the legs of the Smith bird are parallel to each other, while the Kanawha version, much larger than any of the others, stands on a cut log. Grist (plate 117) illustrates an import reproduction of the French rooster made in various clear and opaque colors, but easily recognized by the newness and inferior quality of the glass and the mould detail.

All these roosters occur in many opaque colors, including slag, as well as transparent colors. They range in size from 8 1/4" to 10" high.

The French rooster is hard to find; Westmoreland's are generally available in white, but scarce to rare with painted decoration or in unusual colors. The Smith and Kanawha versions are now becoming somewhat hard to find.

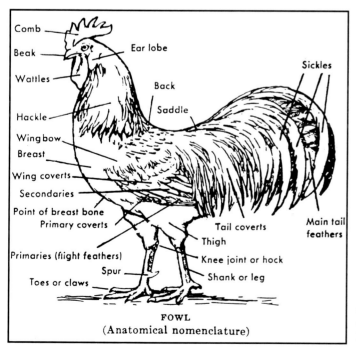

FOWL
(Anatomical nomenclature)

Naming the fowl's parts (for city slickers only) from the *Standard College Dictionary*, Harcourt, Brace & World, 1963, p. 527.

121 - VALLERYSTHAL BREAKFAST SET

Although well known, these attractive, eleven-piece egg servers merit inclusion, especially for their well-preserved cold painted decoration. The large oval tray, notched at one end so that it almost appears heart shaped, has a scalloped rim and rests on three knobbed feet. A woven crisscross pattern covers the surface of the tray, interrupted by six equidistant round depressions with rope borders to accommodate the egg cups. A seventh indentation at the front of the tray is for the two-handled covered basket salt. At the center, the familiar Vallerysthal hen also fits, more or less securely, within a rope edged oval depression. The appealing egg cups are fashioned with the birds' wings extending up each side, as if to support the egg receiver.

Made by Vallerysthal, with most if not all of the pieces in the set signed. It dates from the late 1800s and was continued through the turn of the century, but curiously the set as a whole is not illustrated in any known catalog. The hen itself, the bird egg cups, and the little basket salts, however, are individually shown in several catalogs.

We know it in white and blue milk glass and in clear amber. Tray is about 12" by 10"; egg cups 2 5/8" high; basket salt 2 3/4" in diameter. Scarce in any color, and finding the complete set, without missing egg cups or basket salt, is quite difficult.

122 - MUSTERSCHUTZ BREAKFAST SET

The design of this outstanding hen and egg cup breakfast set is truly unrivaled. The large beaked hen has a nicely moulded wattle and comb, and well-defined neck feathers, all of which are enhanced by the lavish application of burnished gold paint. The large flange of the base has a braided edge and six round slots for the stemmed egg cups, each fitted with a little chick emerging from the cracked shell. On the sides of the base is a basket weave pattern of two long horizontal strands and three short vertical ones. Its early vintage is especially evident in the web of fine hairlines visible throughout the inner surface of both top and base.

The set is profusely marked by the maker, German we assume, about whom we have been unable to find any information. The base is marked "Musterschutz No. 1391." The chick covers are marked "Musterschutz No. 1393," and the cups are marked "Musterschutz No. 1392."

We know it only as shown. Length of hen top 8 1/4", length of base 11 1/2". Height of chick egg cups 4". Extremely rare.

123 - NESTING BIRD COVERED DISH

For sheer artistry, this piece is certainly extraordinary. The conception is of a nesting bird, its wings spread out to cover its eggs, some of which protrude beyond the wings. Below its breast two of the eggs have already hatched and the little fledglings await feeding time. The bird rests on a mass of straw and leaves which fill the remaining surface of the cover. The base is fashioned as the nest itself, composed of coarser twigs and branches, three of which entwine to form leg supports. This piece invites comparison with two other similar and better known covered dishes — the Robin on Nest (F-40) which, incidentally, should not be attributed to Greentown, and the Robin on Pedestal Base (F-3).

Maker unknown, but an early piece and most likely European. Known to us only in white. Overall height 5". Rare.

124 - LOVE BIRDS COVERED DISH

These love birds are best known to collectors in a reproduction made by the Westmoreland Glass Company beginning in the early 1950s. The one shown here is believed to be the prototype, at least in regard to the cover itself. The flared basket weave base, however, is only one of several variants on which the love birds have been found. For a detailed examination and illustrations of all the different versions, see the article by Scott in GCD, IX:4, Dec/Jan 1996, pp. 82-86.

Maker unknown, but believed to be European. The base of the love birds pictured here is identical to the base of the "Plumed Warrior" hen covered dish, shown and discussed more fully in No. 118 of this book.

We know it in white and blue. The base measures 6 7/8" by 5 7/8". Very scarce.

125 - EGG BONBON DISH

A mammoth upright egg set in a wicker basket and topped by a plump, finely detailed short-tailed hen sitting on a straw nest with three small eggs. Most unusual, the smooth egg is embossed in flowing script "Bon bons John Tavernier." The basket is deeply constricted in the middle (2 1/8" from the base) and has a raised crisscross pattern with a braided top and bottom edge. The top portion of the piece fits over a tin insert, presumably removable originally to allow candy to be placed inside. The bottom is concave and embossed "Depose."

Maker unknown, but a French origin seems reasonable.

Known to us only in white. Height overall 12". The hen and her straw emblem measure 2 3/4" and the rest of the 4" top is the upper half of the large egg. Scarce, possibly rare.

126 - BIRD EMERGING FROM EGG COVERED DISH

With its little wings spread out, the fledgling bird breaking through the enormous egg looks like he is about to take flight. It is difficult to appreciate from the photograph alone what exquisite care has been given to moulding the bird whose features are all nicely detailed. The two-part egg has a stippled surface and rests on a low-rising, scalloped base.

It is signed "S V." The resemblance of this piece to known Portieux and Vallerysthal egg covered dishes with different animals as finials is apparent. We know it in blue and green, but it most likely occurs in white and possibly other colors. Length 4 5/8". Rare.

127 - LION ON AN OVAL BASE COVERED DISH

This elegant covered dish is a marvel of classic lines and understated intricacy. The cover is a warm amber glass perfectly mated to the creamy custard base. The lion's massive head is beautifully detailed, as is the rest of its body. A series of rings is moulded all around the central band of the oval base, with a wide, bulging rim above and a slightly flaring bottom. The deeply recessed underside of the base has a crosshatch pattern.

Maker unknown, but almost certainly of foreign manufacture, possibly English. We know it only in the colors as shown. Height overall 5 1/2"; length of base 6 3/4", width 4 1/2", depth 2 1/2". Rare.

128 - LIZARD ON STRAWBERRY

The body of a large lizard, sometimes incorrectly called a salamander, dominates the cover of this dish modeled as a strawberry which divides just below the creature's hind legs. Serving as the finial, its realistic head is deftly moulded and rises almost a full inch above the berry. The lizard's long tail moves sinuously across the side of the base, then curves back before tapering at the end. Tri-foliate strawberry leaves extending above and below the dividing line are moulded in high relief on either side. Eight petaled feet elevate the base about 1/2". Some examples have been found with a notched cover for the insertion of a spoon.

It is illustrated in a 1903 advertisement for a German glass company, Gebrüder von Streit, Moulded Glass Works, Berlin S. W. Alexandrinen-Strasse 22, reprinted in Notley who considers it "a bizarre curiosity" (p. 18). The similarity is obvious between this piece and the French Snail on Strawberry, treated in a "Special Feature Article" in this book. The von Streit brothers advertised for "Home Trade and Export" and may have been wholesale distributors of glass made by other firms as well, but we have found no evidence to suggest a French origin for this piece.

Known to us only in white. Height about 5 3/4", maximum width 4". Very scarce, perhaps even rare.

129 - RABBIT WITH EGGS ON ARCHES BASE

Collectors of animal covered dishes will immediately recognize this base whose sides are formed as overlapping triple arches, because it is the same design used by Fenton for its 5 1/2" hen covered dish. Others will be reminded of the 7" Rabbit with Eggs made by Westmoreland. Although the rabbit cover shown here is smaller, it is nonetheless identical to Westmoreland's larger version in all respects — the ears laid back, the body slightly hunched, the eyes with a small dot indentation to mark the pupil, a round bushy tail, four eggs on each side, the straw or grass design around the animals, and even the striated surface on the underside of the rim — every detail is the same.

Maker unknown. In her article "Turkeys and Rabbits" (GCD, IV:2, Aug/Sept 1990, p. 24), Anne Cook discusses both the large and the small rabbits, and illustrates them in clear glass She also reprints a page from an 1898 U.S. Glass catalog which shows the large rabbit on a typical Challinor-type basket weave base, together with other Challinor animal dishes — the rooster, hen, turkey, and "Wavy Base Duck." It seems fairly certain that Westmoreland's large rabbit with eggs is in fact a copy of the one shown in the U.S. Glass Catalog and may originate with Challinor. We have not been able to trace the origin of the triple arch base of the smaller version, but there is no doubt that it is old. According to a letter written to Francis Price (cited by Cook, p. 24), when Fenton found an old hen on this distinctive base he liked it so well that he decided to create a new mould and reproduce it..

We find it hard to explain why the small rabbit with eggs has not previously been shown in any of the published milk glass literature. Perhaps it is because this rabbit, like its companion hen on the same base, is found more often in clear crystal rather than milk glass. The opaque one shown here is a creamy ivory or light custard color, and the glass is a bit more translucent than may appear in the photograph.

Length 5 1/5". Scarce in clear glass, possibly rare in opaque.

130 - CROUCHING RABBIT

With large ears laid back, this good-looking fellow bears obvious similarities to the Atterbury rabbits whose top and bottom together form the full figure. The posture of the head resting on its legs and its eyes warily cast upward suggest he is hiding rather than preparing to hop away. A crescent mould seam, faintly visible between the ear tips, is the only breach in the mass of fine, almost angora-like hair covering the entire body.

Embossed "Portieux" inside the base, and illustrated in PC (p. 66, No. 978). Belknap (p. 191) states that the Atterbury rabbit was made in three sizes (large, medium, and small), but no collector to our knowledge has seen more than two sizes. Some veteran collectors surmise that Belknap may have confused this French Rabbit as the third size, but actually it is about the same size as the small Atterbury rabbit. An inferior reproduction, probably made in Taiwan, has been found in purple slag.

Known to us in opaque white, blue, and French pink opaline. Maximum length 7"; width 3"; height 3 1/2". Hard to find to Scarce.

131 - LOP EARED RABBIT COVERED DISH

In contrast to the Crouching Rabbit, this one with long ears lying flat against its body appears ready to speed away. The fur detail is well defined. The underside of the base is slightly raised by a broad marginal rim.

Illustrated in VCC (p. 304, No. 3772) as a sugar. See also R.W. Lee, "Antiques Journal," July 1951, p. 19, Plate III. Our example is embossed "Vallerysthal" inside the base.

Known to us in opaque white and blue as well as clear frosted glass. Approximately 6 1/2" long and 3" high to the top of the head. Scarce.

132 - CAMBRIDGE STUBBY RABBIT

This crouching, fat rabbit is adorable, with its long ears laid back and extending to just above its hind legs, large moulded eyes, and plump cheeks. The fur detail is weak, with just a few strands evident at the top and around the legs. The bottom of the base is absolutely flat except for the pads and toes of the feet which are well defined.

Garmon and Spencer (p.14) attribute it to the Cambridge Glass Co., stating that it was made in a 7" size also and produced at two different periods. The older style is the one shown and discussed here.

Known to us in black and reported by Garmon and Spencer in crystal, "Peach Blow," and "perhaps other colors." Length 5 1/2"; width 3 1/2". Approximately 3 3/4" high. Scarce in any color, and very scarce in black.

133 - RABBIT EMERGING FROM SIDE OF VERTICAL EGG COVERED DISH

Most collectors might agree that this is surely among the very finest of the varied and large number of Easter Egg novelties made to delight young and old alike. The mould work is outstanding, with deliberate care given to delineating the rabbit's features and to its coat of fur which is meticulously detailed. The laid back long ears are akimbo, the right one bent slightly down while the left sweeps upward. A striking sense of animation is achieved not only by the posture of the head and ears, but by the two front feet pressing hard against the side of the egg as though trying to propel the body forward. The egg, which divides just below the rabbit's feet, rests in a straw nest supported by three legs formed as masses of thick twigs. The piece illustrated is fortunately well-preserved in the hand painted decoration of gold and varying shades of blue and green which enlivens the slightly off-white satin glass.

Maker unknown, but possibly Mt. Washington, perhaps Gillinder. A companion piece with a chick emerging is also known. See Cook, GCD, April/May 1992, p. 23.

Known to us only in opaque white. About 5" high, 3 1/4" in diameter. Rare.

134 - RABBIT ON AKRO AGATE BASE

Perhaps it is the extreme height of the base that lends a certain grandeur to this rabbit, who fills almost the entire length of the cover. In size, posture, and in many other features, the animal closely resembles the one on a "picket fence" base made by the Westmoreland Glass Company and may well have served as the prototype for this one. The most notable difference is that this rabbit has slightly shorter ears. The body hair is distinct, especially on the head and ears where it is so finely detailed that it almost rivals the exquisite mould work of the McKee animals. The scalloped edged cover may look like it floats precariously atop the matching scalloped rim of the base, but in fact an inner lip on the cover slips down into the base for a very secure fit.

Shown in T-BG, No. 601. The base is marked with a "B" in a triangle, the number 654, and the words MADE IN U S A. These represent a combination of marks: the "B" is for the Guernsey Glass Company, of Cambridge, Ohio, founded in the late 1960s by Harold Bennett (hence the "B"). He began by making some Cambridge Glass patterns (hence the triangle?) and later produced other pieces as well, mostly small novelties. "Made in U S A" and the number "654" were mould marks once used by Akro Agate for this garden dish. Bennett obviously acquired this mould after Akro's closing in 1951 and put it to use as the base for this rabbit cover without removing the Akro markings. An excellent example of a "factory authorized marriage."

We know it only in black milk glass. Length 6"; height 5 1/2". Despite its young age, this piece is more than hard to find.

137 - ANTELOPE JACK RABBIT COVERED DISH

Among the most appealing of all the Easter Bunnies, this fellow sits completely upright, his front legs folded in front of him and his long, alert ears standing absolutely upright, curving only slightly inward to meet each other before their tips part. It might appear to be all of one piece, but the head and shoulders are a separate unit. Probably designed as a large candy or sugar-coated Easter eggs container. This piece is worthy of a place in any serious milk glass collection.

Advertised in 1900 by Dithridge & Co. in *China, Glass and Lamps*, reprinted in F-393.

Known to us only in white. Height overall 9 1/2"; the ears alone are 2" long! Scarce to rare.

135 - STANDING RABBIT ON FLOWER BASE COVERED DISH

Who can resist this full-figure two-part rabbit, standing tall and imposing, but obviously rapt in deep thought. With his long ears (2 1/2"!) lying flat down his back, his right arm raised with the paw touching his cheek, his left arm resting on his chest, and his wide eyes directed upward toward the heavens, he seems to be pondering the mysteries of the universe. Actually, his universe is no mystery, consisting of the flower rock garden nicely moulded around the base.

Maker unknown. Opaque white, painted in natural colors of green and brown. Height 8". Scarce.

136 - RABBIT ON LACY BASE COVERED DISH

This Imperial Rabbit covered dish is included mainly because of its rarity compared to other Imperial animal dishes. In addition to the absence of eggs on the cover, the Imperial version differs from the similar and more familiar Westmoreland large rabbit covered dish (see N-113) in having a smaller body and large bulbous eyes. Like the Imperial Rooster, the ribbed pattern which circles the cover of the Rabbit is consistent with the design of Atterbury's "Ribbed Fox" and "Ribbed Lion," but there is no documentation assigning either the rooster or rabbit to Atterbury. And though the Imperial Lion carries the Atterbury patent date, no such markings are found on either the rooster or rabbit, which would suggest, therefore, that they were Imperial's own original creations or copies of other firms.

The top of the rabbit is not marked in any way, although the lacy base carries the IG logo on its underside, if it has not been removed by someone trying to pass it off as an antique piece. Imperial assigned it the number 157 and produced it during the 1950s-60s. Made in purple slag, as well as white and white painted. 7 3/4" long across the top of the base. More than scarce.

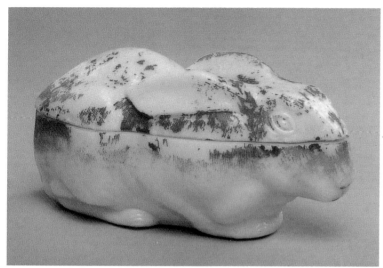

138 - RECLINING RABBIT COVERED DISH

Unlike other full figure rabbit covered dishes that usually divide at the level of the mouth or nose, this example separates just below the eyes, so the base contains the full mouth and nose with well-defined nostrils and whiskers. The details of the legs are not as well moulded, appearing only as four indistinct toes on each foot. The entire body is finely striated to simulate fur. The underside of the base is smooth with an indentation shaped like a bowling tenpin.

Unmarked, this piece may be attributed to the Henner Glassworks of Germany, dating to the 1920s, according to Mary Van Pelt who supplies a sketch of it in her book *Figurines in Glass* (privately printed, copyright 1975, p. 24).

We know it in white and the custard color shown here. Length 7 1/4"; width 3 1/4"; height 3 1/2". Rare.

139 - EASTER RABBIT EMERGING FROM TOP OF EGG COVERED DISH

A delightful piece for any collector, the oversized head of a rabbit emerges from the top of a vertical egg which, though large, seems scarcely large enough to hold the rest of the body. The rabbit's long, upright ears — perfect for lifting the cover — are perky, in contrast to its front legs which rest passively on the jagged top of the cracked egg. One cannot help finding this wide-eyed, fat and contented creature rather droll. The word "Easter" is embossed in large irregular letters on the base which rests on three splayed feet. Circling the top edge, a decorative ribbon, moulded in the glass, forms an oval loop that serves as one foot, then continues to the back where it is tied in a bow, the ends falling down to form the other two feet. This is surely one of the most amusing and desirable of the Easter novelties, probably intended to hold candy eggs.

Maker unknown. Dithridge has been suggested as a likely maker, but needs verification. Illustrated in Cook's "Easter Glass: Mostly Old," GCD, V; 6, April/May 1992, p. 29.

Known to us in white and blue. Height 5 1/4"; diameter of opening 2 3/4"; base diameter 1 3/4". More than hard to find.

140 - RABBITS CUDDLING COVERED DISH

A most engaging covered dish whose cover and base may seem discordant but nonetheless are properly mated. Four arches, one at each end and one on each side, are embossed with fish, curiously out of keeping with the creatures forming the finial, unless we are missing the connection. The flanged rim of the base has a plain upper side, while the ornate underside is moulded with scroll work on a stippled surface. A circle of fleurs-de-lis is centered on the bottom of the base. The cover, with its slightly raised stippled surface and scroll design, continues the motif of the flanged rim of the base, assuring it is a correct match. But instead of fish, we find two cuddling rabbits forming the finial, their heads crossing over and snuggled on each other's back.

Maker unknown. Known to us in white and green. The base is 6 1/4" long, with a 4" opening. Overall height 5 1/4". Rare.

141 - VALLERYSTHAL SWAN COVERED DISH

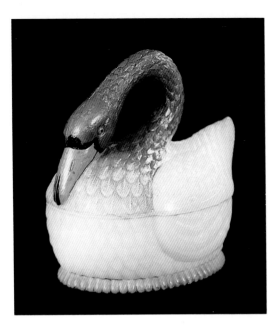

A lovely creation much admired by collectors, this swan with its gracefully curved open neck, head resting on its breast, has been shown previously in other publications. We include it because less well known is the fact that there are at least two variants, differing only in the pattern, or lack of one, on the underside of the base. One of them has a completely smooth indented underside. The other has a design of four embossed flowers, with slanting lines of differing lengths and widths between them. There is also a fruit on the anterior flower. Both variants have been found with and without the name Vallerysthal embossed inside the base.

Illustrated in F-24, N-134, and VCC (p. 307, No. 3803 with four different painted decorations).

Known to us in white, blue, and green, but we have not seen both variants in all colors. The version with embossed flowers on the underside of the base appears to be the older of the two, and it is more frequently found painted. Length 5 3/8", height to top of neck 5 1/2". Hard to find in white. Scarce when painted or in colors.

Note: A reproduction, made in Taiwan from the 1980s, occurs in opaque blue, purple slag, clear crystal, and transparent blue and pink. It is a copy of the Vallerysthal variant with flowers embossed on the underside of the base, but less elaborate and lacking fruits on the anterior flower. The earliest copies were marked with a fake Heisey logo (an "H" inside a diamond).

This reproduction also differs in having a narrower bill, 1/4" wide at tip (1/2" in original); 5/8" wide at base (3/4" in original). The vertical bands around the bottom edge of the base are somewhat longer, 5/8" (only 3/8" in original). The tail is also slightly higher, 2" as against 1 5/8" in the original.

One should note that compared to many Taiwan pieces the feather detail of this reproduction is surprisingly good. These may be the reproductions advertised in the late 1980s by Castle Antiques & Reproductions, Inc., offered in depression glass blue and pink. These swans were also sold — probably from the same Taiwan supplier — by A.A. Import Co. in their 1991 catalog (#56), although some were made at least as early as 1981. A.A. Import Co. advertised them in red (PG16020), blue (PG 16019), pink (PG 16018) and purple slag (PG 1667).

Reproductions readily available.

142 - CERE SWAN COVERED DISH

The name we have assigned to this swan covered dish calls attention to its distinctive "cere" (the fleshy growth at the top of its bill). The ovoid base, continuing the full-figure body of the cover, has a plain underside and a narrow striated bottom edge that elevates the dish about 1/4". The swan's short, blunt tail seems disproportionate compared to the large head and bill. The feathering detail is quite good, if somewhat subdued.

This early piece is shown as #3719 in an 1894 Portieux catalog and is continued in its 1933 catalog as #1006. A full discussion of this swan and a comparison with the better known Vallerysthal swan in the preceding illustration appears in O.N., VI:2, p. 628.

Known in white and blue. Decorated with the head painted gold, it is designated "Cygne #6722" in the 1933 Portieux catalog. One collector reports finding an example with glass eyes, but most likely they were attached by a prior owner, as none of the Portieux or Vallerysthal animal dishes are known to have been designed or intended to have glass eyes affixed. The base measures 5 1/4" by 4 1/8"; the overall height is 5 1/2". More than scarce.

144 - MOUSE ON EGG COVERED DISH

143 - FAN-TAIL PIGEON COVERED DISH

With breast puffed out, wings flaring slightly away from the body, and tail feathers proudly erect, this duck resting comfortably on a bed of straw is a real charmer. The edge of the round base is flanged with eighteen scallops, plain on top and double braided underneath. The basket weave on the sides is a pattern of three vertical and two horizontal strands. On the underside, the pattern is a series of long double strands crossed by very short, but still two stranded stripes.

Maker unknown. Illustrated in L-VG (plate 111) without attribution.

Known to us only in white. Length 5" across the flanged edge of the base. Rare.

A large egg, divided at the middle lengthwise, is supported and elevated by a 1/2" high oval plinth. The entire surface of the egg is deeply stippled. The finial is a large eared mouse crouching atop the egg as if to be hanging on for dear life. The little moulded eyes and feet are about all the detail there is, and the body is perfectly smooth. Curiously, that leaves the mouse's tail as perhaps the most fascinating feature. Curving in a perfect arch, the tail is about 3" long and stands out prominently in high relief on the egg's stippled surface.

Made by Portieux, shown in PC (p. 65, No. 973, designated "Œuf de Pàques"), and apparently not made by Vallerysthal whose egg with a rabbit finial (both in a large and a small size), although similar, does not allow interchange with the Portieux mouse cover.

Known to us in opaque white, blue, a transparent rose colored glass (shown in Grist, plate 67), and possibly in pink opaline. Exactly 5 5/8" long measured across the top of the base; 3 3/4" at the widest part of the egg; 5 1/2" high overall. The mouse finial is about 2 1/2" long *sans* tail. Scarce

145 - MOUSE ON TOADSTOOLS COVERED DISH

This intricately designed piece, a masterful example of fine mould work, is surely one of the most whimsical and amusing of all the French covered dishes. The sides of the tall base are formed as stems with expanded foliate tops of a large cluster of mushrooms. The lid is a continuation of the base, with additional layers of mushroom tops on which a tiny long tailed mouse crouches and appears to be busily eating.

Our example is embossed "Vallerysthal," on the underside of the base. Illustrated in VCC (p. 308, No. 3821); SW (p. 6, next to bottom row); and R.W. Lee, *Antiques Journal*, July 1951, p. 19.

Known to us only in caramel, but probably made in white and other colors. The inner diameter of the base is 3 1/4", the maximum base width across the mushroom tops is 6". The diameter of the mushroom top is approximately 5". Height to top of mouse 4". Bordering on rare.

146 - FROG ON ROCKS COVERED DISH

A most appealing creation, the frog sits upon a mound of rocks which forms the surface of the cover and is continued around the sides of the base. The lid has an inner lip to hold it securely to the base. Fitted with amber glass eyes, finely webbed feet, and a discretely pursed mouth, this alert fellow, although lacking any warts on its body, is very realistic indeed.

Attributed to Atterbury, it is illustrated in F-55B. Known to us only as shown in opaque white with the frog in green cased glass. The base is 4 1/2" in diameter and 2" deep; 5 1/2" high overall. Extremely rare.

147 - SNAIL ON WOODEN BASKET

Modeled as a basket, the base of this attractive piece consists of eighteen staves bedecked with a pattern of long leaves and bound together by two iron bands, each held by three small studs. The cover is formed as six long wooden slats and two crossing ones, each held in place by four small studs. The finial is an upright coiled terrestrial snail emerging from the shell, its tentacles clearly evident, and its body appearing to slither over the surface. The lid has an edge that fits inside the rim of the base and holds it secure.

Maker unknown. Although unsigned it may well be another of the innovative Vallerysthal pieces. Known to us only in opaque green. Height overall about 4"; diameter at the top of base 5", tapering to 3" at the bottom. Possibly rare, especially in this color.

148 - RESTING WATER BUFFALO COVERED DISH

This hump back, great horned Indian buffalo is captured in a resting position with legs tucked under his body, head alert, and tail curling ground to his left side. A creature of imposing proportions and considerable appeal.

Made by Vallerysthal. Shown in VCC (p. 308, No. 3809). Known to us in white, it was reissued by the company in clear crystal and frosted during the 1970s. The top is 10" long and 4" wide; the base maximum length is 10" and the width 4 1/4". Rare in milk glass.

149 - WATER BUFFALO WITH RIDER COVERED DISH

This surely ranks among the most stunning and notable designs ever created for an animal covered dish. The water buffalo's great curving horns are swept back over its head and the fine detailed hair of the mane contrasts with the smooth glistening body. Sitting upright on the animal's back and facing us is a robed oriental figure holding a water jug under his right arm. The rider's shaved head and saffron robe give him the look of a Buddhist monk.

Embossed "Vallerysthal" on the underside of the base, it is shown in VCC (P. 305, No. 3808). Lee (*Antiques Journal*, July 1951) reprints a page of a slightly modified German version of the 1908 French catalog in which the water buffalo is shown with other "Butterdosen" (butter dishes).

Known to us in white, clear frosted, and a warm caramel color which when painted produces a truly striking effect as the caramel glass glistens like the hide of a live animal. The top is 10" long and 4" wide; the base maximum length is 10" and the width 4 1/4". Very rare in any color.

150 - DROMEDARY CAMEL COVERED DISH

This Arabian single humped camel is divided lengthwise to produce a long and narrow covered dish. At rest and with its legs tucked in, the camel's long neck and head dominate the piece. Indeed, the head may be the most extreme example of a "finial," absolutely essential to picking up the top portion because the rest of the cover is almost impossible to handle without it slipping from one's fingers. The bulbous nose, large eyes, wrinkled neck, and mass of hair atop its hump are the camel's most notable features, but careful attention has also been given to the clumps of body hair in the lower portion as well as to the nicely moulded tail. This "ship of the desert" is much more realistic and impressive than the better known two-hump camel covered dish. Many collectors have said that in an antique mall or on a dealer's table, they almost failed to recognize this piece as milk glass, for when painted or in other than opaque white, it can be mistaken as a ceramic item.

Usually signed Vallerysthal on the underside of the base. Shown in SW (p. 6), and in VCC (p 308, No. 3806) together with other butter dishes.

Known to us in opaque white, blue, green, caramel, and in dark cobalt blue. Overall length from tip of nose to tail 8 1/2"; height to top of nose 4 1/2"; maximum width 3". Rare in any color.

151 - TURTLE WITH SNAIL COVERED DISH

This intriguing covered butter dish may well be called "Slow and Slower." The full bodied turtle is painstakingly designed, with the slightly overlapping cover fitted to the base so as to simulate a real turtle's shell. The anatomical features of the turtle's entire body and those of the large hitchhiking snail which serves as finial are distinct and well moulded. The turtle's legs are in a walking stance, giving this otherwise static piece an unexpected sense of motion, however lumbering!

A Portieux product, illustrated as "Tortue #995" in the 1933 catalog. Known in white and blue. Overall length about 8"; base opening 5 1/2" by 4 1/8". Hard to find.

152 - FLY ON WALNUT COVERED DISH

Among the most attractive and desirable of the French designs, this covered sugar is an amazingly detailed and accurate representation of a walnut complete with the ridges, grooves, and clumps of the real object. On top sits a large fly with wings folded flat along its back and eyes so large they cover most of the head, just as they do in real life. The top edge of the base fits snugly into a flange protruding from the inner margin of the rim of the top so the walnut looks as through it were all of one piece.

Illustrated in VCC (p. 304, No. 3766) and SW (p. 3, next to last row) where the editors call the insect a "Locust" which it manifestly is not.

Known to us in white and creamy caramel. It is 5" long, 4" wide and approximately 4" high. Scarce, possibly rare.

153 - LOBSTER COVERED DISH

Amazingly lifelike, this gigantic lobster looking as though it is about to crawl away is one of the most stunning of all milk glass animal covered dishes. The top consists of the carapace and head, with realistic stalked eyes, and an eight segmented tail which curls down to the base in four additional segments. The base consists of a pair of very large horizontal claws, meeting along the midpoint, and the lower half of the carapace which has three odd loops at its lower edge. The underside is flat except for the claws which are deeply concave. The mould work is excellent, and when painted red, the lobster looks ready to serve.

Maker unknown. Known to us only in white. It is a large piece, 9" long from the tip of the claws to the end of the tail, approximately 3 1/2" high and 3 1/2" across the carapace. Extremely rare.

154 - RAM COVERED DISH

This charming miniature dish may be a child's piece or, perhaps, a covered salt. Everything about it bespeaks old age, from the quality and character of the glass to the design features and mould work. The round base, pressed from a three-part mould, has a delicate ribbed pattern running vertically on its sides. A narrow ledge just inside the flanged and scalloped top serves to support the domed cover. As if not to distract from the finial, all the other elements seem muted compared to the impressive figure of the full-bodied ram who commands our attention. It reclines at ease, with one leg outstretched, cushioned by just the faintest hint of grass on an otherwise smooth surface. The animal's features are extremely well moulded

The maker is unknown, but most likely European. It is shown in Millard 184-b, without attribution. An English origin has been proposed, but not convincingly. Both the base and the cover carry cryptic registration numbers. The cover is marked M. S. 2509, and the base is marked [M?]S. 2184, neither of these being consistent to our knowledge with English registry numbers.

Known to us in white; possibly occurs in blue as well. Base is 3 1/4" in diameter; about 3 1/2" high overall. Rare.

155 - BABOON ON GALACTIC BASE COVERED DISH

The baboon on this base, which we have named "Galactic" in keeping with the crossed orbits of the design, is a variant of the base shown in F-114. Because this base is consistent in size, quality of glass, and design impression, as well as being found as the identical base for another Flaccus animal, the Monkey, we accept this variant as authentic. For additional discussion of this piece, see O.N., XI:1, Dec. 1995, p. 9.

Generally accepted as one of the series of Flaccus animal covered dishes and known to us only in white. Length 6 1/8". Rare.

156 - BUTTERFLY COVERED DISH

This hexagonal dish has a large butterfly on its cover. It rests on a two-step surface, the upper portion having an elaborate floral pattern, the lower part plain. The unusually large and deep base is elevated by three chunky double legs. The designs on three of the side panels are all different — a sitting bird, a fine heron, and a group of butterflies. Alternating between each of them are panels bearing a floral design. The underside of the base is equally ornate, suggesting this piece may also exist in clear glass.

Maker unknown. Known to us only in white. It measures 4 1/8" across top of base; 3 7/8" across bottom of base; overall height 6". Rare.

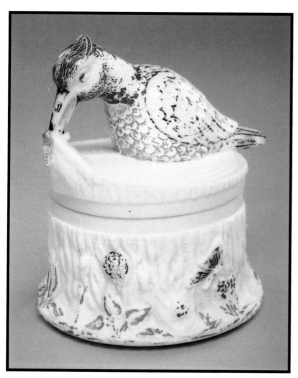

157 - WOODPECKER COVERED DISH

Sitting atop a tree stump, this early bird is enjoying his breakfast of a fat worm. The woodpecker's features, almost cartoon-like, are nicely moulded and highlighted by the painted decoration. The base is embossed with butterflies and floral sprays and grasses, all on a striated background simulating the rough bark of a tree. A multi-rayed star intaglio is pressed on the underside of the base.

Maker unknown, but most likely European. Known to us only in white. Height overall 6"; base diameter 4 7/8". Rare.

158 - TWIN DOLPHIN COVERED DISH

Resting on a mass of scales, two dolphins facing in opposite directions join their tails in a loop to form the finial of this imaginative covered dish. The base, too, carries the scale pattern except for the end panels which have a floral design. The details of the dolphin figures are excellent, especially the texture of the skin and the topknots. The underside of the base is rayed.

Maker unknown. Because the design on the base of this piece is identical to the "Hen on Fish Scale Base" (No. 109 in this book), both of these covered dishes would seem to be products of the same company.

Known to us in only in clambroth milk white glass. Length 5 3/4"; height 4 1/2". Rare.

159 - BOAR ON BASKET BASE COVERED DISH

Although the wild boar resting on a domed lid is only 3 1/2" in length, the impression one gets is of a massive, imposing creature in a defiant stance, its large head straining forward above the thick front legs. The boar's deep set, almost human-like eyes are piercing, and two large fangs protrude from each side of its mouth. The lid is very heavy because the body of the boar is solid glass, except for a small cavity in the hind quarters. The basket weave pattern of the base is rather intricate. At the top is a braid with very slight scalloping, below which is a band of three horizontal strands crossed diagonally by single ones placed at 1/2" intervals. The remaining portion is a weave of two horizontal crossed by two vertical strands. The underside of the base is woven much like the central portion of the sides, but in the middle is a raised rectangle with horizontal lines crossed by three "X" marks in a row.

Maker unknown, but it is one in a series of other animal covered dishes with bases carrying the same triple "X" design on the underside. We rather doubt the Xs are a company trademark.

Known to us in white and in clear crystal. Length 5 1/8", height 4 1/2". Scarce in milk glass; somewhat hard to find in crystal.

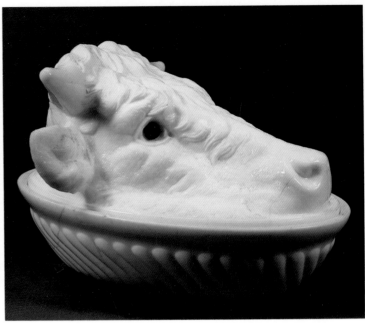

160 - STEER'S HEAD COVERED DISH

Because only a small illustration of this celebrated covered dish appears in F-128, and a mere line drawing in Lee (L-EA, plate 109), the conspicuous absence of this piece in the rest of the standard milk glass literature impels our including it in this book. As noted in Ferson, the Challinor catalog lists it as "Bull's Head" but collectors avoid using that designation so as not to confuse it with the small Bull's Head mustard jar made by Atterbury. Comparison between the Steer's Head and Atterbury's Boar's Head is inevitable, but we shy away from judging which is better, as both have their own spe-

cial appeal. Most collectors agree that the steer's head is particularly expressive, with very fine detail, and when fitted with glass eyes the effect is astonishing. The bases of both these covered dishes are similar in having a ribbed design around the sides — Challinor's ribs running obliquely and Atterbury's vertically. To our knowledge, it has not been determined which company was first to make these covered dishes, each obviously competing for favor in the popular market.

Made by Challinor, Taylor circa 1891. Known to us only in white. Length of base 7 7/8"; maximum height 5 1/2". Extremely rare.

Figurals

161 - "FAN AND CIRCLES" RIBBED COVERED DISH
[Boar's Head Alternate Cover]

This regal covered dish, though often alluded to, has not previously been shown in the standard literature. We have named it by reference to its imposing finial, a design called "Fan and Circle Variant" by Belknap (B-48) for a large tray, shown as No. 207 in this

book, whose edge pattern is much the same. The oval base, marked with a May 29, 1888 patent date, is familiar as the dish for Atterbury's Boar's Head cover. If there are any doubts that this alternate lid may be a "marriage," they can be dispelled immediately by the fact that there are exactly sixty-four ribs in both the base and the cover, hardly a coincidence. Moreover, the design, the fit, the aesthetic proportions, and the quality of the glass are unmistakably Atterbury. We know few if any

other finials that are as ornate, and certainly none that are as large, for it extends over fully two thirds the length of the cover! The fan, consisting of seven plumes, is flanked on each side by a chain of rings. The domed surface, up to where the vertical ribs begin, is adorned with an intricate pattern of fine striated clusters. Classic, elegant, and a prize possession for any collector.

Made by Atterbury, possibly before the Boar's Head cover was created, although we have no documentation to prove that supposition. Rings, petals, plumes, and ribs were favorite elements in many Atterbury designs.

We have seen this only in white, but it may also have been produced in blue. Base measures 9 3/8" by 6 1/4"; cover 8 1/4" by 5"; and 4 3/8" high overall. Very rare.

162 - STRAWBERRY BOWL COVERED DISH

A truly remarkable piece whose top consists of a huge pile of small strawberries arranged in five or more irregular rows. From the middle of what appear to be more than one hundred berries, a tall twig finial emerges. The base is a footed bowl with five fluted margins on either side of a basket handle. Directly below is a circle of drapes on ropes, twenty-four of these, each having a graceful tassel. The surface of the base is a series of alternating diamonds each formed by four convex bars. The bowl sits on a footed base with a rope design at the junction and the same crisscross pattern around the sides.

Maker unknown. Although unsigned it is most likely European and has all the characteristics of a Vallerysthal piece.

Known to us only in white. Height to top of the finial about 6". Diameter of the top of the base 6" (6 1/2" across the handles). Bottom diameter 3 1/2". More than scarce.

163 - CROOKED HOUSE

This is a fascinating piece whose intricacy cannot be appreciated from a photograph alone. Every detail of the stone house is meticulously moulded. No two sides are alike, and all of the masonry work strives to simulate individually hand set and rough hewn stones. Even the single window on each side of the tiled roof is different in size. The front of the building has a two-panel door placed slightly off center; the right side of the building has a single window but the left side is solid stone; and at the back of the house we see a large cathedral arch window which looks much like the opening for a massive wood-burning oven even though the house lacks a chimney. In keeping with its intended rusticity, the entire structure is amusingly out of whack and all its features deliberately asymmetrical.

Maker unknown, but thought to date from the 1920s. Known to us only in the colors shown, white base with blue lid. Height 2 1/2"; length 2 5/8"; width 1 7/8". Rare.

164 - ALPINE CHALET

From its centered chimney to the double steps of the threshold, this house fairly yodels its identity. In marked contrast to the "Crooked House," this one is a classic example of architectural proportion and balance typical of the Swiss chalet. The roof and attic portion forms the lid of this covered dish, nicely detailed with square shingles, attic windows, and gingerbread under the roof. The central double door, front and back, is flanked by shuttered windows. On the sides there is a door, a window on either side of it, and two windows above. A splendid rendition, lacking only the billowing smoke we expect to see coming out of the chimney.

Maker unknown. Known to us only in milk white, both plain and with painted decoration, as shown. Height 5"; length 5 1/8"; width 3 1/2". Very scarce.

165 - GINGERBREAD HOUSE

The inspiration for this outstanding piece may be the German fairy tale, as it certainly looks like Hansel and Gretel standing by the front door and the witch alongside beckoning them to enter. This covered dish has a great deal of minute detail, with a bird on a nest and a cat on the window ledge all embossed in high relief on the left side of the house. Two more windows are moulded on the back and one window on the right side. The design of the tiled roof and the sides is very elaborate, combining hearts, rectangles, and circles. A small chimney sticks out ominously at the far end of the roof.

Maker unknown, but a German origin seems likely (see F-382). If produced when the immensely popular Humperdinck opera *Hänsel und Gretel* was first performed, that would date this piece around 1893.

We know it in opaque white and green. The latter has some obscure marking: "Ges.geschützt / 76.K. No 1." Height 3 7/8"; length 4 3/8"; width 3 3/8". Rare.

166 - TOWN HOUSE

A perfectly square brick house with shingled roof, representing a style of the late nineteenth century perhaps. The formal, detailed central door is set below a flat lintel and surrounded by five windows so placed as to suggest square rooms all of the same size. The steps and surrounding area are carried forward as a flat panel. The

sides and back of the building are less well detailed with brick work and windows only faintly embossed.

Maker unknown. Known to us only in white. Height 4 3/8"; length 4 5/16". Availability unknown, but probably scarce.

167 - BEADED EGG COVERED DISH

Most milk glass Easter eggs are hollow blown, but a few like this are pressed glass — two pieces together forming an egg "box" or covered dish with a flat bottom. The cover fits on a flange raised above the level of the top margin of the base. An elliptical ring of beads, 2 1/2" long by 1 1/2" wide, adorns the cover and frames a group of raised, petaled flowers randomly placed. With long tendril-like stems, they appear to be violets. The glass is of good quality.

Maker unknown. Known to us only in white. Length 4 1/4"; width 2 3/4"; height about 2 1/2". Hard to find.

168 - PERFUME BOTTLES IN A COVERED BASKET

This round covered basket is often found devoid of its contents, although the four vertical projections inside the base hint that something is missing. The insert is a metal tray with

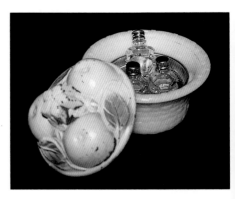

three holes to hold small perfume bottles. Made in a highly translucent milk glass, the base has a broad, single strand basket weave pattern around the sides and the upper edge of the rim. The cover, which appears to be clear acid etched glass painted overall in naturalistic colors, is modeled as three oranges with intervening leaves. An orange blossom at the top with two more below it serves as finial.

Maker unknown. The underside of the base bears the number "13" but no other markings. We assume it may be a souvenir piece, and assume further that the bottles contained "Orange Blossom" perfume; hence, no doubt especially popular for sale in Florida or California, and consistent with Depression-type glassware.

We know it only in white, and painted as shown. Height overall about 3 1/8"; diameter across the top of the base 4 1/4". Somewhat hard to find.

169 - CROWN COVERED DISH

Most of the design elements of this regal covered dish converge at the finial, a cross set on a globe criss-crossed with small blocks. Running vertically on the cover and down the sides are eight strands of pearls with banding on each side. All the intervening surface is completely ridged by fine horizontal threads. Near the bottom of the base are flower blossoms linked to each other by swags, below which is a wide band with evenly spaced alternating diamond and round studs (simulating gems, perhaps), and at the very bottom is a narrow flanged border with fine ribbing.

Made by Vallerysthal, illustrated in SW (4th row, p. 3) and VCC (No. 3750, p. 303). Previously shown in F-636, but without commentary.

We know it in opaque white, blue, and green, though very likely made in clear and frosted colors as well. Height 5 3/4", diameter 4 5/8". Very scarce.

Note on variants: We have found three versions of this Crown Covered dish: one has a plain surface on the underside and is found both with and without the Vallerysthal signature. The other two are similar to each other, but not exactly alike, in having embossed figures on the undersides which looks like a spread-winged eagle or a Phoenix bird. We have not found either of the latter ones signed. In addition, the embossed elements on the sides of the bases and the finials of these two versions also differ slightly from the signed Vallerysthal example. These variants may be products of other companies, or could possibly be alternate moulds used by Vallerysthal.

171 - CROWNED LADIES AND SERPENTS COVERED DISH

For sheer fascination, this covered dish would be hard to surpass. Full figures of crowned and draped ladies stand at each of the four corners, their feet extending below the base to serve as rests for the bowl. The cover has fern leaves running to the finial and four embossed honey bees. These, curiously, are matched by four snails, one on each side of the base. Entwined in the ladies' arms are serpents whose heads face each other, tongues flicking, and their tails looped together. If there are symbolic meanings in all of this, we are at a loss to imagine what they may be. The glass has a grayish cast and is fiery opalescent.

Produced at least as early as 1894, illustrated in a Portieux catalog of that date (*folio* 184, No. 3463) and continued in the 1933 catalog (PC, p. 65, No. 965 designated simply "Carre"). Known to us only in white. Height 5 7/8"; width 5 3/4". Rare.

170 - ARTICHOKE COVERED SUGAR

The foot of this realistic figural is formed as six large petals, each with a central rib, interspersed with smaller petals. A ring of twelve beads marks the juncture of the body of the base which consists of four rows of ribbed petals of increasing size.

The conical top rises in a similar design of two petal rows and a conical top of nine ridged rays.

Illustrated in VCC (p. 305, No. 3775), the example shown here is signed "Vallerysthal" inside the bottom of the base.

Known to us only in white. Height 6" and 4 1/2" across the top of the base. Scarce.

172 - TRUMPET VINE COVERED SUGAR

This sugar bowl is shown in B-225b, but in a slightly larger size if Belknap's measurement is accurate. The two-part piece is formed as a cantaloupe, its ribbed surface laced overall with irregular lines simulating the warty rind of a melon. The inner surface is also ribbed, but smooth. Embossed vines and leaves overlay the sides and continue uninterrupted on to the cover. Three large leaves extend below the bowl to serve as feet. The finial is a large melon blossom, the trumpet nicely arched to form an easy to grasp and graceful handle.

Marked S V inside the cover. The identical piece is illustrated in a line drawing that appears in an 1897 catalog of the Belgian glass company Val St. Lambert (p. 41, #28). This may be a clue to the identity of the S V mark, as several other pieces so marked are also found in this catalog, but additional documentation is needed.

Known to us only in white. Height 5 1/2"; diameter 4". Very scarce.

174 - GRAPE VINE COVERED DISH

Although a very well-known covered dish, we include this example because it has the unusual feature of intricate metal work encasing both the lid and the base.

Made by Portieux and illustrated (without the metal casing) in PC (p. 65, as "Vigne" No. 967). Some examples carry a round paper sticker with "P V France" in blue letters. This covered dish has caused some confusion for collectors because it was extensively reproduced by the Jeannette Glass Co. beginning in the 1950s in their popular "Shell Pink" milk glass and subsequently by Indiana glass in various clear colors. See Weatherman, *Colored Glassware*, p. 207 and N-187.

Known to us in white, blue, green, yellow (pictured), pink opaline, and in clear frosted. Height 5 3/4", diameter 4 1/4". Portieux made this piece well into the 1950s and it is readily available, but not with metal casing as shown.

173 - GRAPES COVERED DISH

The entire cover of this attractive oval dish consists of a huge cluster of grapes and leaves topped by a large knob serving as finial. A discrete pattern of wide ribs circles the upper surface of the flanged shallow base, but what is most striking is the design around the sides and on the bottom. An intricate combination of elements, including plumes and stylized triangular leaves, is unified into an attractive overall geometric pattern by the minute diamond cuts that cover the remaining surface. The milk glass has areas of lustrous translucence, a feature which distinguishes much of the earlier French products and is highly prized by collectors.

Marked Portieux inside the base, it is illustrated in PC as "Fruits" No. 1005, p. 67, and with color decoration No. 6721, p. 327. Known to us only in white. Length 7 5/8"; width 5 3/4" including the 3/16" flange. More than scarce.

175 - BOAT-SHAPED COVERED DISH

This is a beautifully designed covered dish. Nicely proportioned, its graceful lines are complemented by restrained embossed elements consisting of fine vertical ribs above and below a heavily stippled band. The cover repeats the rib pattern around its edge and at the base of the wide-ribbed oval knob finial. At both ends, the handles, quadrangular in cross-section, rise up from the base enhancing the symmetry of the overall design. A pattern of converging ribs is embossed on the underside. The glass is a glossy, deep purple marble, characteristic of its manufacturer.

Made by Sowerby, the inner surface carries the peacock trademark on one side and a diamond registry mark on the other. According to our reading of the design lozenge, it was registered on February 20, 1878, and is so listed by both Slack (p. 168) and Thompson (T-1, p. 31), but incorrectly listed as January 20, 1878 in both Lattimore (p. 169) and Cottle (p. 100). An identical piece, but with a low pedestal base and lacking a cover, is illustrated in Heacock (H-J, #385) as an open salt, but it is more likely the open sugar bowl (#318793) or "stand" (#319794). The piece shown here may be either the covered sugar (#318789) or more likely the butter dish (#318791).

Known to us only as shown, but may have been made in opaque white or other of the Sowerby colors. Length overall 7"; width 4"; height about 3 3/4". Very scarce.

176 - MELON COVERED DISH

A charming piece, the top and bottom together forming a large melon-like fruit whose surface is covered with small rayed flowers. Eight vertical ribs run the full length of the sides. The base rests on an eight-lobed foot, each representing a separate leaf. Above each of these, another leaf extends midway up the sides between the vertical ribs. The lid has an inner lip that fits inside the top of the base.

Unsigned but most likely of Continental origin. Known to us in green and blue. Height 6"; opening at the top 4". Scarce, possibly rare.

177 - "REMEMBER THE MAINE" BATTLESHIP

Generally considered the rarest of the various battleship covered dishes, the "Remember the Maine" has not been illustrated in milk glass in the standard references. The Fersons (F-104) reprint a McKee 1898 advertisement showing a sketch of the ship, and a photograph of it as well, but in clear crystal.(F-104B).

Attributed to McKee, circa 1898.

In addition to milk white, sometimes with elaborate gold painted decoration, it was also made in clear crystal and transparent colors of blue and green. Length 7"; maximum width 2 3/4"; height to top of smoke stack about 4". Scarce in any color, and rare in milk glass.

Reproduction note: In the 1980s reproductions began to appear, known to us in clear crystal, transparent pink and blue (both light and dark), and in opaque black, but thus far none of the copies has been found in opaque white. A detailed comparison of the McKee originals and the reproductions appears in O.N., X:1 Dec. 1994, p. 10. Two readily distinguishing features are summarized here: in the shield's banner at the bow of the ship the embossed stars on the original are lacking in the reproductions. Also, the smoke stacks of the originals are round, whereas those of the copies are distinctly oval. Sometimes found with "Made in Taiwan" paper labels, these reproductions were advertised by Castle Antiques as recently as 1994 in their wholesale catalog.

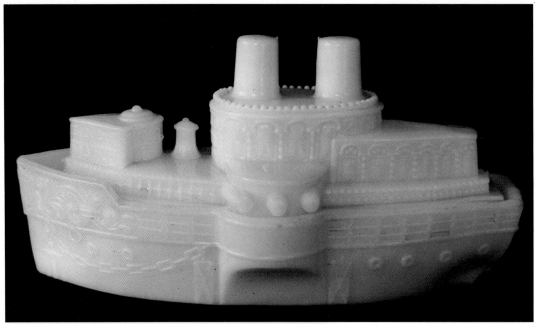

178 - THE BATTLESHIP MAINE VARIANTS

This covered ship, among the best known and most admired of Spanish-American war memorabilia, has been shown in virtually all the major milk glass references: L-EA, p. 183; B-162b; M-300a; Lindsey, No. 477; Marsh, No. 315; and N-172, to name a few. We justify our including two more examples of the Battleship Maine in this book as both are quite extraordinary, one because of the well-preserved original paint which reveals so beautifully the extraordinarily detailed mould work of the embossed elements, and the other because it has a most uncommon feature — a beaded main cabin roof — not shown or mentioned in any of the references cited above.

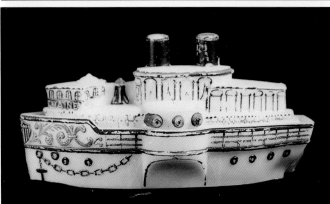

We believe the first comprehensive study of variant forms of this covered dish appeared in O.N. (II:6, Oct. 1987, p. 2-4; and III:1, Dec. 1987, p. 2) where two types are distinguished in many different ways, too extensive to repeat here. Briefly, one notable feature concerns the main cabin roof, with one type having a double rim (seen in the painted example here) versus a single rim (shown in N-172). Another feature concerns the capstan between the forward and the main cabin where one type is "open" and the other type is "closed" — that is to say, "closed" by a thin connecting glass (also seen here in the painted example). In a subsequent study, still another, a third type, came to light and was fully reported in O.N., X:1, Dec. 1994, p. 10-13. This one, shown in the unpainted specimen, has an "open" capstan, and a ring of beads around the upper rim of the double rimmed main cabin roof.

Maker unknown. To date, no reproductions have been reported. Known to us only in white; none has been found in transparent, either clear or colored. Length 7 3/4".

Although listed as "Usually available" by Ferson, prices vary greatly when account is taken of the variant types. In general, the single rim cabin roof with closed capstan versions, like the one illustrated in N-172, are not too hard to find. A painted example like the one shown here is very rare. And the extreme rarity of the beaded cabin roof variant may be attested by its absence from all previous listings, and the fact that only two members of the National Milk Glass Collectors Society report having one in their collections.

Human Figures

179 - OLD WOMAN WITH BASKET COVERED DISH

This intricate covered dish divides at the waist line. The base itself consists of the lower body of a woman seated on a wicker basket (2 1/2" square). She has another round basket (2 1/2" in diameter) with center divider between her legs. Her matronly features, wimple headdress, crossed arms, and hands folded in front convey an air of total complacency. Much of the original paint is still intact.

Maker unknown, mostly likely European. Known to us only in white. This piece measures 7 3/4" overall. Rare.

180 - LITTLE GOLFER COVERED DISH

If this engaging piece were larger and made in ceramic, one might think it was a cookie jar! But it is indeed a milk glass beauty that is hard to resist. The plump little golfer, with eyes cast aslant, stands holding her golf bag at her side. She is dressed in a short, full skirt, a ruff around her neck, and wears shoes that look like booties. Her knitted tam with knob at the top is the lift off cover for this charming creation.

Maker unknown. Known to us only in white, both plain and nicely painted, as shown. Height 6". We believe it is scarce.

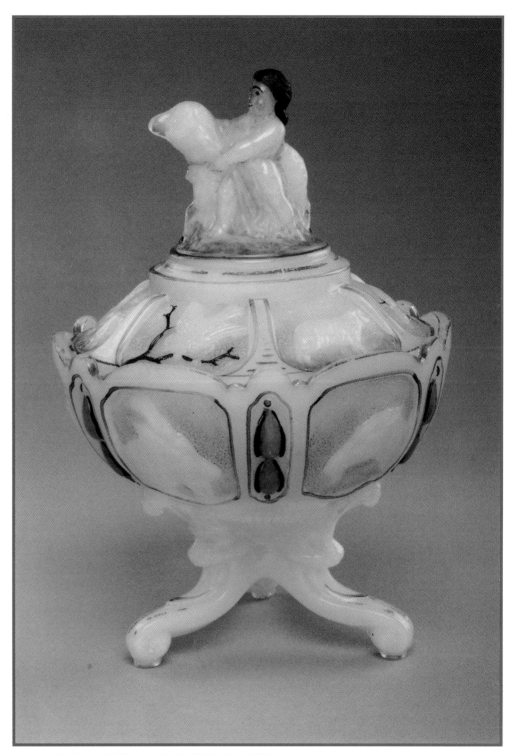

181 - CHILD WITH LAMB COVERED DISH

For variety and intricacy of design, this covered dish is surely a contender. The large base is supported by three splayed feet formed as heads of mythological creatures. Around the sides are six framed panels, each with the head of an animal in high relief — a cow, a bull, a ram, a ewe, a Billy goat, and a Nanny goat. The cover also has six panels — a sheep, a cow, and a goat, with birds on branches alternating between them. The finial is a darling union of a child with its arms around the neck of a lamb. Most appropriately for the design, the entire piece is highlighted by paint in delicate pastel colors.

Maker unknown, but most likely European. Known only in white. The base measures 5 5/8" across the top; 8" high overall. Rare.

182 - INFANT IN SHELL ON REED BASE COVERED DISH

The infant depicted on the lid of this piece, sometimes referred to as "Moses," is believed to be part of an elusive series of covered dishes that includes about seven different covers. One of these, a frog on identical reed base, is shown in F-115. We find it difficult to call the figure on this cover "Moses," however, because the infant seen resting in a large sea shell clearly is winged, and we have found no allusions in religious imagery to support a winged child Moses, although wings do symbolize a "divine mission." Whoever or whatever the child represents hardly matters, for the piece is exquisitely detailed and very difficult to photograph to its best advantage.

Maker unknown. Known to us only in white. Length 5 3/8"; width 2 3/4". Rare.

183 - GIRL EMERGING FROM SEA SHELL COVERED DISH

Truly outstanding, this piece merits praise in all respects. It is ingeniously conceived, skillfully moulded, and of top quality glass. The dish is fashioned as a large bivalve, its upper and lower shells elaborately ridged and scalloped. An enchanting young girl, serving as the finial, presses her arms against the shell as if pushing her body through it, like a chick emerging from an egg! A striking illusion is then created, for the shell itself becomes transformed into a large Victorian hoop skirt adorned with embossed leaves and flowers. The base rests on three legs that appear to be formed as parasitic outgrowths of the shell. Can the young lady's name be anything other than Pearl?

Maker unknown, but most likely European. We know it only in white, beautifully painted as shown. It measures 5 1/4" long and is 6 3/4" high overall. Rare.

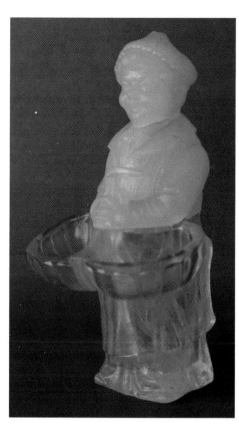

184 - BAKER BOY COVERED DISH

It may seem odd to call pieces such as this — made in the three-dimensional likeness of human or animal figures — a "covered dish." But it is indeed a covered vessel, by virtue of the division into two parts, the lower portion being a hollow receptacle. This example even goes a step further, for it also incorporates two small open baskets, so it might as properly be called a condiment or relish container. A great deal of attention has been given to the young lad's facial features and clothing which suggest he may be Dutch. By no means a ragamuffin, he is dressed in shirt and tie, wide collared coat, and a baker's apron tied in a long bow extending almost floor length at the back. In his tightly clasped hands, he holds a stub handle which serves as a connector for the two shell-shaped condiment containers. The cover has two notches which slip over lugs in the base to assure a secure fit. Although the piece may appear unsteady, it is well proportioned and not easily toppled.

Maker unknown, but probably European and late nineteenth century.

Known in white and in highly translucent milky opal ("clambroth"). It is difficult to give all the measurements of three-dimensional figures, suffice to say the width across the baskets is 4 1/4" and the height overall is 8". Rare.

185 - BAKER MAN COVERED DISH

Similar in conception to the Baker Boy covered dish, this too is an all-in-one condiment server. The full-figure gentleman divides just above the waistline, providing an opening for the hollow base. He holds two large basket salts woven in a single strand design, below which is what appears to be his gathered-up apron whose strings are tied behind in a bow. He sports muttonchops and wears a baker's hat that is pressed down, looking a bit like a military cap. An outstanding piece.

Maker unknown. Known to us only in white. Height overall 8". Rare.

186 - SAILOR ON BOAT COVERED DISH

Reclining on the boat deck, this dapper mustached sailor, with legs crossed, head comfortably propped on his right hand, and left hand tucked inside his pocket, is the very picture of repose. A coiled rope cushions his body, and crossed oars lie idly below. His suit and cap are unmistakably French. The cover of this dish has an inner lip to hold it securely to the base which is nicely moulded to simulate wood.

Maker unknown. Known to us only in white. Height 4 1/2"; length 7 1/4". Extremely rare.

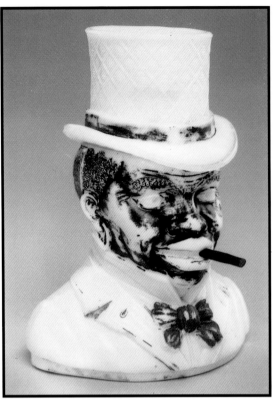

187 - BLACK MAN WITH TOP HAT COVERED DISH

The bust of a stylish gentleman forms the base of this covered dish, possibly a small humidor. He sports an elegant coat, bow tie, and high collared shirt. All of his facial features — wide eyes, full lips, and radiant teeth — are nicely moulded. A small hole in his mouth is intended to accommodate a cigar, probably made of wood. The elegant top hat has a diamond basket weave pattern, with a 1/4" hat band painted black, and brim turned down in front and back. Much of the original paint has been preserved in the example shown here, enhancing the fine details of this attractive piece.

Maker unknown. Known to us only in white milk glass. It is 5 1/2" wide at the base and 7 1/4" high overall. Rare.

188 - MAN IN DERBY HAT COVERED DISH

This portly gentleman looks as though he might have stepped right out of the pages of Dickens' novel, *The Pickwick Papers*. In bow tie, buttoned vest, cutaway coat and velvet lapels, he completes his fine attire with patent leather shoes, Derby hat, and walking stick hanging jauntily from his raised arm. The face, painted in flesh tones, has a dour expression, and the bulbous nose puts the finishing touch on this wonderfully comic character.

Maker unknown. Known to us only in white with painted decoration, as shown. Height 7"; maximum width 4". The bottom portion which ends just above the bent arm measures about 3" high. Rare.

189 - ENGLISH POLICEMAN

This finely detailed English "Bobby" stands with one arm at his side, and the other, club in hand, crossing his chest. His uniform belted coat sports two rows of five buttons, cuffs, a round collar, and shoulder straps. His formal hat has the customary badge, a band around the base, and a chin strap. The full length coat covers all but the tips of his shoes.

Maker unknown. Known to us only in white. Height overall 8"; the base is 3 3/8" high and 3 1/2" wide. Very rare.

190 - SAINT NICHOLAS WITH PACK

A majestic figure resembling the German Sankt Nicholaus is the inspiration for this most remarkable covered dish. With a beard that flows halfway down his body, the venerable saint, clutching a walking stick in his right hand, wears a pointed hat and a cloak that extends to his feet. Laden with gifts for the children, he has a teddy bear in his left hand and a doll dangling from his belt. Other toys appear in his large backpack — an airplane, drum, wagon, and the head of a hobby horse. The lid joins the base at shoulder height, and a threaded rim at the base opening suggests it may have had a rubber gasket to secure the two parts together.

Maker unknown. Probably not too old, as suggested by the airplane among the other traditional toys. Known to us in white and pale blue milk glass. Height 7 1/2"; width 3". More than scarce.

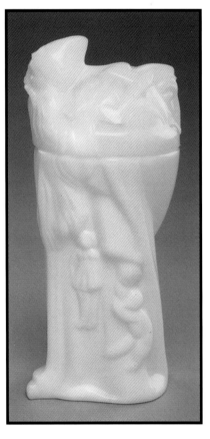

191 - WINTER SCENE ROUND TRAY

Both for its impressive size and the beautiful hand painted scene of an isolated farm house and trees whose branches are laden with snow, this tray merits high praise. Most collectors familiar with the decorated wares of the Boston and Sandwich Glass Company will probably agree that the painting is characteristic of the work of Edward J. Swann, renowned Master Decorator for that company from 1872 to 1895. He was especially attentive to light and shadows and insisted upon absolute fidelity to naturalistic details. The gold trim on the outer border and matching inner one create a wide band to "frame" the painting. Examples of his work, some very similar to the winter scene on this tray, are illustrated in B-K (Vol. IV, p. 249). The old-time "opal" glass is of good weight and top quality.

Maker unknown, but a Boston and Sandwich attribution appears to us quite likely. Known to us only in white. Diameter 13 1/2", with a 1" raised rim. Rare.

192 - SMALL BEAR DISH

A small round nappy or pin holder with six indentations along the rim. At the center, a handsome Grizzly Bear stands imperiously upon a raised bar carrying the words "Mid Winter Fair."

Maker unknown. Known to us only in white. Diameter 3 1/8". Rare.

193 - CLOWN ASH TRAY

No anguished Pagliaccio, this round faced, wide eyed, smiling clown appears thoroughly content with his role as comedian. The expanded angular sides of the tray are formed by his outstretched arms holding wide his pantaloons which taper down to his tiny feet. The glossy milk glass is of very good quality.

Maker unknown. We have found it only in white. It measures 6 1/4" by 3 3/4". More than hard to find.

194 - DUCK OPEN RELISH DISH

We marvel at the wonderful blend of realism and whimsy in the creation of this bird which looks to be a sea gull. The way in which the head is "mounted" on the neck, for example, is indeed curious. Although the proportions may not seem quite right, the overall conception is masterful.

Maker unknown. The mould work and the characteristics of the glass, no less than the affixed red stone for the eyes, all point to Atterbury as a possible origin. Known to us only in white. Length 10 1/2". Very rare.

195 - OWL PICKLE DISH

Pickle dishes of various shapes and sizes were popular best-sellers in the Victorian period. Formed as the body of an owl, this deep oval dish, with protruding ears and tail feathers, is an unusually attractive example. The entire inner surface is a mass of finely detailed feathers and the huge eyes and beak moulded in the glass stand out menacingly. A clever concession to realism is achieved by the slight dips in the edges of the dish to suggest where the owl's body ends and the head begins. An oval collar on the underside supports the concave dish to keep it from wobbling.

Made by the Central Glass Company, it is illustrated as "#732 - Etched Pickle" in an undated (circa 1880s) trade catalog, reprinted in Revi, p. 115, and Baker, p. 120.

Known to us in milk white, deep amber, and clear etched. Measures 8 1/2" by 5 1/8". More than hard to find.

Reproduction note: This dish was reproduced by L. G. Wright from a new mould made by Botson in 1963, as reported in M-R (p. 74), and shown as "Hoot Owl Relish (#77-75) in light amber and blue transparent (p. 120). It was also made for Wright in chocolate glass by Westmoreland, as illustrated in a reprint (M-R, p. 165) of a 1983 advertisement by Jennings Red Barn, West Martinsville, West Virginia.

196 - BIRD ON CENTERED PEDESTAL DISH

One wonders what the mould maker had in mind when this unusual piece was created. The shallow round dish seems to be a bird bath, with a central beaded edged pedestal supporting a bird with spread wings. A very decorative piece, made of very fine glossy milk glass.

Maker unknown. Known to us only in white. Diameter 4 3/8". Scarce.

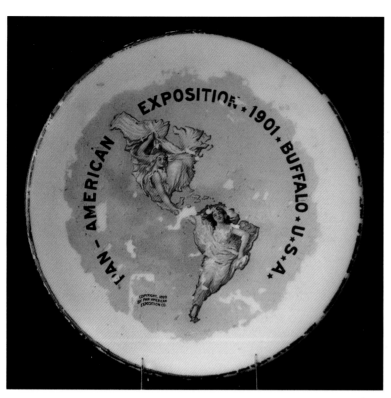

197 - PAN-AMERICAN EXPOSITION PLATE

This large concave/convex plate, with its somewhat worn cold-painted decoration, is one of the many items created for the 1901 Exposition in Buffalo, New York. Well known to collectors is a souvenir novelty modeled as a frying pan and embossed with two frying eggs in the shape of North and South America (Lindsey, No. 490; F-488). Here, the two continents are depicted as lovely ladies whose flowing garments of yellow and red create the map outlines of the Americas. The friendship between them is cleverly conveyed by the extended arms and clasped hands of the two women. Near the bottom, at the left of South America, are the words: "Copyright 1899 by Pan-American Exposition Co."

Maker unknown. The same design has been found in a somewhat larger plate made in ceramic. And a miniature lamp, with the identical painting on both the font and the globe, is shown in S-1, Fig. 309, said to be found with pink or blue backgrounds, as well as "green in a glass textured like an orange skin."

Known to us only in white, as shown. Diameter 10". Scarce.

198 - PANSY BORDER WITH LADY PORTRAIT PLATE

An astonishing creation, the open work of this plate is most unusual as the holes are irregularly formed in accord with the intricate shapes of the large pansy flowers and leaves that make up the border. The portrait of a pensive lady is affixed under a sheet of clear convex glass, all framed within a circle of beads. The example shown here is almost translucent, and when held up to the light the glass is the epitome of what is meant by fiery opalescence!

Maker unknown. The plate without portrait or other decoration is shown in B-6a, and said to have been made in milk white only. We too have seen it only in white. It is slightly over 6 1/4" in diameter. Belknap may be wrong in stating this plate was made in a 7 1/4" size. The plate alone is scarce, and more so with a picture under glass.

93

Left:
199 - BLACK BOY CHASING CHICKEN PLATE

This plate appears to be a companion to the "Watermelon Eater," having the identical open work border design. The youngster firmly grips the leg of the frantic chicken. The detail is noteworthy, particularly in the boy's teeth and hair, as well as the hen's feathers.

Both plates are marked on the underside "Pat. Ap'l'd for" with an "M" below the abbreviation. Long a mystery, the maker (or distributor?) has only recently been discovered by glass historian Tom Felt from advertisements in *Crockery and Glass Journal,* reprinted in his article "Black Collectibles in Glass: Part I," GCD, XII:1, June/July 1998, p. 26. In 1905, the firm of James J. Murray & Co., Philadelphia, Pa. offered these plates, as well as the hollow egg/globe "More Chicken" (see F-678) as part of a series of "Original Easter Novelties in decorated opal glass."

Known to us only in white. It measures 7 1/8" by 6". Rare.

Right:
200 - WATERMELON EATER PLATE

Politically improper to say the least — as are many of the items in the currently popular category of "Black Memorabilia Collectibles" — this amusing plate is greatly admired nonetheless. The large bird perched between the melon eaters appears to be doing them the favor of picking out the seeds.

For attribution and other particulars, see the preceding entry, "Black Boy Chasing Chicken."

201 - "FOURTH OF JULY CHILDREN" PLATE

A toy cannon, a young lad in Revolutionary War costume and tricorner hat, poised ready to light the fuse, and a fearful lass alongside stopping her ears in anticipation of the impending BOOM! — can one want a more delightful piece to commemorate the national holiday? The plate in satin white milk glass is concave/convex with a turned up edge and crimped border all around. The painting, very well executed in brilliant tones and fine detail, is signed by the artist "L. F. Bryant."

Maker unknown, but typical of Mt. Washington or similar blanks for plates to be adorned with painted decoration.

Known to us only in white. Diameter 8 1/4". Very rare, possibly unique?

203 - PENNSYLVANIA TURNPIKE PLATE

The face of this plate proudly carries the words "Pennsylvania Turnpike / World's Greatest Highway" in green enamel paint. The reverse telescoping perspective of the divided lanes emerging from a tunnel in the distance is hardly an aesthetic triumph. The intention is obviously to magnify the expansive highway, so that a bus and a few cars in the background appear scarcely more than fly specks. The picture is not a decal, but seems to have been subjected to some kind of acid etching process. All of the gray airbrush painted areas have a satin-like finish while the white places are glossy smooth. The border is not one which we have found on other plates as "blanks," and may well have been designed specifically for this souvenir plate. It is an attractive pattern of floral sprays and curlicues all done in high relief. A series of five concentric rings are moulded on the slanting surface of the underside of this slightly coupe shaped plate. An unusually heavy plate for its size, the glass is almost a quarter inch thick.

Maker unknown, but if only for political reasons, it seems reasonable to suppose a Pennsylvania company, perhaps L. E. Smith. If made to commemorate the completion of the turnpike, it would date from the early 1960s.

We know it only in white with gray paint, as shown. Diameter 8 1/4". At least scarce, in our experience.

202 - BRIDGE AND STREAM WINTER SCENE PLATE

Many of the beautiful hand painted concave/convex plates which we find today have lost some of their paint over time. The one pictured here in a gilt frame has been well preserved by a thin sheet of clear glass placed over it. The scene is typical of many such "Winter Scenes," with muted colors and fine brush work. The snow banked stream and small foot bridge command the near view, with stark leafless trees and a solitary structure, perhaps a rural church, in the background.

Maker unknown. Diameter 8". Examples such as this are hard to find.

204 - PERFORMING HORSES DISH

This deeply recessed soap dish or pin holder is quite distinctive. The recessed center, framed by a massive wide rim is embossed with four performing horses, each standing with one foot on a pedestal rising from an undulating platform. It may well be a commemorative or souvenir of the famous Austrian white Royal Lipizzaner Stallions.

Maker unknown. Known to us only in white. This is an extraordinarily large dish, 7 1/2" long, 6 1/4" wide and 1 1/2" thick. Weighing 4 1/2 pounds, it may just as well be intended as a hefty paperweight. Availability uncertain, but very hard to find at the very least.

205 - "PHOENIX GLASS" PLATTER

This turkey size oval, shallow tray is simplicity itself, decorated only by sprigs of yellow roses. The glass is heavy, slick, and about 1/4" thick. On first seeing it, we immediately assumed, incorrectly, that it was "Corning Ware." Although it is much the same type of glass, this piece is not nearly as dense white as most of the comparable Corning products.

Made by the British Heat-Resisting Glass Co., Ltd., Birmingham, England, founded in 1934 (See Dodsworth, p. 112.). The company manufactured a type of milk glass appropriately named "Phoenix," to indicate its indestructibility. The tray pictured here is part of an extensive line of tableware. It is marked "PHOENIX" on the underside with the number 129. The company was taken over by United Glass in 1966 and was liquidated by the end of the decade, according to Lesley Jackson, "Automated Table Glass Production in Britain since World War II," *The Journal of the Glass Association* (Vol. 5, 1997), p. 80.

Known to us only in milk white. Length 13"; width 10". Availability unknown.

206 - CARD RECEIVER TRAY

This exquisite small tray is a product of one of the three most distinguished nineteenth-century glass companies in the New England area, a company celebrated especially for its hand blown art glass, cut glass, lamps and chandeliers. We include this tray as but one example of the many fine pieces it also produced in pressed glass. The glossy white opal is tastefully decorated with gold enameled floral sprays. The turned up sides give the tray considerable depth, and the squared off indentations on each side provide pseudo-handles for picking it up conveniently.

This is an example of "Crown Milano," made by the Mt. Washington Glass Works, originally of South Boston, Massachusetts, which merged with Pairpoint Manufacturing Co. in 1894. The tray carries the "Crown Within a Laurel Wreath" mark on the underside and the number "101." According to glass historian Kenneth Wilson, in a letter dated Sept. 27, 1996, "the type of decoration seen on this tray, sometimes called 'Dresden' or 'Colonial,' was introduced in 1893 and continued to be made until about 1897-99, and possibly a little later. The same form of tray with similar, but varying decorations, was also made in an eight inch size."

Known to us only in white. It measures 5" square with a depth of 1 1/2". Scarce.

Belknap devotes a full page illustration to this large platter with a floral decoration (B-48), but its majestic beauty is lost because his photograph of it fails to capture the exquisite mould detail. We hope this picture may reveal something of its magnificence, but perhaps only a hands-on experience with it can confirm why, when at its best, this company's milk glass products are considered the top of the line. The 5 1/2" by 3 1/2" central rectangle with rounded corners is deep set, and the expansive outer border spreads up and out a full 4". The scallops of the outer corners are carried through on the underside of the tray by bold ribs in high relief, slightly cvident in the undulating surface on the corresponding top side. The stately "fan and circle" openwork pattern on the sides was also used with dramatic effect in the finial design of the alternate cover for the Boar's Head Covered Dish (No. 161 in this book).

That it was made by Atterbury is evident both in the unmistakable "White House" quality of the milk glass and in the design itself which might almost serve as a signature mark for this company.

We know it only in white. The tray measures 13 1/2" by 11 1/2". Belknap neglected to give the size, but says "it is unusually large for a Milk Glass piece," adding — in his typical droll manner — that it "would make even stale cookies taste good." Very scarce, probably because its survival rate cannot be very high.

208 - "OLD WOMAN AND MULE" ROUND TRAY

This large tray is a smooth slab of opaque white glass called "Vitrolite," characterized by "curf marks" or ridges on the underside. According to Edelene C. Wood (GCD, VII:2, Aug/Sept 1993, pp. 59) "Vitrolite" was the name given to this type of milk glass in 1908 by George R. Meyercord, a Chicago industrialist, who first produced it at The Meyercord-Carter Glass Co., in Vienna, West Virginia. Almost indestructible, it is best known by milk glass collectors in the Fersons' frontispiece, the Harper's "Here's Happy Days" advertising plaque — "a combination of a ceramic transfer fired onto the glass" (see O.N., VI:2, March, 1991, p. 626). In this instance, the scene is not a happy one, however, as it depicts an old woman standing in a two-wheeled cart with a huge head of cabbage at her side and a cage filled with cackling hens and geese loaded in back of the cart. The mule pulling the cart apparently needs a bit of persuasion. A gaggle of geese swimming nearby and a horseman in the distance seem to be regarding the woman and her stubborn mule with vast amusement. The milk glass is set in a cherry wood frame with two brass handles. Another member of the Milk Glass Society reports a rectangular tray with the identical scene.

The plywood backing on this glass tray is imprinted "ROCHESTER STAMPING CO." and the number "11576." This company, in Rochester, New York, may have replicated Vitrolite glass or more likely had it supplied by the manufacturer. It also produced an extensive line of casseroles, ramekins, and bean pots under the name "Royal Rochester" Metal Mounted Earthenware. In a recipe booklet, dated 1914, the company guaranteed it to be near fire-proof, acid proof, and "absolutely sanitary."

Known to us only in white. Diameter 17 1/4". Very scarce.

209 - FISH-SHAPED TRAY

Formed as a large fish, this deep tray is unremarkable except for the embossed features of the face. Its large eye with bulging pupil and its mouth turned down and slightly open combine to give the creature a look of wary vigilance. The ribbed tail and fins are conventional, but the seven spiked ones on the dorsal side seem odd, though they may actually be found on a real fish for all we know. The milk glass is white, smooth, and glossy on the upper surface, but slightly crinkled on the underside.

Probably fairly recent, it carries a round white paper label with "Made in Sweden" printed in blue ink. Known to us only in white. Length overall 10 3/8"; width of opening 3 1/4". Availability unknown.

210 - LADY SEATED WITH OPEN APRON — TRAY

It may appear somewhat odd to call this piece a tray, but that is indeed what it is. Though hollow, it is a heavy figural item not easily toppled. The amiable woman, seated on a straw box, wears a long, amply pleated smock. Her outstretched arms pick up her apron to form a shallow cavity which is the tray proper, or perhaps the largest master salt we've ever encountered. Her maid's cap, tied with bows at the top and behind, suggests her station in life, but her fine features and head tilted slightly upward denote a proud spirit nonetheless.

Made by Portieux, it is shown in PC (p. 329, No. 7343) with painted decoration and is designated "Vide-poche sujet" (dresser table tidy or pin tray).

Known only in white. Height 6 1/4"; 3 3/4" across at the widest part. Rare.

211 - THREE KITTENS TRAY

An appealing rectangular wickerwork pattern tray with three kittens, in high relief, emerging from a cloth-lined straw nest. The raised margins of the tray are irregular.

Maker unknown. Known to us only in white, both plain and painted. Length 7 3/4"; width 5 1/2". More than hard to find.

212 - PHRENOLOGIST'S HEAD INKWELL

This remarkable piece holds a fascination not only for milk glass and inkwell collectors, but for anyone intrigued by what we are supposed to discover about our mental faculties and character traits simply from examining the shape of our heads. Exquisitely moulded, the hollow glass head, securely fitted in a wreath-like collar, is supported by a metal stand, about 7" wide, formed as a cluster of leaves and branches. Demarcated areas on the head identify the location of various parts or functions of the brain, such as "SPIRITUAL," "INTELLECTUAL," "LIVELINESS," "COMBATIVE," and "CAUTIOUSNESS," and embossed boldly across the top is the word "GODLINESS."

Embossed around the sides of the inkwell opening are the words: "WASHINGTON MANUAL." The outside of the hinged metal cover bears an eagle emblem on a stars and stripes shield; inside are the words — somewhat indistinct — "[?S]EE WASHINGTON MANUAL / JOHN HECKER / N Y ". The head has been said to resemble portraits of our first president, but that may be pure coincidence. We have also seen larger L. N. Fowler's phrenologist's model heads in ceramic, some of which look like recent reproductions, but none in milk glass.

Known to us only in opaque white. The head alone, apparently without the metal frame, is shown by Warman (PLATE 1) who says it is of "Sandwich origin," but we have found no documentation for such an attribution. Height overall is about 6 1/2"; the milk glass head itself measures 4 3/4" high. Extremely rare.

213 - BEVELED BLOCK ["Cherub"] INKWELL

This milk glass inkwell is formed as a large and heavy rectangular hollow block with beveled corners. The well is not removable, but moulded directly in the glass, and fitted with a domed cover with a large knob finial. Two step-up extensions on either side at the front serve as supports for ink pens. Usually found with the cover painted in pink or other pastel shades, and with a floral or other decoration to give the austere design a feminine touch. The example shown here also appears in W-67, but Warman's small black and white photograph does not do justice to this piece. The glass is of excellent quality and the delightful figure of a winged cherub sporting with butterflies seems just right for a Victorian lady's escritoire.

Maker unknown, but it has a European look about it. Known to us in white and in blue, invariably with some decoration. Length 4"; width 3"; diameter of inkwell 1 1/4"; height overall about 3 3/4". Scarce.

215 - ORIENTAL INKWELL

We include this small square inkwell mainly as an example of many other pieces you will find with this distinctive decoration — invariably including at least two green palm trees with hazy purple mountains in the background and orange trim. It is exceedingly heavy, as it is almost solid with the inkwell cavity scarcely large enough to hold an ounce of ink. The domed cover, embossed with scrolls and palm leaves, is beaded around the edge as is the finial.

Identified by Ruth Grizel as a Westmoreland Specialty product, it is listed in the company's 1915 Price Guide as #901 Ink Well and Cover for $.80 per dozen. She illustrated this and other items with the same pattern in *Heirlooms* (cover photo and plate 3-B), and again in *The Original Westmoreland Glass Collectors Newsletter* (IV: 8, Aug. 1996) where she lists almost forty other items as "Oriental Souvenir Novelties" with "Fired Decoration," including puff box, mug, pin tray, hatchet, and the like. Grizel also reprints a Butler Brothers 1918 catalog ad offering an assortment of a dozen or so of these novelties with "Oriental" decoration.

We know these pieces in white, almost always with satin finish, as well as in clear frosted. The inkwell measures 2" square and about 3" high. Individual items range from fairly available to scarce.

214 - HEMISPHERICAL INKSTAND

An unusual ink modeled as a half-globe. The hinged brass rings secure the shallow convex cover to the inkstand. A separate transparent cup to hold the ink fits into the broad hollow base. This example is nicely decorated with large red diamonds, trimmed by gold dots, alternating with broad dark bands. On the lid and front panel a royal sportsman is hailed by three lovely maidens.

Maker unknown. Probably European. Known to us only in white. Height 2 3/4"; diameter of base 4 3/8"; diameter of lid 2 3/4". Scarce.

216 - WORLD GLOBE ADVERTISING INKWELL

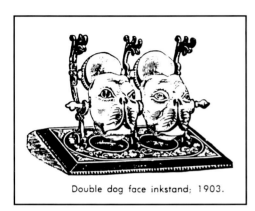

Little is known about the sponsors of this globe set on a short standard with square base. It appears to be an inkwell, and bears the inscriptions: *[Front]* THE NATIONAL STOCKMAN & FARMERS / THE / WORLD'S GREATEST / FARM PAPERS / PITTSBURG *[Back]* THE / FARMERS' REVIEW / CHICAGO.

Maker unknown. Known to us only in white. Height 3"; base 2 1/2" square. Rare.

Double dog face inkstand; 1903.

Tower Manufacturing Co. catalog illustration (circa 1903)

217 - DOUBLE DOG FACE INKSTAND

Not a little frightening, especially when painted, these milk glass inkwells formed as bulldog heads are characteristic of many such decorative inkstand figural novelties popular from about the 1870s through the 1920s. On the desks of hapless scriveners, they provided a welcomed diversion from the drudgery of putting pen to paper. The hollow glass receptacles are supported by rods that fit into grooves at either end, allowing the wells to rotate forward to give access to the opening for the pen. When not in use, the wells are turned backward and rest against a metal back piece in the frame. The pen rack holders were set either above, as in this example, or in front of the inkwells.

Made by The Tower Manufacturing and Novelty Co., New York City, 1903. See John Mebane, "Novelty Inkstands," *Spinning Wheel*, April 1968, p. 14, from which a catalog illustration is reprinted here. This inkstand sold for $12 a dozen. It was also made in a single dog head version.

Known to us only in white. The glass receptacles are a little over 4"; the metal stand measures 5 3/4" by 4 1/2". Very scarce.

218 - INKWELL AND PEN HOLDER TRAY

When found without the inkwell cover, this piece is sometimes mistaken as a combination match-holder and ash tray, for the deep well has an attractively beaded top rim, giving no hint that a cover might be missing. The tray's scrolled and curlicue border is elongated to support several fountain pens, and its center is nicely painted with a flower and leaves. The inkwell cover has a complementary scroll design.

Attributed by Heacock to U.S. Glass, circa 1900-1905 (HCC, Premiere Issue, Winter 1982, p. 28).

Known in milk white and light custard or "ivory," usually decorated with green or blue edging. Length 7"; width 5 1/8"; height overall 2 5/8". At least scarce.

219 - HORSESHOE INKWELL

A fine example of a milk glass inkwell fitted in a metal frame, not an uncommon occurrence, the most famous of course being the Phrenologist's Head inkstand. The ink container has an elaborate metal top fitted by flanges into a metal, possibly copper, horseshoe frame with nails protruding to serve as pen holders.

Maker unknown. Known to us only in white. The inkwell is 1 1/2" square. Hard to find.

220 - SWALLOW INKSTAND

A deep triangle of two steps with sheared corners forms the base for this attractive octagonal inkwell fitted with a ringed, hinged metal closure. Swallows sit peacefully on a wire in the middle of the "well" and along the base, while a pair are seen in graceful flight on the flat upper surface of the base.

Maker unknown. Known to us only in white. Height 3 1/4"; width 4 1/2". Scarce.

Jars

221 - MASCOTTE THREE-PART DOMED COVERED JAR

Here is a majestic piece consisting of three separate components — a wide ribbed round platform base, a cylindrical body with a pattern of three rows of diamonds-in-squares, and a domed lid bearing the identical pattern — a single row around the edge and a double row around the pointed finial. The lid has a lip that fits securely into the jar. We cannot be sure of its intended use, but it is part of an extensive table service, perhaps a pickle jar. The quality of the glass as well as the fine mould work bespeak old quality glassmaking of the highest order.

Attributed to Ripley & Co., of Pittsburgh, Pennsylvania. The Mascotte design on numerous table pieces, plain or etched, was continued at Factory "F" [Ripley] by U. S. Glass Company well beyond the turn of the century (see H-3, p. 123; L-VG, plates 42, 43; and Revi, pp. 290-294). Of all the early pieces, only this jar, according to Jenks and Luna (JL-PG, p. 358), carries the May 30, 1873 patent date. The word PATENTED as well as the date is embossed in reverse on the underside of the jar, explainable by the fact that when made in clear glass, the lettering of course would be normal when viewed from above.

Sketched in a triple-tier size, it is illustrated among an assortment of "apothecary jars and globes" in a catalog of the supply house Whitall Tatum Co., which suggests it was prob-

Triple-tier apothecary jar (sketch from a catalog of the supply house Whitall Tatum Co.).

ably adapted for such use by drug stores. (See Munsey, p. 178.)

In opaque glass, we know it only in white. Overall height 9 1/2". Base element 1 1/4" high, 5 3/4" diameter; Jar 4 1/4" high, 4 5/8" diameter; Lid 4" high to top of finial. Very scarce in opaque, especially if complete, as the base is often missing.

223 - NESTING HEN ROUND POMADE JAR

The body and feathers of this small fat hen are nicely detailed. Its head is raised and the solid tail is sharply turned up. The requisite eggs, of course, are safely guarded under its wings. On the underside of the wide reed basket base is a paper label that reads "Pomade Fine-E. Coudray, Parfumeur," and "Depose-AT-836" is embossed on the rim of the raised foot.

Maker unknown, but assuredly French. Known to us only in white. Height 4"; width 2 5/8". Rare.

222 - OLD KING COLE MUSTARD JAR

Whether this jar was intended to represent the nursery rhyme character is uncertain, but the jolly, rotund figure with crown on head certainly looks like him. That it was a mustard container may be assumed from the marking around the base "COURONNE DE DIJON," a name which may also explain the choice of a crowned figure to advertise the product. The lid has lugs which fit into notches on the jar to hold it secure.

Maker unknown, but most likely French. We know it in green and white, sometimes with painted decoration. Height 5 1/8". Scarce.

224 - PARROT POMADE JAR

Tiny raised diamonds cover the surface of this round jar. The long tailed parrot, bending forward slightly, forms the finial. A smooth band where the cover and base come together gives the appearance that the fit is not quite right.

Maker unknown, but unquestionably an old piece. Known to us only in blue. Height 1 1/4"; diameter 2". Hard to find.

225 - PAPPY AND MAMMY JARS

The main portion of both these highly collectible pieces is the head and neck, which form the base whose covers are a straw hat for Pappy and a kerchief tied in front for Mammy. Bright eyed and exceedingly amiable, they are striking examples of popular figures less often found in milk glass than in ceramic, and usually intended for use as tobacco and cookie jars.

Maker unknown, but probably American. The Pappy jar was previously shown only by Millard (M-295b) but without the straw hat cover and designated as a cigar holder.

Known to us in white, and usually painted as shown here. They measure about 6" high with base opening of 3 1/2". Both are very scarce.

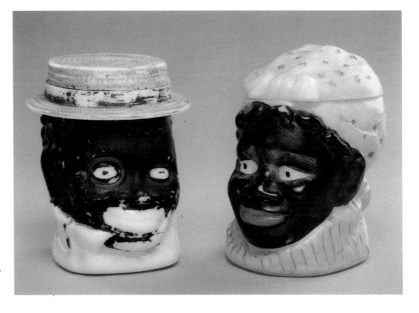

226 - MONKEY MARMALADE JAR

A seldom seen piece in this well-known and avidly collected pattern. It differs from others in having a broad band at the top with a plain rather than a scalloped edge. The bottom is similarly designed and the underside of the jar is deeply impressed.

Attributed to George Duncan & Sons. but see also Heacock (HCG-3, p. 54) where a pitcher is shown in this pattern and said to be a product of the "short-lived Valley Glass Co., of Beaver Falls, Pa."

We are aware of two variants of the marmalade jar, one with bottom completely smooth, the other with deeply pressed converging rays also found on most other monkey pieces.

Jenks & Luna (p. 374) note a reproduced Monkey Spooner (4 3/4" high) in clear, amber, and possibly other colors. The only piece we have seen is a deep reddish-amber and is the base of the sugar rather than the spooner. Fersons (p. 56) note reproductions, presumably by L.G. Wright, of the monkey pattern in vaseline and clear. Height 4 3/4"; base diameter 3 1/2". More than scarce.

227 - DRUM WITH HAT FINIAL POMADE

The base of this covered jar is modeled as a drum and the cover's finial is a military drummer's hat set on a round three-tier platform.

An unmarked English product, dated circa 1885 and attributed by Slack to George Davidson & Co.

Shown here in milk white, it was also made in opaque blue and in a marbled green. Height 4 1/2"; diameter 3 1/2". Very scarce in any color.

228 - FOX AND FISH COVERED JAR

This is a splendid piece, similar to the somewhat more familiar Elk's Head and Steer's Head jars attributed to the Flaccus Company. It bears a nicely detailed fox head with a fish in its mouth, framed by a ring of beads, and the words "Hirsch Bros. & Co. Louisville, Ky. & Pittsburg, Pa." The rest of the surface carries a floral pattern, possibly a rose with leaves. The milk glass lid insert is also elaborate, with the same fox head surrounded by two rows of beads and embossed with the same words.

Maker unknown. Known to us only in white. Height 6 1/4"; diameter 3". Rare.

229 - "REMEMBER THE MAINE" JAR

Lindsey illustrates two covered dishes, three plates, and four tumblers all commemorating the Battleship Maine whose sinking in the harbor at Havana in 1898 helped precipitate the Spanish-American war (Figs. 462-466; 471-474). Other commemoratives were also made, and Lindsey's omission of this covered jar may suggest something of its rarity. The name of the vessel does not appear on the jar, but the likeness to the Maine and its location in Havana are unmistakable. This piece is discussed in Ferson (F-434), but we include it here together with an artist's sketch to show the extraordinary detail of the embossing. One can but faintly discern mould marks at 2 13/16" intervals around the jar whose circumference is 11 1/4". The embossing appears on three sections of the four-part mould, while the fourth (the back of the jar) is plain. Notice the ominously turbulent waters buffeting the hapless ship as it steams into the harbor, with Morro Castle in the background. The degree of minute detail makes this jar nothing short of a marvel.

Maker unknown, but because of the identical screw cap with its Eagle milk glass insert, it is assumed to be a product of the same company that made the Owl Fruit Jar (F- 510).

Known to us in milk white and clear crystal. Height 5 1/2"; diameter about 5 1/2". Extremely rare.

A commissioned artist's precise rendering, exclusively for this book, of the embossed design on the "Remember the Maine" jar.

Lamps

230 - LIGHTHOUSE LAMP

This charming lighthouse with an attached building behind the main tower is formed by thin glass panels set within a metal frame. The various elements are nicely proportioned. Similar structures in various shapes and sizes are popular sellers. This technique of framing thin sheets of semi-opaque or translucent glass in soft metal bands is perhaps best known to collectors in the popular window "sun catchers" of brilliant colors imitating stained glass.

Identified by a metal plate, inserted inside the tower, imprinted: Centuryville "TM" Co., ["c" in circle], Century Classic 1993, S.N. Meyers [in script], Limited edition No. 02492.

Known to us only in white. Height overall 6"; base width 2", depth 3 1/2"; house height 2 3/4"; length 1 3/4". Obviously recent, usually available in gift and souvenir shops.

231 - FELS POINT GLOBE

Although at first glance this may look like a large flask, it is actually a lamp globe. It bears an oysterman's shallop under sail with the word "Fels" embossed above the sails and "Point" near the base. Fels Point is a famous shipping area of Baltimore, Maryland and boats of this type were common in Chesapeake waters. These globes presumably were used on street lights in Fels Point.

Maker uncertain. Probably Baltimore Glass Works. There was a short-lived Baltimore Flint Glass Co. located at Fels Point and acquired by the Baltimore Glass Works. (See McKearin, p. 50 and *passim*.)

Known to us only in white. The globe is 16 1/2" tall, 12" wide, and 9" deep. Rare.

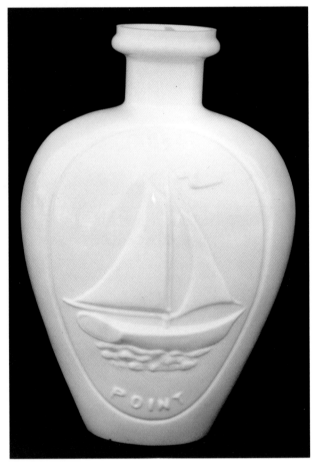

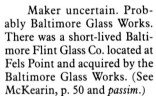

232 - CAT AND MICE LAMP

This lamp globe formed as a full-figure cat rests on a separate round black milk glass platform. Open mouthed, the cat can almost be heard bellowing "Meow!" as it clutches two hapless mice in both paws, the catch of the day. The demure pink bow around its neck, however, tells us the owner of this lovable pet does not prize it simply as a rat catching predator.

Maker unknown. Known to us only in white. Height overall 8 1/4". More than scarce.

233 - CAT LAMP

We cannot tell whether this is the Cheshire cat because it has no indication of a mouth to grin with! Those are actually his paws, not enormous teeth, which you see under his face. The sleeping beauty is almost a ball, with its body curled around so tightly that the large, fat tail nearly touches its cheek. Lacking any handle or protrusion to grab on to, it is very difficult to pick up, nor does it help that the glass is sleek and slippery. It is hollow, of course, and will hold a good quantity of lamp oil. A single curving mould mark runs the entire length of the body from just below the right ear to the base of the tail.

Maker unknown, and difficult to date. The burner shows some signs of age, but the cat looks like it might belong to the Art Deco period.

Known to us only in white. Maximum diameter 5 1/2"; height to the top of the brass collar 3 1/4". It apparently is more than hard to find.

235 - SANTA CLAUS LAMP

A most attractive electric lamp, this jolly Santa Claus sports his familiar red and white suit with large black belt girding his ample paunch. The lamp, all of one piece, portrays the eagerly awaited Christmas visitor as he makes his way down the chimney bearing a gift box and a doll in his arms.

Maker unknown. Known only in white and invariably appropriately painted. Height 8 1/4". Scarce.

234 - MAMMY LAMP

Set on a separate black milk glass support, the globe of this milk glass electric lamp is a full-figure Mammy, nicely painted. Her blue dress with yellow collar, white and gray apron, and of course the polka dot bandanna are traditional. She stands with her hands in her pockets and appears to have a quizzical look on her face.

Maker unknown. Known to us only in white with painted decoration. Height 7 1/2". Scarce.

236 - SANTA CLAUS OIL LAMP

This early miniature two-piece lamp is much prized by collectors. The lower half is the oil reservoir, measuring 3 1/4" high and 3 3/8" across the bottom. The Nutmeg burner, with round metal platform to hold the 6" high Santa globe, is marked PAT. FEB·Y 27 1877. Arms crossed and rather gaunt, he is more formidable than our contemporary rotund images of jolly old St. Nick. From his characteristic black boots on a mound of snow to the rest of the traditional painted decoration, this lamp is a classic example of an Old World Santa.

Attributed to Consolidated Lamp and Glass Co., Pittsburgh, Pennsylvania, circa 1894. It is similar to another Santa lamp, probably made by the same company, but that one is identifiable by an indentation found on the underside of the base and is generally regarded as less well made. See S-1, Fig. VII, and S-2, Fig. 349; also Solverson, Fig. 165.

Known to us only in milk white, variously painted. Overall height 9 1/2". Rare.

237 - BANANA SPLIT LAMP

Objects such as this are often the reason why some purists raise their highbrows in disapproval at the mere mention of "Milk Glass." Though obviously a commercial piece, probably intended for an ice cream shop window, we admire this delightful recreation *in milk glass* of a traditional soda fountain favorite! The globe of this electric lamp is realistically moulded as a platter holding chunks of bananas and, of course, the obligatory three mounds of ice cream dripping with sauce. The side of the platter is embossed "Pat Appl. For." No one will ever call this piece aesthetically profound, but one collector remembers his mother bringing it out of the deep recesses of her closet and displaying it conspicuously when she was told by a veteran dealer that he knew of only three in existence. When gaudily painted it is indeed "something else."

Maker unknown. Known to us only in white. Length 8 1/4"; height 3 1/2". More than scarce, possibly rare.

238 - HAM AND EGGS ON A PLATTER LIGHT GLOBE

To entice the hungry worker on his way to work, here is an advertising piece just right for the window of the popular diner that used to be down the street. Its intended use as a light globe is evident from the small notch at the back to allow passage of an electric light cord. Wonderfully modeled, it appears to have been sufficiently important for someone to protect against reproduction, as the words "Patent Applied For" appear underneath, on the side.

Maker unknown, but quite possibly by the same manufacturer as the Banana Split lamp. Known to us only in white, realistically painted with reddish-brown ham and yellow egg yokes. Length 12"; height 2 3/4". Rare.

239 - EAGLE MINIATURE LAMP

Framed by rows of beads forming a diamond, the embossed eagle with wings spread and holding two arrows in its claws appears on the front and the back of the shade as well as the base of this miniature lamp. The rest of the surface is adorned with leaves and scrolls. According to Smith (S-1, #275, p. 130-31) the painted decorations on these milk glass lamps always have the eagle done in gilt, but the background color combinations vary, including yellow and blue, orange and brick red, green and white, green and pink, and possibly others. Because the paint is not fired on, finding specimens with the original paint intact is not easy. The nutmeg burner in this example is marked "A & P M.F. CO."

Maker unknown. Smith, cited above, reports that this lamp was advertised in Butler Brothers catalog "Our Drummer" for Feb. 1900 and was offered for sale at $2.25 per dozen. (In the Smith and Feltner 1987 price guide, the lamp is valued at $400.) Height 7 3/4". Scarce.

240 - OWL MINIATURE LAMP

Miniature lamps formed as figurals are especially well-suited because the separation of the shade for a head and the base for a body is neatly achieved by having the burner element serve as the connecting "neck." The proportions are sometimes a bit strained, as in this example where the head of the owl seems rather large for the body. The surface of the globe and base is feathered all over, with the face of the owl appearing on both sides of the globe. The base, however, is not reversible, as the owl's feet appear in the front while the back has the tail feathers. According to Smith (S-1, #497, p. 205) this milk glass lamp with fired on paint occurs in black and grays with orange eyes, in various shades of reddish brown, and in light and dark green, the latter seen in the example pictured here. The nutmeg burner is marked "MADE IN U.S.A."

Maker unknown. Height about 8". Very scarce. In the Smith and Feltner 1987 price guide, the lamp is valued at $1,800 - $2,000, a reflection in part of the desirability of figural objects among milk glass collectors.

241 - FISH AND SHELLS LAMP

A stately lamp with elegant lines, it combines a fish motif with sea shells in a backdrop of cascading waterfalls. The base has three equidistantly placed fish swimming downward with large shells in between. The fanciful fish appear to have the body of a scaly eel, with large rayed fins on each side, and a spheroid head. The oil font has an unrelated but appropriately designed pattern of vertical ribs crossed by a rope twist. We suspect the base may also have been used to support a candlestick top as well, because the font is a separate element cemented to the base. The depressed underside of the base has an intaglio of converging rays. The screw top burner appears to be of foreign manufacture.

Maker unknown. Known to us in both blue and white opaque. Height to top of font 8". Scarce.

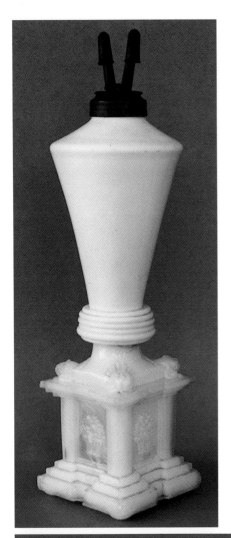

242 - LION AND FLOWER BASKET WHALE OIL LAMP

This impressive early lamp is sometimes called "The Monument" because of the monumental character of the base. It is of heavy pressed glass, with ribbed pillars at each corner rising from a triple stepped plinth. Flower-filled wicker baskets are embossed in high relief on each of the four panels. Above each pillar is a lion's head resting on its front paws, all extremely well detailed. The free blown oil reservoir comes in various shapes, either as a sphere, a cylinder, or a cone, the latter sometimes with moulded ribbing. The glass can vary from dense milk white to fiery, almost translucent opalescence.

Well documented, these lamps have been attributed to Sandwich, but specimens marked "N E G CO" (New England Glass Company) have also been found, according to McKearin, p. 380. He further suggests, "It may be that the Boston and Sandwich Company made those which are unmarked, or that the New England Glass Company had two moulds for the base." Wilson also attributes this lamp to either Sandwich or NEG (*New England Glass and Glassmaking*, p. 257). In examining several examples, we have found one notable difference in two of the bases. One version has a large knob moulded at each corner on the underside, elevating the base about 1/4". The other has a perfectly flat underside. McKearin may be right in suggesting that NEG had two moulds.

We know these lamps only in white opaque and opalescent, but they are reported and shown in clear as well (McKearin, plate 196, No. 9).

Depending upon the type of font, the height will vary, ranging from about 7 1/2" with spherical font to almost 10" with the conical one. Extremely rare.

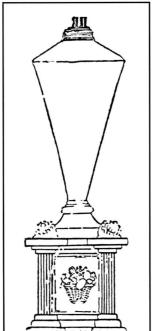

Monument Lamp sketch, from C. W. Dreppard, *ABC's of Old Glass*, Award Books, New York, 1968 ed., p. 81.

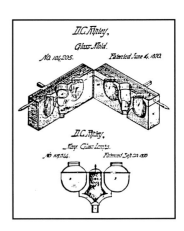

Patent application drawing for Ripley's double font "Marriage Lamp" Shown at bottom left.

243 - RIPLEY MARRIAGE OR BRIDE'S LAMP

Noted for his lamp designs, Daniel C. Ripley received a patent (No. 104,205) on June 14, 1870 for the glass mould design of this highly prized lamp. The glass lamps design, comprising double side-by-side oil fonts and a connecting cup, was granted patent No. 107,544 on September 30th of the same year (see patent drawings). The intricate process of joining the two fonts required two glass blowers working together. It was quite a risky operation, and sometimes resulted in the separation of one of the fonts — an example of such a mishap is shown in F-525 — and of those that survived intact, stress cracks are not unusual. The hollow cup between the fonts served as a matchholder and was originally fitted with a metal lid that is missing in the example shown here. The twin fonts were connected by a brass collar to a pedestal base which apparently can be found in a variety of shapes and sizes, according to Loris Russell (*A Heritage of Light, Lamps and Lighting in the Early Canadian Home*, Toronto University Press, 1968, p. 210). A No. 1 Queen Ann burner is customary on these lamps.

The lamp pictured in Ferson (F-525) with one of the fonts missing is said to be marked PAT[T] PENDING, apparently an early effort which did not fare well. The one seen here is marked on the matchholder, PATENTED SEP 20 1870.

According to the patent papers "... glass of different colors may be used in the different parts so as to add considerably to the neatness of its appearance" (quoted by Peterson, *Glass Patterns and Patents*, p. 172). Known to us with fonts made in clambroth blue or white and affixed to milk glass or clear glass pedestal bases of various designs. Height to top of fonts 12 3/4"; width across the two fonts about 9". Rare. One made with blue fonts on a tall clambroth two-part stem with a brass connector was sold at a James D. Julia auction on October 10, 1997 for $4,140.

245 - SAINT NICHOLAS BONBON

The name "ST NICOLAS," as spelled in French, embossed on the front of the pedestal of this satin finish bonbonniere, identifies the saint, but we should recognize him immediately anyway from the presence of the three children by his side. Legend recounts how he once discovered a wicked innkeeper stealing children, killing them, and serving them as meat to his guests. St. Nicholas, finding three of the children dead in a basket, made the sign of the Cross and they were brought back to life. This miracle served to make him the protector and patron saint of children. In addition, his bishop's attire and staff are traditional for this legendary 4th-century saint of Myra.

Maker unknown. It is embossed on the back "BON BONS JOHN TAVERNIER LES MEILLEURS!" No doubt of French manufacture, it probably dates from about the turn of the century. Known to us only in white. Height 16 1/2". Rare.

244 - SAINT ANTHONY BON-BON

This candy container is a beautiful rendering of the thirteenth century patron saint of Padua, capturing the essence of the figure whose image frequently is painted on the robes of the Franciscan Order. Of fine quality, glossy milk glass, and fitted with a metal base closure, this example still shows traces of brown paint on the head and back. The facial features are excellent, both of the saint and the Infant Christ whom St. Anthony is often depicted carrying, especially after the Renaissance period. Notice that he holds a spray of lilies, a frequent offering symbolic of purity.

Maker unknown. Embossed "BON BONS JOHN TAVERNIER" on the back; most likely French, dating from about 1898 to the turn of the century. Known to us only in white. Height 16 1/2". Rare.

246 - SAINT CATHERINE BONBON

Identified as "SAINTE CATHERINE," embossed on the front of the pedestal, this is yet another of the impressive John Tavernier bonbon candy containers. The sword she holds in her hand as well as the wheel embossed at her feet are emblems of the instruments of her martyrdom by the emperor Maximim II because she spurned his offer of marriage, so we know it is the third century St. Catherine of Alexandria, not the much later saint of Siena. Like the others in this series, it is beautifully modeled. The words 'BON BONS JOHN TAVERNIER LES MEILLEURS!" are embossed on the wheel at her feet.

Maker unknown. French, dating from circa 1898 to the turn of the century. Known to us only in white. Height 16 1/2". Rare.

248 - THIMBLE SHOT GLASS

A humorous little shot glass formed as a thimble. On the band around the top are embossed the words "JUST A THIMBLE FULL" in large block letters. The pimpled surface of the rest of the piece is, of course, what makes it a "thimble," tapering to a rounded semi-flat bottom which allows the shot glass to stand upright.

The trademark inside the bottom identifies it as a circa 1885 product of the English company George Davidson, shown in brown glass by Lattimore, p. 65. A similar one was made by Sowerby.

We know it in purple marble and clear crystal. Height 2 1/2"; diameter 2" across the top. More than scarce.

247 - RABBIT HUNTER CANDY CONTAINER

This lad, with plump cheeks, pursed lips, and wide eyes, is as adorable as he can be, standing proudly with his trophy, a large rabbit held by its hind legs. The painted decoration enhances the details of his garb, a soft green felt hat with a wide red band, hip-length mustard colored coat with V-neck collar and buttoned down the front. A large brown pouch, slung from his shoulder, hangs waist high on his right side. On the left behind him, a rifle is suspended by another shoulder strap. Hollow and fitted with a screw cap at the base, it would seem to be a container for candy, but no larger than jelly beans as the constriction near the bottom of the trousers is quite narrow.

Maker unknown. What appears to be a trademark is faintly embossed on the back, in the shape of a bell bearing a design of some sort which we have been unable to identify. See O.N., XI:4, Sept. 1996, p. 6.

Known to us only in white. Height 8 1/4"; base diameter 2 1.8". Rare.

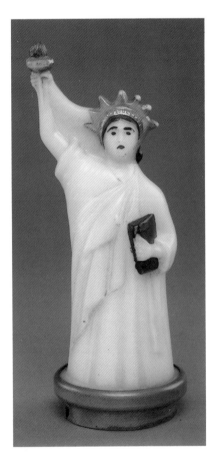

249 - STATUE OF LIBERTY FIGURAL

An enigmatic piece whose round, hollow base suggests it might fit over the top of some type of cylindrical object. It is sometimes found with a metal cap at the bottom, suggesting perhaps a candy container, though uncommonly large if it is. The notions that it may be a light signal attached to the roof of a taxicab or the cap of a radiator on an early automobile are intriguing, but undocumented to our knowledge. Although far from an exact replica, it is designed, of course, as the Statue of Liberty with flame held high in her right hand.

Maker unknown. See Kaye, Vol. I, p. 47. Known to us only in white. Height 6" to the top of the flame, on a base 2 2/8" in diameter with a 3/8" rim. Scarce.

250 - HAIR RECEIVERS

Although hair receivers were undoubtedly an essential part of Milady's dressing table, they are not as easily found today as are the pin trays, boxes, or cologne bottles. Two examples shown here are nicely decorated. The one with a painting of Niagara Falls appears to be an individual souvenir item. The other, with painted flowers and the customary gilt to enhance the embossed scroll work, is more typical and more likely a part of a dresser set

Makers unknown. Known to us in white, but undoubtedly found in other colors. Average height 3" with hole in the cover about 1 1/4". Somewhat hard to find.

251 - VICTORIAN LADY CURTAIN TIEBACK

This fetching young lady, with a broad rimmed sun hat in her right hand, is seated outdoors in a garden, perhaps, for crooked at the elbow of her left arm is a basket for gathering flowers. Because the piece is fitted at the back with a metal casing which is threaded to accept a screw, we assume it is intended to be a curtain tieback. But in design, size, weight, and quality this impressive ornament far exceeds such limited functional use. The figure as well as the scroll work of the border is so deeply embossed as to appear almost three dimensional. If asked to define "elegance" by example, one would unhesitatingly point to this wonderful creation.

Maker unknown. Known to us only in white. Length 5 5/8"; maximum width 4 3/4". Very scarce.

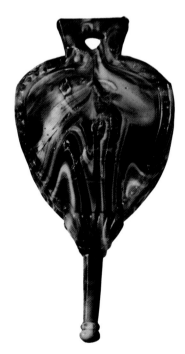

252 - BELLOWS WALL POCKET

Formed as a pair of bellows, this wall pocket is said to be a "hair tidy," or flower holder, or perhaps a matchholder as the back side is heavily stippled and could well serve as a match strike. The front is moulded with the figure of Little Jack Horner, very difficult to see in the marbled glass, seated on a stool, with pie in one hand and the other hand raised high holding a plum, of course. Like others in this series of nursery rhyme subjects, it is modeled after designs by Walter Crane (1877). There are holes on both of the tabs at the top, so it can be hung with either side facing away from the wall.

Made by Sowerby. The accompanying sketch is item No. 1285 from the Sowerby 1882 *Pattern Book IX* (p. 5). See also Slack, p. 58.

We know it only in purple-brown marbled. Length 5 1/2"; maximum width 2". Rare. One was sold at an auction in England in 1989 for £160 (about $250).

Sketch of Little Jack Horner "Bellows Wall Pocket," from the Sowerby *Pattern Book IX* (1882), p. 5.

254 - HOLY WATER FONT

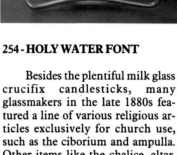

253 - BEARDED FIGURE WATCHSTAND

Among ornamental figural pieces in milk glass designed for specific uses, this is an outstanding creation which never fails to elicit enthusiastic admiration from collectors. The kneeling, bearded figure is naked but for a draped cloth discreetly placed, and may represent the Titan Atlas. Within a large beaded circle, the watch lies flat against the support which rests on his back and is balanced by his upraised arms. The ornate base is slightly elevated by small knobbed feet, and at the front is a long, narrow groove which probably is meant to hold a watch fob. The mould detail is extraordinary, and the glass typically French.

Made by Portieux, it is shown in PC (p. 329, No. 7342) and designated "Porte-montre sujet" (figural watch stand). Known to us only in white. Height approximately 7". Extremely rare.

Besides the plentiful milk glass crucifix candlesticks, many glassmakers in the late 1880s featured a line of various religious articles exclusively for church use, such as the ciborium and ampulla. Other items like the chalice, altar trays, ewers and basins, and holy water fonts also found their way to the private homes of devout Catholics. The two specimens of holy water fonts shown here demonstrate the wide extremes in which they were designed, from ornate to starkly plain.

The painted example with two angels holding the font is illustrated in VCC as No. 4159, p. 312. The maker of the undecorated one, formed as a crucifix and embossed "Patent Applied For" inside the basin, is unknown but probably American. Individual examples vary in size and range from hard to find to rare.

255 - COIN SORTER

Here is a most unusual application of a milk glass wide rimmed dish with a central shallow well, designed to hold a metal tray insert. The tray, with sixteen spring loaded slots for coins of varying sizes, ranging from 1/2" to 7/8", is easily removed by lifting the thin, curved metal handle; when the tray is put back in place, the handle folds down flat.

The underside of the milk glass plate is marked "Stratford-Cookson Company," obviously an English product and designed to accept British coins. It measures 5 2/8" in diameter and is 1 5/8" high. Scare, possibly rare.

256 - NIGHT LIGHT CLOCK

The face of this clock is milk glass, about 1/4" thick, with the numerals etched and painted. It is set in a gilt metal frame with two supports in front and a swivel bracing arm extension attached at the back. A cylindrical open socket at the end of the bracket could allow a candle to be inserted, but by the turn of the century the illumination was more likely supplied by fitting it to a gas jet.

Made by several companies, the maker of the one shown here is not identified but the clockworks are marked with a series of five patent dates, the earliest is Jan 16, 1878 and the last is May 29, 1894. The lithograph illustrations are from an Ansonia Clock catalog dated 1901. The clock is advertised as having a one-day movement with an "Opaloid Glass Dial, Finished in Gilt." It sold for $4.75.

Known to us only in milk white opalescent glass. Diameter 6". Scarce.

257 - PENDANTS AND BROOCHES IN MILK GLASS

Cameo jewelry made in gem stones, marble, bisque, glass, plastic and other materials abound, of course, and it often takes some expertise to distinguish among them. The three illustrated here have been examined by an expert jeweler and certified to be "just glass." The owners of these pieces were delighted to know that their "gems" are definitely milk glass! From left to right:

(1) A profile cameo brooch in a bronze colored setting. The lady wears roses in her hair done up in ringlets that curl down around her neck. The chain she wears comes through two holes at either side of her neck and hangs loosely in front while at the back it is folded over to secure it. The stone is meant to look attached to the chain, but it is actually recessed and glued in. The pin is a simple pin and C shape hook, not a safety catch. Marked in back "Made in Czechoslovakia," the broach measures 2" by 1 1/2".

(2) Worn either as a brooch or pendant, this piece is custard colored and set in an open-work wreath of silvered leaves, measuring 1/2" at their widest point. The full-figured lady in a flowing gown has a bird perched on her left hand while two more birds flutter nearby. A small flowering plant is by her feet. Fitted with a safety catch, it measures 2 1/8" by 2 1/2". Maker unknown.

(3) Also worn either as a brooch or pendant, this is a traditional profile cameo in custard milk glass. It is signed with one of the various trademarks of "Hobé" jewelry whose origins date back to the late 1800s in Paris, France. Descendants of Jacque Hobé brought the tradition to America where it continues to the present day. The mark used on this particular piece dates it as made between 1958-1983. It is set in a 1/4" gold frame with safety catch, and measures 1 1/2" by 2".

Depending upon their origins and dates of production, milk glass jewelry items such as these are very collectible and can vary from readily available to quite rare.

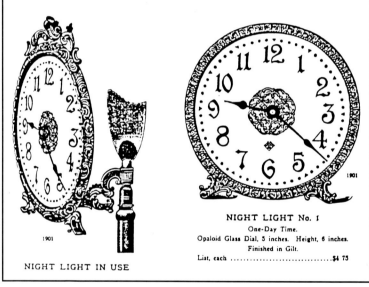

Lithograph illustrations of the Night Clock from a 1901 Ansonia Clock catalog.

258 - NEWEL POSTS

These ornamental fixtures were used at the ends or corners of stair handrails in the stately homes of the affluent. The descriptive term "newel" derives from the Latin, meaning "nut" or "nutlike," and passed into the French language as *noyau*, meaning "fruitstone." The oval knobs of those pictured here are in opalescent glass with a hobnail pattern, applied while hot to a blue glass collar. The whole is then cemented onto a solid brass stem with a hole underneath, so that it would slip into a dowel attached to the handrail. Later ones are sometimes threaded so they could be attached by a screw.

Maker unknown, but in the tradition of Boston and Sandwich or Cape Cod Glass Companies of Sandwich, Massachusetts, circa 1850-1870.

Newel posts generally are conical or round and exist in various colors or color combinations. Height 8". Quite scarce.

259 - EMBOSSED EASTER EGG ASSORTMENT

Very desirable, blown milk glass Easter eggs such as these were made by the thousands as many different companies took advantage of their immense appeal during the late nineteenth century and well into the early 1900s. Many of these eggs are designed with flat bottoms so that they can stand alone, but others are fully rounded. Shown here is a group of eggs all of which have embossed designs. Clockwise from bottom left: (1) "EASTER" in a scroll with floral spray, 4"; (2) "EASTER" and large chick with painted flowers, 5"; (3) "EASTER" and large anchor with painted flowers, 6"; (4) "EASTER" and eggs in a basket with painted trim, 4 3/4"; (5) "EASTER" and chick on a grassy mound, 3 3/4". And in the center, a winged cherub within a garland, 2 1/2".

Various makers, among them Gillinder, Dithridge, Eagle Glass, and others. Generally found only in milk white glass, often decorated with much gilt or colors hand painted on the embossed designs as well as the plain surfaces. Usually available, but some of the more elaborate ones are very hard to find.

260 - GOLF BALL LIQUOR CADDY

Golfers especially may appreciate this novel design for a liquor set, marked at the top of the cover "The 19 TH Hole," where the day's frustrations are traditionally soothed by appropriate restoratives. The two-part container modeled as a huge golf ball rests on a round base simulating turf, painted green, and girded by a metal band for added weight and protection. Inserted at the top of the base is a metal tray, imprinted "Czechoslovakia," with holes for a small carafe and six shot glasses.

Maker unknown. This piece was illustrated and discussed by Albert Christian Revi (*Antiques and Collecting Magazine*, Oct. 1995, p. 6) who states "Many of these handsome pieces in different forms came from Bohemian glass factories in the late 19th and early 20th centuries... and probably sold well in this country and abroad, especially in England where golf is still a popular sport, as it is in the United States." He believes it was made "soon after World War I (1918) when Czechoslovakia was formed, and certainly before it was annexed by Germany in the 1940s." Incidentally, we have encountered a similar set made in lightweight plastic.

Known to us only in white, as shown. Height about 10"; diameter 7 1/4". Very scarce.

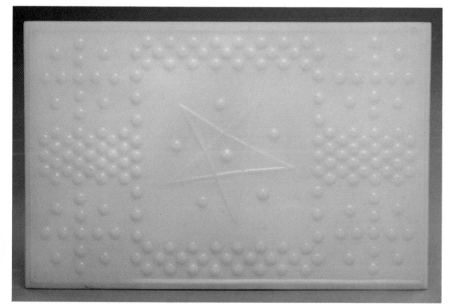

261 - STAR AND DOTS HOT PLATE HOLDER

This large rectangular slab, elevated by six stubby angled legs, serves as a hot plate holder. The center is dominated by a large star outlined by rows and blocks of raised semi-circular dots. The back is embossed "Patent applied for GTH".

Maker unknown. Known to us only in white. Length 10 3/8"; width 7 1/2"; height about 1". Rare.

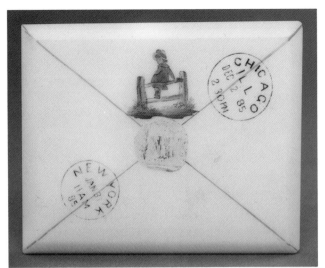

262 - ENVELOPE TILE

A plain slab of milk glass with beveled edges is given a precise identity only by virtue of its painted decoration. The crossed lines create the back of an envelope and a heavy application of enamel creates a *faux* glob of sealing wax impressed with the initials WHS. At the center is a charming miniature painting, really exquisitely done, of a young girl sitting on a split rail fence. Two postmarks signal "Chicago, Ill Dec 2.85 2:30 PM" and "New York Jan 31 11 AM 85." The year "85" in these postmarks is somewhat curious. The piece is not old enough to be 1885 and does not appear to us new enough to be 1985, so do not know what to make of the postmarks. The back side has a waffle pattern of the type common to glass tiles.

Maker unknown. Known only in white, as shown. It measures 4 1/2" by 3 3/4". Rare, and possibly unique in this decoration.

263 - TELEPHONE POLE INSULATOR

Beginning in the 195]0s, as telephone lines went underground, this once essential component of telephone poles has virtually become extinct. These insulators have already become very collectible, particularly the older and rarer specimens; one in yellow glass dating from the 1870s sold recently at auction for $10,000. Most, however, are still plentiful and can be bought for as little as two or three dollars. Those in milk white glass are only slightly less common than the majority that were made in clear and colored glass of green, blue, red, brown, amber — in varying shades, shapes, and sizes — and frequently bearing a patent date. We are always amazed and delighted to find so many purely practical, commonplace objects made in sturdy milk white glass!

The undated example shown is marked "MAYDWELL - 20 / U.S.A." It is threaded inside and the wooden pole seen in this example is actually screwed in.

We know of milk glass specimens in white only, but they may occur in other opaque colors as well. Height of the glass insulator itself, 4"; diameter 3". Somewhat hard to find.

264 - TAXICAB LIGHT

Milk glass has long been a favorite medium for illuminated advertising pieces because of its clean look and the fine light it gives. Here it is formed as a long hollow cylinder with "TAXI" in large contrasting red letters. It is attached at both ends to a metal holder that was bolted to the top of a taxicab, in use during the 1930s-1940s. A transparent, conical green or amber globe is attached at each end presumably to indicate whether or not the taxi was available.

The entire assemblage was made by "Mac Ellis 258 Columbus Ave. Boston 16, Mass." Who made the glass elements is unknown.

Presumably occurs only in white. The cylinder is 6 1/4" long with a circumference of 8 1/4"; total length 11 1/2". Scarce in our experience.

265 - OWL BOOKEND

As a symbol of wisdom and knowledge, the owl is of course an apt figure for a bookend. Weighing nearly five pounds, this horned owl is something of a marvel for its elegant and detailed mould work despite its tremendous bulk. Three books of increasing size are set behind the full-figure owl standing vigilantly on a tree stump whose roots reinforce the overall impression of stability. The original rhinestone eyes and protective green felt on the underside may still be found intact. Few of these bookends appear to have survived, and considering the difficulty of making such a heavy piece, probably not many were made.

Illustrated in a 1924 catalog of the Westmoreland Specialty Co., reprinted by Weatherman, *Colored Glassware*, p.369. It continued to be made into the 1930s. See also Grizel (*Heirlooms*, p. 73), and G-S (p. 208).

Besides opaque white, it was made in crystal and various colors with and without a satin finish, and possibly in green and black opaque. Height 6"; base 4 1/4" by 4 3/4". Rare.

Note: Pictured here alongside the bookend, to show the difference in size, is a familiar small novelty of an almost identical owl, 3 1/2" high, standing on two books. It too is a Westmoreland product issued over many years and continued to be made after its closing by Summit Art Glass Co. A reproduction of the Westmoreland small owl was made by Degenhart in a vast array of colors, beginning in 1967. According to Gene Florence (*Degenhart Glass and Paperweights,* 2nd ed. 1992), "Aside from the Degenhart mark, the owls can be distinguished from Westmoreland counterparts by looking at the eyes of the owl. The Degenhart owl's right eye is dropped slightly, whereas the Westmoreland owl's eyes are straight across from each other" (p. 20).

266 - SEWING "MAKE-DO" PINCUSHIONS

Spill the wine or spoil the milk and there is no remedy. But drop the compote, crack the candlestick socket, or overturn the oil lamp, and presto! — a perfect stem for the thrifty housewife to fashion a new sewing needle or hat pin holder. With a wad of cotton wool, a piece of velvet or homespun fabric, perhaps adding a bit of fine silk tassel to dress it up, what was lost is recovered with a new identity. These examples of milk glass standards refashioned as pin holders are testimony to the good husbandry, not to mention the ingenuity, of those who appreciated and preserved even the fragments of some of "yesterday's milk glass."

The makers of such pieces are known only to the heirs of their estates. Both appear to be the bases of oil lamps. The taller, filled with matted straw, is 7" high; the smaller is 4 3/4." Availability? — if not easily found, easily made!

267 - OPEN BACK SWAN

As every collector of glass swans knows, those created by the Cambridge Glass Company are distinctive in having the swan's feet sticking out behind. After Cambridge closed in 1954, the swan moulds passed through several different hands, including Mosser, Imperial, Levay (by Imperial), and Summit Art Glass. (See Clyde E. Ingersoll's meticulous discussion of various modifications to the moulds, in *Glass Animals*, by Garmon and Spencer, p. 16) The one shown here was made by Boyd's Crystal Art Glass of Cambridge, Ohio, who acquired the moulds upon the liquidation of the bankrupt Imperial Glass Company in 1984. Beginning in 1985 and through the present, Boyd has produced the swan in the 3" and 4 1/2" sizes. The latter is also made as a candleholder. The detail is superb and the glass of excellent quality.

Marked B in a diamond, as are most of Boyd's products — much to their credit, we might add — the swan shown here was made in 1986 in a light green milk glass called "Seafoam." It is beautifully hand painted and signed "CL." Mr. John Boyd informs us those are the initials of Charlie LaCroix. You may also find the initials "SJ," another artist whom he identifies as Scott Jones. Incredible as it may seem, Boyd has made these swans over the years in more than fifty different colors, including opaque, transparent, vaseline, and carnival! Shown here is the 4 1/2" size. Usually available.

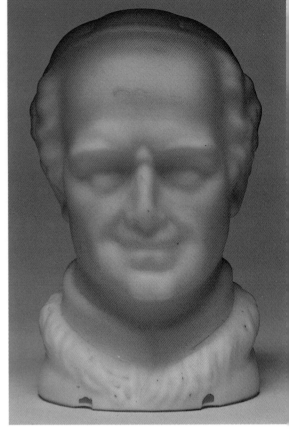

268 - CARDINAL'S HEAD

The prelate represented by this wonderfully modeled head may be an actual historical personage, but we have not been able to identify him. Nor can we determine what the piece was designed for, but since the back of the head is open and six small holes appear around the base, it would seem to be a part of some other missing element. With fired on red paint — suggesting a cardinal — and a fine satin finish to the glass, the head has a startling appeal as it combines both dignity in the broad forehead and warmth in the affable smile.

Maker unknown. Known to us only in white. Height 6 1/2" with a base diameter of 3 1/2". Rare.

269 - WICKER AND FLOWER, HANDLED BASKET

This is an outstanding old piece, with crisp, minutely detailed embossing over every inch of its surface including the underside. The oval basket, a tight waffle weave, is restricted at the center by a high arching handle formed by the braided cords around the top edge that come together and are bound higher up by two small twines. Flanking each side of the handle, in both front and back, are a large flower and three leaves. The underside is fashioned as two branchlets, each bearing three leaves alternating with large flower buds. Remarkably heavy, it is not at all a fragile piece.

Maker unknown. We know it in plain white, white decorated, and in a rich dark blue of the same quality as the "Jolly Moor" matchholder (No. 374 in this book) which is marked "S V," hence suggesting this basket is a product of the same company. Length 5 3/4"; width 3 1/2"; height 5 1/2". Scarce.

270 - FLORAL SCROLL STEIN

German beer steins are commonly found with elaborate decoration, but rarely in milk glass. This is a beautiful example with intricate floral scroll on the sides and a shield topped by a helmet and crown in front. The pewter top is a nicely designed outdoor tavern scene showing a seated gentleman extending his purse to a serving girl with her pitcher in hand and key ring at her waist. In the background is a small chalet and a castle in the distance.

Maker unknown. On the underside it reads "ORIGINAL - BMF - BIERSEIDEL / "Made in Germany" and the number "5." Known to us only in white. Height 6 1/2". Hard to find.

272 - DEER AND COW CHILDREN'S MUG

This handsome mug features an embossed cow's head with upright pointed horns on one side and the head and shoulders of a noble looking antlered stag on the opposite side. Both figures are elegantly detailed. The mug has a single step foot and a handle similar to the type used by Atterbury in the Eastlake (bird) mugs, but the vertical portion of the handle on this mug is swollen in the middle and each end has two round bands.

Maker unknown. It is illustrated in clear glass by Lechler (M-16, p. 29). Besides clear crystal and milk glass, Lechler (p. 138) states it is found in amber and blue as well. It is 2" high with a top diameter of 1 7/8". Scarce.

271 - FIGHTING SWAN CHILDREN'S MUG

A delicate mug with a finely embossed narrow-necked swan on each side. Delineated by a pebbled surface, the bird with wings upraised is in the threat position used by Mute Swan males in defending a nest, as it is indeed sitting on a nest. An aquatic floral design appears in front of and behind the bird. The evenly curved handle is very slender, almost wire-like in appearance.

Maker unknown. Although difficult to be certain from the indistinct illustrations in both Millard (74-B) and Lechler (#M-54), the Millard mug depicts either a crane or heron; Lechler's mug, shown in blue, has the same slender handle but the embossed figure is totally obscure, nor does she name or describe the figure.

Known to us only in white. It is 2" high, with a top diameter of 1 3/4". Scarce.

273 - PUNCH AND JUDY MUG

This mug was inspired, of course, by the famed puppet characters. Both husband and wife, moulded in great detail on either side, stand out in extremely high relief within a circle of beads; in fact, the figure of Judy almost appears three dimensional! In between are scrolls and sunburst florets, while circling above is a border of three fine vertical bands intersected by wide horizontal ones running obliquely. The handle is ribbed with a rosette at the top of the elbow. The glass is of fine quality, and the workmanship superb.

Shown in F-203 without attribution. No doubt of its English origin, it has been ascribed to Henry Greener (circa 1875-80) on the basis of the style of the portrait medallions (see Slack, p. 96).

Known to us only in milk white. Height 4"; diameter of the base 3 1/4". More than scarce.

274 - CLASSIC LADY'S HEAD MEDALLION SHAVING MUG

This is a much larger shaving mug than others we have found in milk glass. The interior has a glass divider creating two compartments: the front one is open all the way down to the bottom for the water; the one behind goes about half way down to hold the soap. The embossed designs are all in the classical Greek or Roman manner, with large oval beaded medallions on each side. The profile of a stately matron with a laurel wreath binding her hair is beautifully moulded, but in very low relief. The handle, hexagonal in cross section, is appropriately austere. This mug is very heavy and made in excellent quality milk glass.

Maker unknown. Listed previously in Kaye, Vol. I, p. 31, who notes its resemblance to the Ceres design mugs, and states that the specimen she shows is marked on the underside "Henry Tetlow & Bros. Phila.," a barbershop supply house.

Known to us only in white. Height 3 3/4" and almost 4" across the top. Rare.

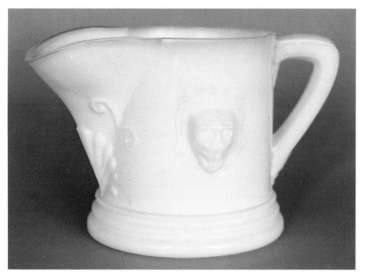

275 - PITCHER-TYPE SHAVING MUG

This shaving mug, shaped much like a cream pitcher, is most unusual. The handle, too, is formed proportionately to match the contour of the spout. A plume or fan design and scroll work are embossed at the front, while the sides have an enigmatic figure head in high relief. Powell says it "appears to be the head of the Gorgon Medusa...although the detailed features leave a lot to be desired" (p. 57). We think it looks more like a monkey, or a shriveled skull reminiscent of McKee's Rameses III matchholder.

Maker unknown. It is marked on the underside "Yankee Shaving Mug — 1876." Powell suggests that since "Yankee Soap" for shaving was registered in 1876, together with the coincidence of the year marking the Centennial, the mug may have been advertised both for the soap product as well as the Centennial celebrations (p. 37).

Known to us only in white. Height 3". Rare.

276 - LION HEAD SHUTTLE SHAVING MUG

A plain shaving mug in what is called the "shuttle" shape, i.e., having an extended front giving access for the shaving brush to get at the water in the mug. A separate (and often missing) milk glass cup, 2 3/8" in diameter, is inserted in the top to hold the soap. A finely moulded lion's head is embossed in high relief on each side. The only other decorations are some faintly embossed leaves around the front and the shuttle portion.

Maker unknown, but marked on the underside "PAT. SEP. 20. 1870." Shown in Powell, p. 56, who states: "Several types of mugs bearing this patent date are evident, but this is the only one known to exist in milk glass."

Known to us only in white. Height 3" and base diameter 3". Scarce.

Lithograph trade catalog illustration of the Lion Head Shuttle Shaving mug showing the often missing milk glass cup insert.

277 - ANGEL WITH HARP MUG

Except for the oval in front, this milk white mug is painted overall in burnt orange. The classic figure of a winged angel, standing among billowing clouds and playing a lyre, is finely etched within the medallion, framed by enameled beading. A ring of beads also circles the top rim, and two enameled flowers are painted on each side. It has a wide arching applied handle that runs almost the full length of the mug. A faint indentation on the underside suggests a pontil mark, but it is completely smoothed and polished.

Maker unknown. It appears to be an early piece, mid-1800s perhaps. Known to us only in white. Height 3 3/4"; diameter 3". Rare, possibly unique.

Novelties

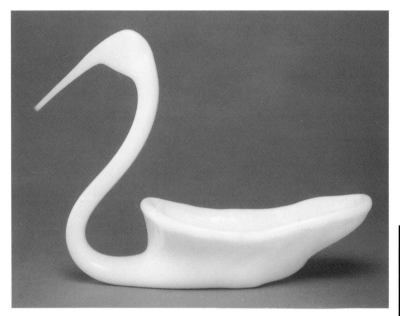

278 - SWAN WHIMSY

Wonderfully proportioned, this swan may look as though it were a one-of-a-kind piece made by an idle craftsman. Not so, however, because we have seen more than one example of it; therefore, though hand crafted it is an established pattern. A much smaller version exists with a short and more realistic applied bill. The long boat-shaped bowl has a flat bottom and heavy hand-worked, rounded sides. Gracefully curved, the long neck ends in a vertically flattened head from which extends a very long evenly sloping bill. It is like no bird that flies, or as Shelley says of his blithe spirit, "Bird thou never wert!"

Maker unknown. Known to us only in white. The bowl is 7 3/4" by 3 1/2"; height about 8 1/2" to top of head. At least scarce.

279 - OPEN BOAT ORNAMENT

Collectors may be familiar with this open boat in a version that is intricately moulded with an inkwell reservoir centered inside it. The boat inkwell, shown here directly above the open boat, is fully described by Revi (pp. 256-257) and Ferson (No. 187), both noting it was a design of Henry Whitney of the New England Glass Co., and patented on Aug. 9, 1870 (the patent date appears inside the rear of the boat). They state that the boat inkstand occurs in white, opaque blue, and crystal. The open boat without an inkwell is the same size, though it appears larger because it is placed closer to the camera. In all respects they are virtually identical, except for a slight difference in the area where the patent date should be but is lacking. The glass is of the same high quality in both boats.

Like the boat inkstand, it seems likely this open boat ornament is also a product of the New England Glass Co.

Known to us only in white. Length 5 1/2"; width 1 1/2"; height 1 7/8". Probably scarce, having escaped mention by both Revi and the Fersons.

280 - NOVELTY MILK GLASS BATTERY LIT LAMPS

Rabbits, ducks, chicks, and dogs are but a few of the animals modeled as milk glass globes for these fascinating miniature lamps. A Halloween pumpkin, a laughing clown, and an eerie skull each has its own special appeal. Also illustrated is an extraordinary array of Christmas related themes — Santa Claus in particular, both full bodied and head only versions — as well as a snowman and a holly wreath with a big red bow and "Noel" painted in bold Gothic letters. Many of them are fitted with flashing bulbs, or as they are called "Winkers," adding a suggestion of animation to the figures.

Most of these novelty lamps date from the 1940s and 1950s, though some may be earlier and others of more recent vintage. The vast majority come from either Japan or Hong Kong and are usually marked in some way: for example, "AMICO Made in Japan;" another bears an "A.A.A." trademark imprinted on a banner with an eagle behind; and a crown trademark was used for "Crown Electric Works, Ltd.," also from Japan. "Rose," "Hil Co" and "Cosmos" are examples of some trademarks on pieces made in Hong Kong, occasionally also bearing the words "British Empire."

In size, they range from 3" to 5" high, and most are about 3" in diameter across the metal base, which can measure a mere 7/8" to as much as 1 1/2" high, generally just adequate enough to hold two size AA batteries. They vary greatly from "generally available" to "very scarce," and prices for some of them can be extraordinarily high, especially if the particular subject happens to be a "hot" collectible.

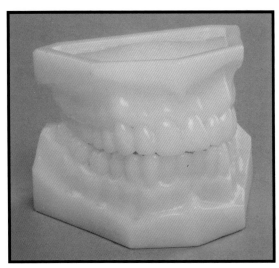

281 - FALSE TEETH

This full complement of thirty-two teeth may be a dentist's model or a display piece. Fitting together nicely, the upper portion has the concave roof of the mouth, and the lower a space where the tongue would lie. Embossed within a circle on each side are the letters "D" and "E" with another "E" between and above them in the upper center of the circle. Below is an ampersand and in the lower quadrant of the circle an ellipse with a small circle in it. Outside the lower part of the circle it is marked "No." on the left side and "1" on the right, and "Pat. applied for" is embossed directly under the circle. All of these elaborate markings suggest it was not intended to be a mere novelty. For milk glass collectors today, of course, it is a choice item.

Maker unknown. Known to us only in white, naturally. Overall about 2 1/4" long, 3" wide; the teeth are about 1" high. Scarce.

282 - LARGE TOOTH

Like the false teeth in the preceding illustration, this single tooth with two large roots may be a professional model or display piece. The biting surface is recessed 1/2" with the gum line visible on the tooth.

Maker unknown. Known to us only in white. The entire tooth is 2 1/4" long; the roots are 1 1/4" long. Rare.

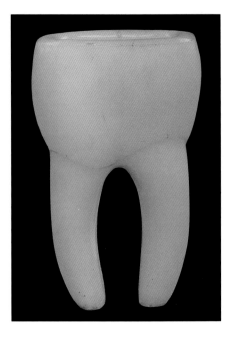

283 - GALLOPING HORSE NOVELTY

Difficult to categorize and surreal in conception, this is indeed an unusual piece. The amount of handwork required to create it is apparent, as each of the individually blown anatomical parts are applied by reheating to the main torso. The end result is no minor achievement, as the proportions are aesthetically pleasing and the sense of motion is dynamic. Even the exaggerated features, such as the bulging eyes, pointed nose, and spatula-like tail are in perfect harmony with the fleet movement of the slender, tapering legs which seem almost to disappear in a gallop.

Attribution given by Ruth Grizel (*The Glass Animal Bulletin,* May 1997, p. 3) as the creation of Martin Haber, Williams Glass Works, England, in 1950.

Known to us only in white. Measurements will vary slightly, but approximately 10" long and 7" high. We do not know how many were made, but we assume they are scarce at least.

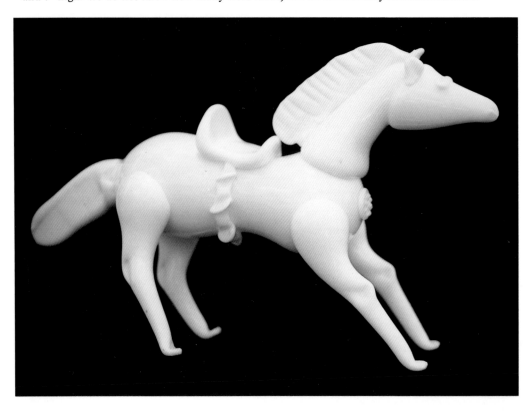

290 - LION ON BRITANNIA SHIELD ORNAMENTAL

The English origin of this aristocratic piece can scarcel[y]
Intended as a paperweight, as it usually is classified, or sin[ce]
ment for the fireplace mantel, the lion is regally poised, its pa[w on]
the shield of Britannia whose sweeping drapery fills the a[rea beneath the]
animal. The lion's immense mane is nicely detailed, in sha[rp contrast to]
the smooth surface of the rest of the body. Its eyes, moulde[d]
brow, and partly open mouth convey a mixture of gentlen[ess and vigi-]
lance combined. The two-step plinth has an upper ring of [?] and a
customary band of vertical ribs below.

Shown by Slack in translucent green glass (plate XXV[?])
marked and dated circa 1890. Slack attributes this, and an [almost iden-]
tical but slightly smaller version, to Henry Greener, and s[ays it is]
probably unmarked because it dates "from the period after H[enry Greener]
& Co. was acquired by James Jobbing" (p. 94).

Known to us in opaque white, and the translucent gr[een re-]
ported by Slack.. It measures 7" by 4 1/4" across the bottom, [and is]
6 1/4" high. Scarce.

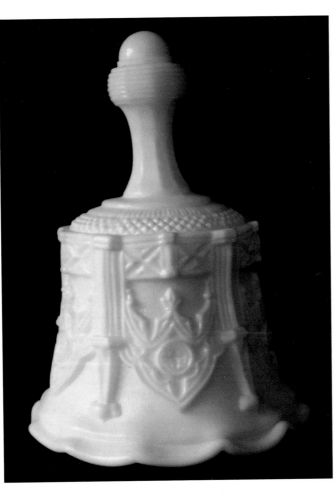

284 - RED-CLIFF-FENTON "SABLÉ ARCH" BELL

This impressive bell is upside down, so to speak, the reason for
which will become clear subsequently. Viewed upright, the design in
high relief around the sides consists of five Gothic triple-arches and
alternating ribbed pillars resembling the interior of a medieval cathedral. The ground area is heavily stippled, and a band of fine diamond
cuts surrounds the upper surface. An unusually heavy piece, it has a
clear glass ball clapper which produces a pleasant if somewhat muted
tinkle.

The identity of this bell first came to light when the eminent glass
historian Kyle Husfloen disclosed the strange circumstances of its creation (see *Collector's Guide to American Pressed Glass*, p. 50). Briefly,
the fascinating story is this. From 1950 to 1980, the Red-Cliff Company,
based in Chicago, produced an extensive line of reproduction china and
ironstone ware. To complement their table pieces, they commissioned
Fenton to make a series of five different glass goblets which were reproductions of old flint pattern glass, though Fenton clearly marked the
goblets "Red-Cliff." When Red-Cliff went out of business, Fenton acquired the goblet moulds and a few years later used them to make a line
of unmarked bells. The one pictured here, according to Mr. Husfloen, is
"a close copy of an early French lacy glass goblet, circa 1840, which was
called *Sablé Arch. Sablé* in French means 'sanded' and refers to the
sanded or stippled background design typical of lacy glass." As is evident, Fenton altered the goblet mould, converting the stem to serve as
the handle, and then further embellished it by slightly flaring and fluting
the plain lip of the goblet.

Made by Fenton, early 1980s. Known to us only in white. Height
5 3/4"; diameter 4 1/8". More than hard to find today, if not scarce.

285 - HUNTING DOG CARD HOLDER

This card holder is most attractive with a
hunting dog deeply embossed on each side. A
floral design extends from the corners down to
the base where it continues slightly outward to
form four feet.

Maker unknown and perhaps of recent origin. Known to us only in white, but reportedly
found in crystal also. Length 3", width 1 1/4",
height to end of feet 2 1/2". Hard to find.

286 - MANATEE FIGURAL ORNAMENT

Also called the "sea cow," this endangered mammal of the
coastal waters of Florida and the Gulf of Mexico is captured in an
exceptional instance of the glassmaker's artistry. The figure is designed to allow free movement when lightly tapped, for it will spin
around or wobble back and forth as though floating or swimming in
water! Despite all efforts, we have not been able to determine precisely what glassmaking techniques were used to create this wonderful conversation piece. The definition of its features, though minimal, is exacting in its eyes, mouth, and skin creases on the fins and
under the head.

Maker unknown, but evidently the work of a contemporary
glass artisan and not a mass production item. The underside of one
of the fins has etched markings in script which are difficult to make
out. They appear to read "Reufe" followed by the numbers "64" or
"84," quite possibly dating when it was made. Perhaps in a future
printing of this book, the identity of the maker will be known.

We have seen this piece only in white. Length 5 1/4"; width
across the fins 3 1/4". Possibly rare.

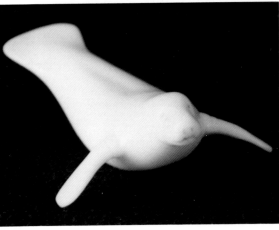

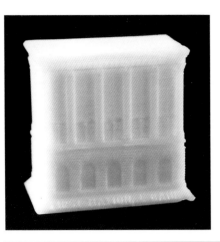

287 - "FIRST [...]

Milk gla[...]
common and [...]
landmark wh[...]
BANK" emb[...]

The own[...]
she was able t[...]
research here [...]
what it takes[...]
each piece in [...]

The banl[...]
its 50th year a[...]
fanfare, as it [...]
structures in t[...]
m[...]
A[...]
3 [...]
en[...]
m[...]

St[...]
un[...]
by[...]

tu[...]
an[...]
to [...]
giv[...]
190[...]
tio[...]

3 3[...]

Sk[...]
bui[...]
Cha[...]

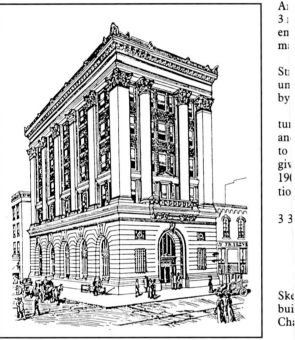

Paperweights/Figu[...]

288 - DRUMMER BOY FIGURAL

This young boy is not a drumme[...]
a commercial sense, as he has a bag o[...]
he appears to be dispensing "goodi[...]
"Our Drummer" is embossed on the [...]
York & Chicago" is embossed on the [...]
may not know, Butler Bros. was the l[...]
great variety of merchandise, includin[...]
Westmoreland, and many other glass [...]
Perhaps this was a piece made for the [...]
pany conventions.

Maker unknown. Known to us o[...]
basc diameter 2". Scarce.

292 - ST. BERNARD DOG ORNAMENTAL

This is a heavy piece of milk glass, well suited for use as a paperweight. The dog, resting on a surface that feels almost like velour, is beautifully moulded with a thick coat and front legs widely spread apart. Its head, turned slightly to the left, is well detailed, with long, drooping ears, and its tail is thick and large. The sides of the high plinth are embellished by a series of raised, elongated ovals. The underside has a 1/2" edge and is deeply hollowed.

Embossed "Vallerysthal" on the bottom, it is illustrated in VCC (p. 312, No. 4054) and in SW (p. 8, second row). Known to us only in white. Length 5 1/2"; width 3 1/4"; height about 3 3/4". Scarce

293 - "THE ONLY LOVE YOU CAN BUY" FIGURAL

Nostalgic and tender, this piece captures an idyllic moment in the life of a young lad with his dog. With his curly-tailed pet beside him licking his face, the barefoot country boy is seated on a mound of rocks. He wears a broad brimmed hat and holds a round lunch pail in his lap, preparing for his noon meal — which accounts, perhaps, for his dog's abundant show of affection.

Made by Gillinder. It is embossed "Gillinder & Sons Centennial Exposition 1876." Known to us in white, clear, and frosted. Height 4 3/4"; base 5 3/8" by 3". Rare.

294 - GREYHOUND FIGURINE

This appealing ornament, perhaps a tiny paperweight, catches all the latent power and speed of a greyhound who, though appearing to be relaxed, also gives the impression of straining for the command to spring into action.

Illustrated with the prosaic generic name "Chien" (dog) in PC (p.149, No. 2116) and also shown in color (p. 329, No. 7359). The piece seen here is embossed on the bottom "Portieux" and "France."

Known to us in blue and white. Only 2 3/4" long and 1 5/8" wide. The height to the dog's uplifted nose is 2". More than scarce.

295 - GIRL WITH LAMB ORNAMENTAL

Seated on a tall sheaf of wheat, this pensive barefoot peasant girl has long braided hair and wears a dirndl dress with flaring skirt. Tending the lamb beside her, she seems relaxed and contemplative, a study in tranquillity.

Maker unknown. Probably French. Known to us only in white. Height 6"; base 4" by 2 3/4". Rare.

296 - AMERICAN INDIAN CHIEF FIGURE

This Indian may be simply a traditional type or a representation of an historical personage; if so, his identity is not known to us. That he is indeed a Chief is evident from the impressive feathered headdress. That he is stoically self-assured may be surmised from his crossed arms. The excellent mould work is enhanced by the painted decoration.

Maker unknown. Impressed on the back of the figure's right leg is a mark which we have not been able to track down. It looks like a "C" or "G" marked inside a diamond.

Known to us only in white. Height 6 1/8"; base diameter 2". Rare.

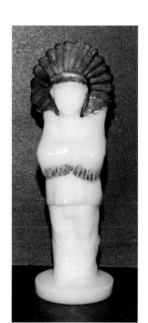

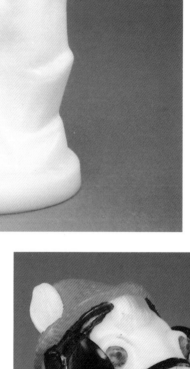

297 - POLAR BEAR PAPERWEIGHT

A formidable looking bear standing almost upright on a block of ice. It is a heavy piece with a round base. The fur detail is rather faint.

Maker unknown. The age is perhaps questionable. Known to us only in white. Height 4 3/4"; diameter at the base 3". Hard to find, perhaps scarce.

298 - HORSE HEAD PAPERWEIGHT

One of the really charmingly droll pieces that many milk glass collectors find especially "collectible." It is a true peddler's horse, fitted with bridle, blinders, and a conical hat with holes for the ears to protrude through. He is by no means a despondent beast as the mouth is set in a broad grin, the large teeth gleaming and the nostrils flaring. Down the back of the head hangs a braid of hair. The elliptical base has a pair of depressions, one dome shaped the other crescent shaped. Appropriately painted, it is indeed a delightful piece of milk glass.

Illustrated in O.N., X:2, March 1995, p. 6 & 14. Known to us only in white and black. Hard to find to scarce.

299 - BEAR PAPERWEIGHT

A squatting bear on a stippled mound is seen holding what looks like a valve in his front paws. Its teeth, claws, and fur are all nicely detailed. Around the irregular octagonal base are embossed the words, "The Firm of John Matthews New York."

Maker unknown. Known to us only in white. Height 4"; base 2 3/4" across. Rare.

Plaques

300 - RABBIT EASEL

This is a splendid piece which may surprise you. As you look at it, you see a yellow chick inside a huge egg clasped by a squatting rabbit between its front paws and hind legs. When you come close to it, however, you find that it is not fully rounded as it might appear, but flat with an easel stand behind it to hold it up. The survival rate of pieces like this is obviously low.

It is marked "M," and "PAT AP'L'D FOR." See No. 199 in this book for details. Known to us only in white. Height 7"; maximum width 3 3/4"; and about 1/2" thick. Scarce.

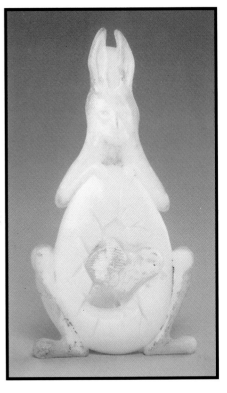

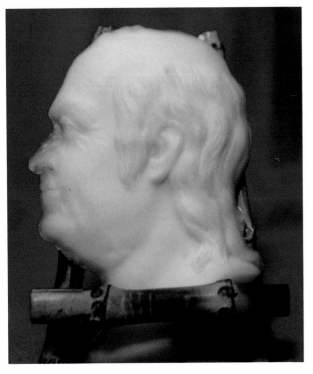

301 - BENJAMIN FRANKLIN PLAQUE

The illustrious American statesman is faithfully rendered in this beautiful profile plaque. Each detail is meticulously moulded, with extraordinary care given to make every feature accurate and true to life. The milk glass is matte white, lending both warmth and dignity to a man whose accomplishments were unexcelled in so many fields of endeavor.

Maker unknown. Known to us only in white. It is very slim, only 1/4" to 3/8" thick. Dimensions are 4 3/4" by 3". Rare.

302 - GENERAL ULYSSES SIMPSON GRANT PLAQUE .

This plaque is a massive piece of milk glass, almost 3/4" thick and weighing over 5 pounds. The surface is satin finished on the front and glossy on the back. The Grant profile measures 7 1/2" high, and is beautifully detailed in very high relief. We believe the plaque may have been designed to be placed inside a frame for hanging, as there is no way it can be displayed on a wall without some sort of casing. A prize for any collection, especially those devoted to historical figures commemorated in milk glass.

Maker unknown, although Gillinder is a strong possibility. We have seen various plaques such as this, but without any embossed figures, in pages of an undated Gillinder catalog, housed in the Jones Museum of Glass and Ceramics, Sebago, Maine. Grant's death in 1885, a time during which Gillinder & Sons was a thriving company, would appear to suggest a probable date for the production of this plaque.

Known to us only in white. Diameter 10 1/2". Very rare.

303 - "TEDDY" ROOSEVELT PLAQUE

Another historical item which both Lindsey and Marsh appear to have missed. The portrait of President Theodore Roosevelt, elevated above the plaque's surface, shows him as a young, vigorous man, no doubt in his "rough rider" days. The front of the plaque has a satin finish; the back is smooth and polished.

Embossed on the back, "Copyright 1904 by Chicago Carrera Ware Co." with the letters "E.J.L." in reverse.

Known to us only in white. It is 1/2" thick and about 3" in diameter. Very scarce.

304 - McKINLEY PLAQUE

A great many campaign items and assassination memorial tributes, including plates, tumblers, statuettes, bottles, and trays honor our 25th President. This round plaque, with the words "Wm. McKinley" inscribed below the coat lapel, is especially notable for its excellent mould work. The border simulates a wooden frame with a hole at the top for hanging. The profile in high relief is finely detailed, even to the presence of a birthmark on his cheek.

Shown in Ferson (F-546), where it is said to be "probably made by the Canton Glass Company in 1901-1902, at the Marion, Indiana site." Also shown in Lindsey, Plate 334, without attribution.

Known to us only in opaque white. Diameter 7 5/8". More than scarce.

305 - GEISHA GIRL PLAQUE

An attractive octagonal plaque or dresser tray bearing the figure of a lovely Japanese girl in full billowing costume and holding a large parasol. Paper lanterns adorn the sides of the tray and lamp-like figures are set in the corner panels.

Maker unknown. The girl with parasol is the same figure as shown on a bottle pictured in Belknap (B-239c). See also K-II, p. 55.

Known to us only in white. Length 9 7/8", width 6 7/8". Hard to find.

306 - CUPID PLAQUE

Framed by a circle of beads, the cherubic child, naked except for a discreetly placed bit of drapery, is embossed in very high relief. He looks like he may be Dan Cupid because in addition to his wings, he carries a small bow in his hands, though no arrows are visible. It is no exaggeration to say the details are simply exquisite, not only in the features of the figure itself, but in the way the entire surface surrounding him, from about the waist down, undulates irregularly to simulate billowing clouds! The rose and scroll design of the border, beautifully moulded, is further enhanced by shallow depressions alternating between the elevations at each corner and both sides. Just above the head of cupid, in the example shown here, a hole is cut out for hanging. Even those we have seen without the opening still show a small indentation where the hole would be made. The milk glass, though fairly thick, has a fine translucence and is unmistakably the product of a topnotch glass factory.

Maker unknown. This piece is shown in Ferson (F-410) where it is called "Cherub Tray," and thought to be "possibly English." We doubt its use as a tray, since nothing could possibly be placed on it without spilling or tumbling off. We also doubt it is English. It may be possible to deduce the original maker from the fact that this plaque was reproduced by Kemple, probably around the 1950s. It was one of a large number of moulds purchased from Mannington Art Glass, some of which are known to have originated with Gillinder. (See Burkholder and O'Connor, p. 15, and p. 73 where the plaque is shown in amber glass.) Judging from the subject matter, the characteristics of the glass, and the excellence of the mould work, we think the piece may well be ascribed to Gillinder.

We know it only in milk white. Length 10 1/2"; width 7 1/2". Very scarce, possibly rare.

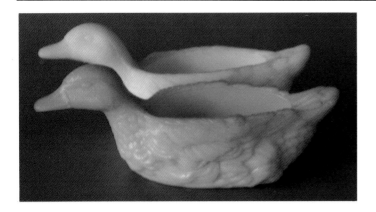

307 - DUCK OPEN BACK SALT

Shown here are two duck salts: the one in blue is signed Vallerysthal, the one in white is an unsigned close copy made by Westmoreland. The mould for the reproduction piece does not appear to have been made directly from a casting, because the feathering on the sides, although excellent in both examples, is quite different. The tail of the original is somewhat wider as well. When not signed, the easiest way to tell the difference is to examine

Salts, Open

the inside area. Running your finger along the surface just behind the duck's neck, you will find the French version has a slight indentation near the top and then slopes back gradually, whereas the Westmoreland piece lacks the indentation and goes straight down.

The original, sometimes signed "Vallerysthal" though but faintly, is shown in SW (p. 7, bottom row) and VCC (p. 300, No. 3289 in various decoration). It is also shown in PC (p. 328, "Saliere Canard" No. 7189). The Westmoreland copy, first issued in 1926 and continued for many years thereafter, has been reissued after its closing in many different colors, including milk white, by Summit, who now owns the mould (see Grizel, *Our Children's Heirlooms*, p. 30).

The Vallerysthal original is known to us in opaque white, blue, and green, and in amber. The Westmoreland copy and the Summit reproductions come in a wide array of colors, including milk glass and slag.

Length from tip of beak to end of tail ranges between 5" and 5 3/8", depending upon the sag of the head in annealing. The French piece is somewhat hard to find; Westmoreland copies less so; Summit reproductions readily available.

308 - ROOSTER OPEN SALT

A full-figure fowl, most likely a rooster from the shape of the tail feathers, formed with an open back serves as a salt dip. The two-part mould is replete with crisp, realistic feathering, and nicely detailed legs and claws tucked in close to the body. In contrast, the shape and dimensions of the head and tail look like a cartoon figure. The scrawny long neck, fat beak, and bulging eyes stand out ridiculously compared to the discrete little wattle and the trim and proper comb.

The initials S V are embossed on the underside. Known to us only in white milk glass. 4" long overall; 3" high. Hard to find.

309 - FIGHTING ROOSTERS DOUBLE OPEN SALT

Although these two birds have sometimes been described as "kissing," the position of their beaks suggests otherwise. One of them is nipping at the other's comb, while his adversary, in turn, is nearly devouring his opponent's wattle. It certainly looks more like a cock fight to us. These birds bear a strong resemblance to the single rooster open salt in the preceding illustration, and they all are undoubtedly the creation of the same mould maker. In this piece, however, the feathering and other details are less well defined.

Embossed S V on the underside. Known to us in blue and in white. 6 1/4" long overall; 2 3/4" high. Hard to find.

310 - DOG WITH BASKETS, DOUBLE OPEN SALT

This open salt is found in two sizes, the one on the left being a bit smaller than the other. The dogs are almost identical, however, lying with outstretched legs on a grassy mound. The rectangular baskets flanking their sides are held by straps crossing over the dogs' backs. Apart from very minor variations in the mould detail, the most obvious difference is in the position of the head. The smaller dog's head is turned only slightly to the left, whereas the larger dog's head turns sharply, almost at a right angle. The mould work in both is very good.

Both of those shown here are marked "S V" inside one of the baskets.

Known to us in white and blue milk glass. The small one is about 3" long; 3 3/4" wide across the baskets; and 2 1/8" high. The other is only fractionally larger. Both are scarce.

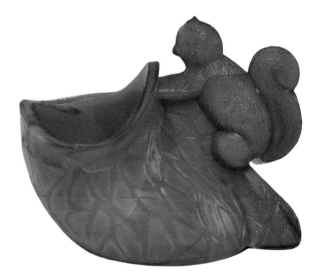

311 - SQUIRREL ON NEST OPEN SALT

Climbing a branch to peer into a broad leafy nest, this squirrel may be on its way home for the night or looking for birds' eggs. You decide.

Maker unknown. Known to us only in blue. Length 3"; width 1 7/8". The upright squirrel is about 1 3/4". Hard to find.

312 - WALNUT DOUBLE SALT

The two halves of a large walnut, held together by a looping tree branch serving as a handle, make up this most appealing double salt dip. The ribbed and pebbled surfaces of the walnut and the bark of the tree simulate the real thing. Leaves, two on each side, fill the area between the walnut halves, no doubt for the aesthetic effect as well as a practical way to lend the piece greater stability. The outer surfaces of the leaves are perfectly smooth, but the backsides are realistically veined, evidence of course that the piece was also made in clear and transparent colors.

Unmarked, it is shown as item #8, p. 21, in an 1897 Val St. Lambert (Belgium) catalog in the Rakow Research Library of The Corning Museum of Glass. Also illustrated in H-J, #794, without attributing the maker but dating it circa 1890.

Found in grayish white fiery opal, shown here, and in clear glass with a faint yellow tint as shown in H-J. Length 6", height 3". Scarce.

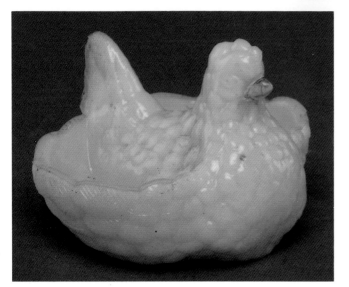

313 - HEN DOUBLE SALT

A most attractive item in the shape of a hen with wings spread out forming two large cavities to serve as salt dips. Although hollow, it is uncommonly heavy for such a small piece, and the glass is so slippery that picking it up by the head or tail is near impossible. The mould work is quite good, especially the embossed shafts and barbs of the wing feathers.

Marked S V deep within the cavity of the underside.

Most often found in blue, but no doubt occurs in white and other colors. About 3" long from beak to tail, 4" wide, and 2 1/2" high. Hard to find.

314 - ROOSTER DOUBLE SALT

Double salts, in metal and ceramic as well as glass, were often designed with animals, and even with human figures, to serve as handles in lieu of the more usual knob or post. This one is a fine example of the genre. The centered full-figure rooster standing on what appears to be a pile of rocks is flanked in front and behind by square simulated wood baskets.

Maker unknown. Shown in H-J (# 4765), who remark about the small size of the two salt dips and suggest a European origin, circa 1890.

Known to us in opaque white and blue,; possibly occurs in crystal and transparent colors as well. Length 4 3/4"; height 2 1/2". More than scarce.

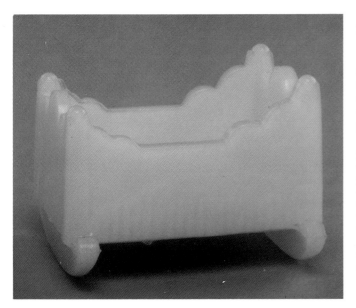

315 - CRADLE SALT

Modeled as a cradle with rockers at each end, this open salt has an appealing austerity. A series of vertical stripes go around the lower third of the "box" and six wide bed slats appear on the underside. Its vintage is evident in the design of the headboard and footboard which feature a centered high arching loop, reminiscent of old fashioned beds and early gravestones.

Two of these cradles are illustrated in Heacock and Johnson; one in dark amber (H-J # 854) said to be a later reproduction and the other in light amber (H-J # 855) regarded as the original (circa 1900) but without attributing a maker. The original measures 1 7/8" high, while the later copy is about 1/4" taller. Heacock's co-author, Patricia Johnson, in an "update supplement" (Oct. 1988) was able to attribute this cradle to the Co-Operative Flint Glass Co., so it might well date from as early as the 1880s.

Known to us only in opaque white and light amber. Length 2 7/8"; width 1 3/4"; height 1 7/8". Heacock believed that both the original and the copy are rare, and from our own experience we would tend to agree.

316 - SWAN MASTER SALT IN SILVER CHARIOT

Objects combining glass and metal, either permanently fixed together or, as in this example, separable, are not too common and seem to have had rather limited appeal. An exceptionally successful union is evident in this swan master salt set in a silver open chariot. The glass and metal components nicely complement each other, as Dan Cupid high aloft guides the swan with a delicate linked chain curbing its neck. The swan's large spread wings together with cupid's own give the entire piece an amazing sense of movement. For grace and elegance, this particular mating of glass and metal is hard to surpass, but the swan itself is an outstanding piece by a justly famous glassmaker.

Previously shown only by Millard (276b) who incorrectly attributed it to Sandwich. It is a product of Gillinder, illustrated in an undated catalog (circa 1870?) housed in the Jones Museum of Glass and Ceramics, Sebago, Maine.

Known to us in white, blue, and clear frosted. Measurement of the swan at its extremities, 5 1/2" by 2 3/4"; height of frame 7". The swan alone is somewhat hard to find; as shown, very scarce.

317 - SQUIRREL ON BRANCH DOUBLE SALT

The handle for this charming double salt is a roguish squirrel, clinging to a tree stub with its long curled tail extending beyond the top of its head. The sides of the salts are ribbed and the bottom has a pattern of converging rays meeting in a small button at the center. The upper rims are smooth and slightly expanded. The glass is opalescent.

It is embossed "S V" on the underside of the element connecting the salts.

Known to us only in white. Height to the tree top branch 3"; maximum width 5"; the salts are 2" in diameter. Scarce.

318 - TURTLE OPEN SALT

The turtle's back looks like it has been caved in to create this open salt because the inner surface is not smooth but bears the impression of the outer shell. Its legs are formed as large round striated globs, and the tail merely a smaller and narrower version of the legs. With head uplifted, the frog's eyes appear to be looking up attentively. The milk glass is of good quality, and it appears to be an early product.

Maker uncertain, but very similar to a turtle relish dish illustrated in Revi (p. 190), designed and patented by William Leighton, Jr. (June 15, 1875), and made by Hobbs, Brockunier & Co. in both a large size and as a salt dip. The one shown here in opaque glass appears to be identical to one illustrated in crystal by Bredehoft (*Hobbs, Brockunier & Co. Glass*, p. 48). We have also seen what we believe may be a recent reproduction of this piece judging from the newness of the glass and a slight difference in the depth of the cavity.

Known to us only in white. Length 3"; maximum width 2"; height 3/4". Scarce.

Note: Another turtle salt, quite similar but with legs better detailed and a much rounder head, has been traced to Findlay Glass (see Measell and Smith, p. 74).

319 - TURTLE OPEN SALT DIP

Another full-figure turtle salt, it makes a charming novelty piece and is remarkably realistic. Its scaly head, feet complete with toes, and diminutive tail are all extremely well detailed. But, of course, some distortion was necessary to make the turtle serve its intended purpose. The arching carapace is leveled perfectly flat so when the turtle is turned on its back, it stays put. The body cavity is almost large enough to serve as a master salt.

It is shown in PC, #618, p. 38. We know it in opaque white and blue and in clear frosted, but possibly made in other colors as well. Length 4 1/2"; width 3 1/2"; depth 1 1/8". Hard to find.

320 - OPEN SWAN SALT [Meisenthal]

Of high quality glass, the glowing fiery opal almost gives this piece an overall lavender tint. It is more skillfully moulded than are similar swan salts of more recent vintage. Like the Cambridge swans, the cere (i.e., the fleshly growth on the bill) is finely detailed, though somewhat more elongated, and the feathering is crisp and discrete. Each wing feather is separate, so that the ends form an irregular upper margin.

It is embossed "Meisenthal," a French glass company located in the Moselle region just north of the Vallerysthal factory with which it was at one time affiliated in the 1850s. This swan also bears some resemblance to one designed and registered (8 January, 1885) in England by Burtles, Tate & Co. See Lattimore, plate X.

We know it only in white and in several sizes. The one pictured here is 4" long, and 3" high. At least scarce.

Salts, Shakers

321 - RABBIT SALT SHAKER AND TOOTHPICK

An attractive salt shaker, it is embossed with tall grass blades and four floppy-eared rabbits. They are caught nibbling on carrots, two of them facing forward and two in profile. Also shown, the same piece designed as a toothpick holder with beading around the opening (see H-1, p. 62, fig. 398).

Maker unknown. Known to us only in white. Height 2 1/4"; diameter 2 1/4". Both are very hard to find.

322 - COLUMBUS AND ISABELLA SALT SHAKERS

Even to have one of these in one's collection would be extraordinary, but to have the pair is barely imaginable! The bearded Columbus, wearing an elegant cloak with ruffled collar, has a pendant cross on a gold chain around his neck. Isabella, with a queenly headdress that flows down to her shoulders, also wears a crucifix hanging from a gold chain. The pedestal bases are embossed COLUMBUS and ISABELLA, respectively. Whether in regard to the superb mould work detailing their features or to the excellence of the glass itself, the quality of these pieces is outstanding. And to find the pair with the original painted decoration so well preserved is a marvel.

Maker unknown. Both shakers are illustrated in Peterson, (P-2: Columbus Fig. "J", p. 25; Isabella Fig. "F," p. 164) and Lechner (Columbus, p. 213; Isabella, p. 235) without attribution and dated circa 1892-1900.

Known to us in white, and shown by Lechner in a brilliant opaque green. Each measures about 3 3/8" high. Both are extremely rare.

324 - MAN WITH TOP HAT SALT SHAKER

This portly gentleman looks like a nineteenth century story book character. The mould work is excellent, with such details as a frock coat, high collar, and bow tie complementing its most prominent feature — an enormous top hat. The underside is deeply recessed, but the piece is still large enough to contain a large quantity of salt. In addition to the salt shakers, an identical version is found without a screw top, quite possibly intended as a toothpick holder.

Maker unknown. Known to us only in white. Salt shaker measures 4" high; toothpick version 3 1/2" high. More than scarce.

323 - YOUNG COLUMBUS SALT SHAKER

What he lacks in facial hair, as seen in the bearded Columbus shaker, is amply compensated for by the full head of hair in this piece. The milk glass is translucent and very heavy. "Columbus" is embossed on the front of the base.

Maker unknown. Previously shown in Peterson, P-2, Fig. "I," p. 25, without attribution. Height 3 3/4". Rare.

325 - FITZHUGH LEE [?] SALT SHAKER

Despite our best efforts, it has been impossible to determine with certainty the identity of this American Army General. On the sole authority of Lindsey, a quite similar salt shaker shown as No. 380 in her book is said to represent General Shafter. Both Marsh (No. 201) and Peterson (P-2, Fig. "E", p. 162) picture that same shaker and simply repeat Lindsey's identification. The salts illustrated in all three of these sources, however, are plainly not the same as the one shown here. Those which are said to be Shafter reveal a clean shaven face, whereas this one has a full mustache. Moreover, the uniforms are different, and the shoulders of the Shafter bust are less broad.

Who, then, might this bust represent, if it is not General Shafter? A strong possibility is General Fitzhugh Lee, a nephew of Robert E. Lee. A contemporary portrait of him in a jewelry store ad and a decal portrait on a plate shown in Lindsey (No. 378) bear some resemblance to this bust, the eyes in particular, although the face of the shaker is less plump. Fitzhugh Lee served as a Major General of the U.S. Volunteers during the Spanish American War. He retired from the Army in 1901, and it is quite possible this shaker may have been issued as a commemorative at the Pan-American Exposition of the same year. We leave it to others more knowledgeable than we are to sort this out.

Maker unknown, but this salt is so similar to the one said to represent Shafter as well as another depicting Dewey that all of them would appear to be products of the same company.

The Shafter salt shown in Lindsey is said to be 3 3/4" tall and made in "opaque white glass, natural finish." The one shown here is only 3 1/4" tall and has a satin finish. All these salts are considered rare.

An undated complimentary flyer by Schleghter's Jewelry Store, of Reading, Pennsylvania, honoring Fitzhugh Lee who is referred to as "Major General of Volunteers, U.S." This would date it about 1898, when Lee was one of three ex-Confederate generals who were made Major Generals of U.S. Volunteers. Lee retired as Brigadier General of the U.S. Army in 1901. (*Reproduced courtesy of Russell Eaton.*)

326 - CHICK ON PEDESTAL SALT SHAKER

Although shown previously in Peterson (P-2, Fig. "N", p. 156), and Lechner (p. 119), we could not resist finding room for these beautiful chick salt shakers, as they would grace any table and, we trust, delight the readers of this book.

Long believed to be products of Mt. Washington/Pairpoint, owing to their similarity to that company's "Chicken Head" salts, the attribution of these pedestaled chicks to C. F. Monroe of Meriden, Connecticut, was discovered by Wilfred Owen in two trade ads in *Keystone Jewelers Magazine* (February and April 1903), and reported by him in GCD (IV:5, Feb/Mar 1991, p. 59). The ad has the following amusing verse to accompany the illustration of its "Easter Chicken Salt:"

> An egg fresh and nice once was I,
> But a chicken now I be;
> And if you watch me long enough,
> A nice, fat hen you will see.
> *Then I will be too late*
> *for Easter.*

Known to us only in white, decorated. Height 2 1/2". Rare.

327 - THRUSH SALT SHAKER

Much admired by salt shaker collectors, this mould blown rarity features a large bird perched on a leafy branch, all done in high relief. With its large wings and beautifully moulded tail feathers, the creature appears to be ready to take flight. Dense and absolutely white, the milk glass is of excellent quality.

Made by Daizell, Gilmore and Leighton Company, about 1890. Warman (plate 124b) called it "Thrush Salt" and the name has been continued by Peterson (P-2, Fig. "K," p. 175) and Lechner (p. 58).

Known to us only in white. Width 2 5/8"; height 2 3/4". Extremely scarce, if not rare.

Tableware, General

328 - CAT HANDLED CREAMER

A winsome creamer with stippled surface and fluted top. It rests on three ribbed petal-like feet. The handle is formed as an upright cat with finely textured fur.

Maker unknown; most likely English. Known to us only in white. Height 4". Rare.

329 - LOUIS XV CREAMER

For so small a piece, this attractive creamer is quite heavy. On a stippled background, the top portion consists of scrolls and the lower portion of alternating vertical stripes and hexagonal "circles".

It is shown in PC (p. 60, No. 983) and in color (p. 329, No. 7349). Neither of our examples is signed.

Known to us in white and blue. Maximum height 4 1/2"; diameter of the base 2 1/2". Usually available.

Note on the Louis XV design: This creamer is one of a series of pieces with the same design. Among them is a large ornate candlestick with a circle of beads midway along the stem and a gargoyle face near the base (see PC, p. 131, No. 1842). The same candlestick is also fashioned with a round globe at the top to hold lamp oil (p. 137, No. 1941). Other items bearing the Louis XV design include a tooth brush holder (p. 92, No. 1303) and a handled coffee or tea cup with saucer (p. 149. No. 215). Additional pieces were made with this design, but apparently not in opaque colors (see PC, p. 233).

A massive covered sugar bowl is also labeled "Louis XV" in PC (p. 324, No. 6659), but it does not appear to us to be the same design as the creamer or the aforementioned pieces. The finial is a three coiled snail and the design of the cover includes four large scallop or oyster shell-like figures embedded in a maze of fancy work. The same design is repeated on the base and on the foot. It is a heavy piece, and the glass is fire opal.

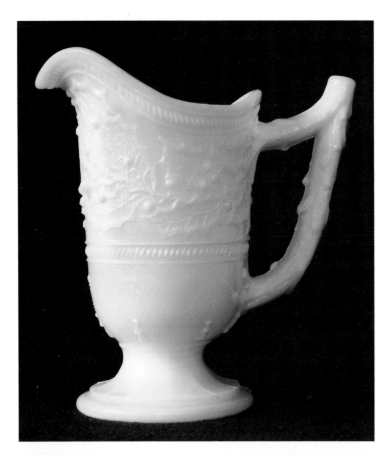

330 - HOLLY CREAMER

This pattern is illustrated by Belknap (B-222d) in a piece he calls a sugar bowl, but which may be a spooner. He says it is of English ancestry and further notes that "there are two different Holly patterns in Early American pressed glass, but this piece does not match either." Because these pieces are not marked in any way, Belknap may have assumed an English origin based mainly on his observation that it was "typical English chalk white Milk Glass." But the matching creamer shown here is highly opalescent leaded glass, nearly translucent in some spots, and quite typical of much Sandwich glass. Ruth Webb Lee (L-EA, Plate 116) shows only three items in this pattern — a covered compote, goblet, and egg cup — and describes it exactly: "...little round berries stand out in clear relief and the leaves are lightly stippled" (p. 436). A fine cable cord runs along the upper edge and another circles the center of the body. The lower portion features an additional embellishment of drapes and tassels, not seen in the pieces sketched in Lee, however. The sturdy handle is formed as a high arching holly branch. The underside has a classic pattern of deeply pressed converging rays.

Although we cannot with certainty attribute it to Sandwich, Lee states "a few fragments in this pattern have been excavated at Sandwich but not enough pieces were found to justify the belief it was produced there in large quantities" (L-EA, p. 436). See also, Barlow, *The Glass Industry in Sandwich*, Vol. 4, p. 237, where an obscure pattern in a Sandwich design book is listed as "Vintage Holly."

Known to us only in white, but also made in clear glass, according to Lee. It measures 5 1/2" high and 2 7/8" in diameter at the base. Very scarce, possibly rare.

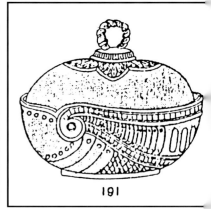

191

331 - CASQUE (HELMET) SUGAR AND CREAMER

Although shown by Belknap (B-212) and correctly identified as English in origin, no attribution is given. Belknap calls special attention to the workmanship as "correct down to the very finest detail." The surface has a "fuzzy" feel owing to the fine stippling, and the glass itself is more like Atterbury's than the typically English milk glass. Belknap also calls attention to "how small the creamer is in relation to the sugar." This feature seems characteristic of many English cream and sugar sets, as the creamer fits neatly inside the sugar bowl, no doubt saving space on the cupboard shelf.

Made in the 1880s, the original moulds for this set were created by W. H. Heppell, and later acquired by George Davidson. Assigned the number 191, a sketch of the covered butter dish is reprinted here from an undated Davidson catalog. As the pieces are unmarked, they could be of either company's manufacture.

Known to us only in white. Creamer 4" high; sugar 4 1/4" high and 5 1/8" across the top. More than hard to find.

Casque (Helmet) Covered Butter Dish, from an undated George Davidson catalog.

332 -HEART AND SCALE CREAMER

An outstanding design, beautifully executed, this creamer made in highly opalescent milk glass is sensational. The top portion has a pattern of dots and dotted diamonds with two large hearts embossed just below the high arching spout. The handle creates an illusion of the upper half joining the lower half at an angle. Fifteen vertical rows of scales cover the sides, separated by a smooth band crossing at the middle. The scales on the upper half slope downward, those on the lower half slope upward. The foot is broad and round and depressed on the bottom. One might compare this design of overlapping scales with the design on the base of the Sandwich Hen covered dish.

This is one of the many masterworks that have made Sandwich and New England glass products so respected throughout the world. Illustrated in milk white by Spillman (p. 78, No. 194) from the Corning collection and dated circa 1830-1845. Wilson (*American Glass*, p. 421, No. 634) shows it in translucent light blue from the Toledo collection and gives descriptive notes. Despite the finding of fragments at the Sandwich site, Wilson suggests a possible European origin because of the non-leaded, though heavy glass. Wilson says it was also made in Moonstone and electric blue. Height to top of spout 4 1/2"; base diameter 2 3/4"; transverse mouth opening 3". Very rare.

333 - DOLPHIN FOOTED CREAMER

An unusual bulbous creamer on triangular feet bearing a dolphin head with tails extending inward and intertwining to form a narrow stem. The body proper expands abruptly with iris-like leaves curling and twisting toward the rim. The handle is also formed as entwined leaves. The top rim is undulate with a deep spout and an elegant band of narrow vertical bars below the rim.

Maker unknown, but probably nineteenth-century English. See Lattimore, p. 108. Known to us only in white. Height 5 1/4"; diameter at the top 2 1/2". Scarce at least.

334 - PRINCE OF WALES FEATHERS SUGAR BOWL

Pressed from a three-part mould, the embossed elements framed within circles around the sides of the bowl consist of three feathers rising from the royal crown, flanked on each side by the floral emblems of England and Scotland — the rose and the thistle. The scalloped base has a series of rays converging on the underside.

Neither this sugar nor the matching creamer, shown in black milk glass by Lattimore (p. 64), is marked, but Lattimore reports the design is illustrated in the circa 1885 Davidson catalog where it is given the number 126. Height 5 3/8"; top opening 5 1/2". Scarce.

335 - RENAISSANCE COVERED SUGAR

A heavy, footed sugar in one of Portieux's two similar patterns both called "Renaissance." On the sides of the bowl a series of vertical raised ribs, framed by a string of small beads, are separated by an elevated carinate ridge. The top of the base is fluted. The double stepped octagonal and scalloped foot is joined to the bowl by a pattern of sixteen formal pleated "leaves," and surmounted by a circle. The cover and round finial incorporate the same elements of ribs, beads, and pleats.

Embossed "Portieux" on the underside of the base. Illustrated in PC (p. 64, No. 938) and in color (p. 324, No. 0646).

Known to us only in blue and black. Presumably also occurs in white. Height overall 6 1/2"; diameter of opening 5"; height of base 4 3/4"; diameter of foot 3 3/8". Availability unknown.

Note on the Renaissance pattern: Used for a variety of table pieces, this design is shown in the following additional items in the Portieux 1933 catalog: two different shapes of open compotes, each in four sizes (p. 53, Nos. 786 and 787); a bowl (p. 85, No. 1201); a very low bowl or plate in four sizes (p. 98, No. 1251); candlesticks in two sizes (p. 132, No. 1867); a candleholder (p. 133, No. 1879); and a bobeche (p. 133, No. 1876).

336 - IVY LEAF SUGAR

The sides of this bizarre little sugar, with a motif of nicely detailed leaf clusters, taper from top to bottom. The dome lid, with an inner lip that fits inside the base, has the same leaf design, in marked relief and covering almost the entire surface. The finial, almost impossible to lift without having it slip from your fingers, is a cone of converging leaves.

Illustrated in VCC (p. 305, No. 3776) and SW (p. 4, fourth row). Known to us only in white. The base is 2 1/2" high, with diameter 4 1/4" at the top and 3 1/8" at the bottom. Overall height 4". Scarce.

337 - DOG AND CAT COVERED SUGAR DISH

This amusing figural depicts a pair of dogs treeing a cat. Serving as the finial, the terrified cat's arched body appears ready for either flight or fight, as the dog "handles" on each side of the fluted base pursue their prey. The dogs, tethered by chains on their collars, strain to free themselves. A chain runs around the edge of the cover next to a circle of beads matched by similar ones at the top of the base. The base, too, has a chain crisscrossing the stippled surface.

Made by George Davidson, it is shown as No. 26 in a circa 1885 catalog. See O.N., X:4, Sept. 1995, pp. 6-7 for a fuller discussion and reprints of sketches from the Davidson catalog, including the matching creamer.

Known to us only in a chalky white. Height overall 5 1/2"; the base alone is 3 3/4" high and 4 1/2" wide. Rare.

338 - HIBISCUS FLOWER COVERED SUGAR

Square with rounded corners, this is an elegantly designed piece. The sides are slightly concave, each embossed with an exotic flower in high relief on a stippled surface. It has five large petals with four long stamens, framed by delicate vine-like tendrils bearing two young buds. A leafy border graces the bottom edge of the base which is arched to create feet at each corner. The convex top is rather imposing, with an "S" and bead border around the lower edge and an upper portion consisting of thirty-two lanceolate "leaves" framed in a beaded border. The round finial appears to be a budding flower. The cover has a flange that fits inside the edge of the base to hold it in place.

Signed "Vallerysthal" across the center inside the base, or near the edge of the underside, it is illustrated in VCC (p. 306, No. 3781).

Known to us in white and in bluish green. Base is 3 1/4" high, and 3 1/2" across top. It is 5 1/2" high overall. Scarce.

339 - CHERRY SQUARE SUGAR

Somewhat top heavy, this large sugar has a base that slopes inward sharply about a third of the way down and bears a small raised star-burst design on the underside. The pattern overall, both on the base and the cover, is of embossed clusters of cherries hanging from leaflets all on a stippled ground. Graceful smooth lines run down each corner ending as rounded feet that elevate the bowl slightly. A recessed inner ledge at the top of the base serves to receive the cover which is convex, its finial consisting of a large twig.

Illustrated in VCC (p. 306, No. 3780). It is found unsigned as well as signed "Vallerysthal" inside the base near the edge.

Known to us only in white. Base 3 1/4" high and 4 1/4" across the top. Overall height 5 1/2". Scarce.

340 - ROSE COVERED SUGAR BOWL

The base of this attractive sugar bowl narrows markedly from the top, then bulges a bit near the bottom. A large rose and two serrated leaves flanked by small rose buds are embossed on the sides. The underside of the base has a formal pattern of twenty-four converging rays. On the slightly convex lid, fitted with a flange to fit into the base, are panels, each bearing a leaf and a long stemmed rose. A large ribbed, conical rectangle forms the finial.

Maker unknown, but probably French. The base lacking its cover is illustrated in N- 360 where it is called a "planter bowl."

Known to us only in white. 5 1/2" high; 4 1/4" wide at top of base; 2 3/4" wide at the bottom. Hard to find to scarce.

341 - QUINCE SUGAR BOWL

Unpainted, this piece takes on the appearance of a rather amorphous "glob," but when painted, it is revealed to be a studied and beautifully designed fruit with delicately moulded ridges and depressions. Top and bottom together form the large fruit. The finial consists of two upraised leaves attached to a branching stem. This projecting leaf motif is carried through to the bottom of the base where three large leaves and a thick stem attached to two flat leaves all combine to form the "feet" on which the upright quince stands. These leaves are sometimes differentiated by the application of "gold leaf," rather than the more common "bronze" (painted gold}.

It is illustrated in VCC (p. 304, No. 3765). Known to us only in white. The irregular shape makes measurement difficult. The opening at the top of the base is 4" by 3 1/2". The maximum foot separation about 4 1/4". The total height about 6". Very scarce.

343 - JEWELED OVAL SUGAR SHAKER

The simple pattern embossed at the top and bottom of this large sugar shaker consists of long pointed ribs alternating with slightly rounded ovals. Marking the front of the shaker is a star burst formed by pointed ribs and alternating tear drops, with a red stone affixed at the center. It is fairly heavy and of fine, glossy white milk glass.

Previously unlisted to our knowledge, the maker is almost certainly Atterbury, evidenced by two features typical of many products made by that company. The red stone is the same as used for eyes on some of Atterbury's animal covered dishes. Equally telling is the marking "PAT^T APL^D FOR" embossed on the underside. We suspect a reworking of the top portion may also have produced a syrup in this pattern.

Known to us only in white. Height 6"; maximum width about 3 3/4"; base diameter 2". Possibly rare.

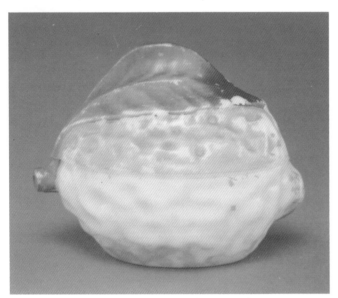

342 - LEMON SUGAR BOWL

A nicely delineated lemon covered dish that lies horizontally. The finial, which actually originates from a stem projecting from the top edge of the base, is a large leaf with one edge uplifted and extending almost the full length of the cover. The surface overall is a motley of well-defined blunt impressions. A most engaging piece.

Illustrated in a German version of the 1907 Vallerysthal catalog, Tafel 8 (second row) as a "Zuckerdose Citrone" (Lemon Sugar bowl).

Known to us only in white. The flat base measures 3" long by 2 1/4" wide. The maximum length of the lemon is 5 1/2", and the height to the raised leaf margin about 4 1/2". Scarce.

344 - PEAR SUGAR BOWL

This fine piece probably was produced using slightly different glass formulas at various production runs as the top of the example shown has a much denser stark white color than does the base. Three leaves radiate from the protruding stem finial. The bottom of the base is formed of hexagons that meet in a depressed center.

Illustrated in VCC (p. 305, No. 3779) in two colors. Called simply "Poire," it is also shown in PC (p. 65, No. 962) and in two colors (p. 326, No. 6683). The example seen here is signed "Vallerysthal" on the inside bottom of the base.

Known to us in opaque blue and white. Height 5 1/2"; maximum width about 3 3/4". Scarce.

345 - APPLE SUGAR BOWL

An attractive apple with excellent details, as is usual in these French pieces. Three delicate branchlets extend from the twig finial, two bearing three leaves and one with only two. Near the bottom are eight elongated indentations such as may be found on real apples.

Called simply "Pomme," it is illustrated in PC (p. 65, No. 961) and in two color versions (p. 326, No. 6682).

Known to us only in white. Height 4 3/4"; diameter of opening 4 5/8". Scarce.

346 - AVELLAN COVERED SUGAR

This piece with its three paneled finial has a "busy" pattern, the cover consisting of ten arrow-shaped extensions radiating from the center, each filled with twenty-five diamond points. Between the arrows are ten diamond-shaped areas each bearing an elaborate cross and between each of these are marginal fans. The body of the bowl has a similar pattern but the arrows are shorter with three diamond-like rows, and the base is a repetition of the top in miniature. The glass is fiery and semi-translucent.

Embossed "Portieux" and "France" on the underside, it is illustrated in PC (p.64, No. 935) and in color (p. 325, No. 6667).

Known to us only in white. Height 4 3/4" with a 5 1/2" opening and a 4" diameter base. Scarce.

Note on the Avellan design: This sugar is part of a table set. Others shown in PC are the butter (p. 67, No. 1000); tall and short open compotes in four different shapes, each of them in two sizes (p. 54, Nos. 798, 799, 800, 801); a covered mustard (p. 33, No. 490); and a low bowl (p. 88, No. 1249).

347 - ROOSTER HEAD FINIAL COVERED SUGAR

This covered dish appears to be a matching sugar for the Rooster Head Finial butter dish (see next entry). With nearly identical covers, the only difference between them is the deep bowl with an elongated dart pattern around its sides rather than underneath. And like the butter dish, the bowl is slightly elevated by four knobbed feet.

Maker unknown, but the red stones set in the eye sockets suggest Atterbury as the probable maker.

We are perplexed by the color of this glass, as it is very like French yellow opaline. An Atterbury Bird and Wheat [Eastlake] mug, however, is shown in F-486 and appears to be made in this color, as does the unattributed "Dart and Bar" Pitcher (F-157). Indeed, that pattern may well be the motif for an expanded table set which includes the pieces with rooster head finials on the covers. Height 5 1/8"; diameter top of bowl 4 3/4". Rare.

348 - ROOSTER HEAD FINIAL BUTTER DISH

The high domed cover of this butter dish is remarkable for the impressive rooster's head, measuring 1 5/8" inches, that serves as finial. The features are extremely well detailed, both comb and wattle luxuriously moulded and almost fleshy in appearance. The cover is impressed with an austere pattern of elongated darts framed above and below by a circle of beads. It rests on the inner lip of the dish whose upper surface is plain, but its underside repeats the elongated dart pattern, minus the beads, and is supported by four knobbed feet.

Maker unknown. As stated in the preceding entry, the flat eye sockets are characteristic features of Atterbury animal covered dishes and may signal its maker.

Shown here in a rich lavender milk glass, this butter dish has also been found in milk white with the rooster's head in blue, both colors and color combinations quite typical of Atterbury products, lending further support to that attribution. Height overall 6 1/4"; diameter of the base 6 7/8". Rare.

349 - PLAIN MELON FLAT BUTTER

The flat, slightly elevated base of this handsome covered butter dish is made of very thin glass, more "fire-translucent" than most Atterbury products. The top edge of the base is undulate with twelve loops and an inner shelf on which the broad lid fits. The design on the lid is the same as that of the pedestal butter and the compote.

It is marked PAT'D 8 1870 (with the "7" reversed), presumably the same date as the pedestal butter with the month omitted.

Known to us only in white. Height overall 4 1/2"; height of base 1 2/16" with a diameter of 6" across the top and 2 3/4" across the bottom. Scarce.

350 - "PATENT MELON WARE" TUREEN

This attractive and highly collectible pattern is illustrated in three different items (covered sugar, covered butter, and tureen) in a reprint of an 1881 Atterbury catalog page by Innes (p. 399, plate 441). All are marked PAT'D APRIL 23, 1878 on the bottom of the base. We can not resist including at least one example, the large and very impressive tureen. Exquisite in mould work, some pieces may be found decorated with fired on paint enhancing the finely detailed leaves at the base of the melon.

We are aware of the tureen in clear crystal and frosted as well as milk white. It has a basal opening width of 5 1/8" and is approximately 6 3/4" tall to the top of the small melon finial. All of the Patent Melon Ware pieces are more than hard to find, and the tureen is indeed scarce.

351 - PLAIN MELON PEDESTAL BUTTER

Another example of Atterbury's beautiful, patented tableware items. Ferson (F-355) shows the base of this butter and indicates that the lid is like that of the Plain Melon compote (F-336). The design is the same in both, but the top shown here on the pedestal base is much narrower and thus relatively more conical than is that of the compote.

Known to us only in white. Height overall 6 3/4"; the cover is 3" high to top of finial, and 4 1/2" in diameter. Scarce.

352 - FISH PITCHER

A well-known but by no means common milk pitcher which we include here because of its fine painted decoration.

Made by Atterbury, it is shown in the company's 1881 catalog. See F-328 and 341 for full details, and F-341b for a reprint of the catalog page.

Known to us only in white. Height 7 1/4". The identical item was also made in a creamer size, 4 3/4" high. Possibly rare wirh painted decoration, as shown.

353 - TREE OF LIFE BUTTER DISH

Although this is a familiar pattern, we include it because the butter dish is found much less often than the bowls, compotes, and other pieces of this tableware. The wide flange of the base is embossed with a mass of leaves and flowers which also adorn the sides. Inside the center of the base is a large multi-petal flower and leaves, all done in high relief. The undersides of both flange and base are plain. The dome cover, embossed in like manner, is separated by narrow vertical ribs into three equal segments . High on the dome, a series of chevrons circle around, interrupted by three equidistant blossoms. The tall round finial is finely ribbed on the sides, with a striated surface above and a small nipple at the top. This is fine quality glass that has a nice ring to it.

Made by Challinor, Taylor and designated as their #313 ware, popularly called "Tree of Life," and dating from 1885-1893 (see Lucas, p.73). For additional commentary on this Challinor pattern as it relates to a similar one by Sowerby, see the article "Patent Ivory Queen's Ware" under Special Features in this book.

Known in white, blue, green, and according to Lucas, possibly pink as well. The base is 7 1/2" in diameter, and 1 7/8" high. The domed lid is 5 5/8" in diameter. Overall, it measures 6 3/4" high. More than hard to find.

354 - FISH FIGURAL TABLE SET

This creamer, covered butter, and open sugar bowl ensemble is surely one of the most inventive adaptations of a fish pattern in pressed glass. Unlike the Atterbury fish pitcher shown in the preceding entry and the Entwined Fish covered dish (F-51) which have embossed fish patterns, this set is made as full figurals exacting great ingenuity on the part of the designer and the skill of an expert mould maker. The creamer poses the least amount of difficulty, as the wide-mouthed, upright fish simply turns its tail up to form the handle. The sugar bowl, too, is

substantially the same, except for the expanded mouth opening and the disproportional small tail that loops up to form a finger handle. The cover of the butter dish, however, is absolutely astounding, as the enormous head of the fish dominates the main portion. The tail rising high at the end of the contracted body flips down forward to create an open loop finial. The base of the scalloped edged dish has forty tapering ribs and rests on four scrolled feet. Each piece was made from a four-part mould, and all of the detail is minutely defined, crisp and clean. The glass itself unmistakably speaks an English accent.

Made by W. H. Heppell, Newcastle Flint Glass Works, Newcastle-on-Tyne, all have the design registry mark for November 24, 1882. The fish "pitcher" illustrated in F-204, without attribution, is the same size as the creamer shown here, but it has a turned down spout. The latter and an identical one in a smaller size are called "milk jugs" and are shown in Slack (p. 104).

We know this table set only in white. The jugs and creamers also occur in marbled purple, however, probably made by Davidson from Heppell moulds. Creamer height 5 1/4"; sugar bowl height 5"; the butter measures 5 1/2" by 4 3/8" across the top and is 5 7/8" high overall. Very scarce.

355 - MARQUIS AND MARCHIONESS OF LORNE BUTTER DISH

This beautifully moulded pattern is shown by Ferson in a large covered sweetmeat and a creamer (F-315, 316), and mention is made there that a covered sugar has been reported. To that, we may add a spooner, and a butter dish, both shown in Lattimore who echoes the universal opinion that *"This series is one of the finest designs ever produced in pressed glass"* (p. 132). Like all the other covered pieces in this pattern, the butter dish has a crown finial and carries the two portrait medallions in high relief around the sides. There is also a shield bearing the words: "MARQUIS / & / MARCHIONESS / OF / LORNE / LANDED / AT / HALIFAX . N . S. / 25TH NOVR 1878." The cover rests on an inner ledge of the base whose wide flange has three equidistant round knobs to keep the lid from sliding off. Less often mentioned, however, is the splendid design embossed on the underside of the butter dish. Its outer arched surface bears England's floral emblems (English rose, Scottish thistle, and Irish shamrock) with a rayed star burst in the central area. The dish rests on sixteen knobbed feet.

Made by Henry Greener, the inside of the cover carries the first Greener trademark, a lion holding a star in its paw. As Jenny Thompson has noted "Although the visit was in November 1878," the diamond registry mark which appears inside the base of the dish is for June 8, 1878 (T-1, p. 80).

Known to us in white, the pieces in this design were also listed in *The Pottery Gazette*, January 1, 1880, p. 23, as made in "Flint Glass, Opal, Malachite, and Blue and Black Majolica" (see Slack, p. 96). "Flint" glass probably used here to mean simply clear crystal, and "malachite" is an alternate term for marbled glass, mosaic, or slag. Diameter of the base 7 1/4"; overall height about 5". Rare

356 - EARL OF BEACONSFIELD SUGAR BOWL AND CREAMER

Like the Marquis of Lorne design in the preceding entry, this too is a justly famous commemorative which surely ranks among the finest examples of press-moulded glass. The portrait of Benjamin Disraeli is faithfully rendered within a wreath of laurel on both the creamer and sugar, with England's floral emblems filling the remaining area. The back of the large sugar bowl carries the embossed inscription, also set within a laurel wreath: "EARL/BEACONSFIELD/THE HERO OF THE / CONGRESS / BERLIN / 1878." Beautifully conceived and masterfully executed, a treasure for any collector of historical glass.

Made by Henry Greener, design registered Aug. 31, 1878. The diamond registry and first Greener trademark are pressed inside both pieces.

We know it only in opaque white, but also reported in clear (flint) by Slack (p. 98). The sugar bowl is 5 5/8" high, with a top diameter of 5 3/8". The creamer is 4 3/8" high. Very scarce.

357 - MELON BUTTER DISH WITH RADISH FINIAL

Typical French whimsy is evident in the splendid design of this mould. With fifteen branching leaflets and a prominent stem, the flange of the base is formed as a large scalloped leaf below which is a plain recessed bottom about 1" high. Resting on the leaf is the lower part of the melon itself, which, with the cover in place, looks much like a football! The dominant pattern altogether is of horizontal rows of cut crescents. The ones on the cover are separated on each side by a deeply cut groove that runs the entire length of the cover. Topping off this creation is a finial formed as a radish or small beet, complete with a bit of leafy green at one end and a long tapering root at the other.

Illustrated in VCC (p. 307, No. 3800). Known to us in white and varying shades of caramel. The maximum length of the floral flange is about 8". The melon is 6 1/4" long and 4" wide. The height overall is 4 1/2". More than scarce.

358 - PINWHEEL AND FANS WATER JUG

A heavy, sturdy piece, this water jug is not familiar to most milk glass collectors in this country, but is illustrated and much admired in books on English pressed glass. The deeply embossed pattern of circular swirls set within a ring of beads resembles pinwheels in three sizes, placed one above the other. In alternate rows are two fans, the lower one larger than the one above. Notice how the graduated sizes of the embossed designs serve to magnify the height of the jug, and how the low placement of the beaded handle further reinforces that illusion. A great amount of oxidizing agents must have been required to produce this glass which appears totally black by reflected light, but is a deep cobalt blue by transmitted light, as you can see in the photograph.

Made by Henry Greener, it has no registry mark but bears the earlier Greener mark (a lion with a star in its paw) at the center of the intaglio on the underside, thus dating it circa 1875-1885.

Known to us only in the color shown, but see Manley, fig. 390, p. 107, who pictures one in a somewhat lighter blue, and Murray, plate 63, p. 76, where two examples are illustrated, one in amber and another in light amethyst. Height about 6 3/4", base diameter 4"; top diameter 3 3/8". Very scarce.

359 - OVAL MEDALLION WATER PITCHER

This well-known pattern is often shown as a four piece table set (sugar, creamer, butter, and spooner), usually with various floral decorations. Kamm (Bk. II, p. 120) mentioned the existence of a large water pitcher as well, but Lucas expressed some doubt because the catalog which shows pieces in this pattern "does not illustrate or list a pitcher" leading him to conclude, "It is possible that other pieces exist, but my guess would be that [the table set alone] made up the complete line in this pattern" (p. 78). The pitcher does exist, in fact, and is illustrated here for the first time.

Made by Challinor, Taylor in the No. 28 "Oval Sett" pattern pieces as shown in Lucas (p. 79) and Ferson (F-242-245).

Although the table set is also found in marbled glass, the pitcher is known to us in white only. It measures 8" high to the top of the upper lip, and 5" across the arched feet. The mouth opening is 6" by 3 1/4". Apparently rare.

360 - DUTCH MILKMAID CHILDREN'S PITCHER

Heavy for its size, this miniature pitcher is embossed on one side with a Dutch girl holding a pail, and on the opposite side with a windmill, trees, and a resting cow. Elaborate scroll work frames the figures, and vertical bars of varying lengths border the lip and handle. A row of circles on the handle is continued on the upper edge of the pitcher up to the spout which is smooth and slightly turned down. The underside of the pitcher has a pattern of sharp rays extending outward from the center.

Maker unknown. It is part of a seven-piece "chamber set" according to Lechler (p. 131), who illustrates the pitcher in white and opaque blue (p. 23) and reports that it is also found in clear and green. Height 2" to the center of the rim. Hard to find.

361 - FLORAL BEVERAGE SET

Shown here is a fine example of a type of "refreshment set" produced for the masses, especially during the 1920s-1930s. There is a particular elegance in this example, evident in the graceful form of the blown pitcher with its turned and pinched lip and the applied elongated handle. The purple floral spray and leaves are heavily enameled, and the thin gold band which trims the tumblers and pitcher is typical of many of the products made by this relatively short-lived company. The glass is of good quality and has a nice ring to it.

Made by the Dunbar Flint Glass Corp., of Dunbar, West Virginia, probably in the 1930s-1940s. The company, founded in 1913, closed in 1953 (see Weatherman, *Colored Glassware*, p. 54). The underside of the pitcher and tumblers are marked in gold "Hand Painted / Original" with the name Dunbar set inside an artist's palette.

Known to us only in white. Height of pitcher 9 1/4"; tumblers 2 3/4". Somewhat hard to find as a complete set.

362 - COCOA OR TEA CADDY

With an expanded swollen base, this otherwise plain four-sided box is something of an enigma. Our best guess is that it was intended as a caddy of some sort. It is perfectly plain except for the familiar scroll pattern along the sides and around the central painted figure.

Maker unknown, but it is probably American dating from the early 1900s when the scroll design was a great favorite for dresser boxes and trays.

Known to us only in white. Height of base 5"; height of top 1 3/4"; Base at the bottom measures 3 1/2 " by 2", and at the top 2 1/2" by 2". Hard to find to scarce.

363 - PEWTER HANDLED SYRUP

A beautifully proportioned syrup, its upper portion, rising from a bulbous lower third, has a raised band at the top just below the wide pewter sleeve. The convex lid has a knob finial. Its graceful pewter handle curves outward from the sleeve and extends down to just above the swollen base. The illustrated piece is beautifully painted with a winter scene.

Presumably a product of the Mt. Washington Glass Co. whose fine glass pieces often have similar winter designs.

Known to us only in white. Height to top of pewter finial approximately 6 1/2". Height of swollen basal area 2 1/4", milk glass cylindrical area 2 1/2". Base diameter 2 1/2". Rare.

364 - EGG SERVICE SET

An eight piece breakfast set, consisting of six low stemmed egg cups, a large divided master salt on high pedestal, and a round tray whose pattern is designed to mark the places for the salt and egg cups. The tray, resting on six knobbed feet, has a double scalloped outer rim with an inner pleated ribbon embossed all around in high relief. The depressed face of the tray is heavily embossed in an elaborate pattern of baroque scrolls arranged so as to form six evenly spaced recessed areas to hold the egg cups. At the center of the tray, a slightly elevated round platform has a raised rim to secure the divided salt. The cups and salt are patterned as overlapping leaves and petals, the tips of which form an irregularly scalloped edge.

This set is shown in VCC (p. 306, #3949) and again in PC (p. 328, #7331). Other references: SW (p.8); H-J (#4650); and Spillman (plate 1460).

We know it in grayish white opal and blue milk glass. Diameter of the tray 10 3/4"; cup 2 1/8" high; divided salt 2 3/4" high. Heacock considered it rare; we think it is at least scarce.

Toothpicks/Matchholders

365 - FROG AND SHELL TOOTHPICK HOLDER

A bizarre figural, either a toothpick or, as Ruth Webb Lee called it, a matchholder (L-VG, Plate 127), modeled as a frog straining to pull a gigantic coiled shell. The tension is palpable, as the frog's front legs bend back pulling the top of the shell while the right hind leg bends forward to provide leverage. The frog's skin is grainy and the shell has evenly spaced rows of beads around its sides. The figures rest on a convex pebbled aquatic leaf, with a smooth underside.

Illustrated without attribution by Heacock and Griscom. If the maker of this piece is identified elsewhere we are not aware of it. Heacock, who dates it circa 1885, shows three examples [in milk glass H-1 No. 302; amber No. 355; and transparent blue No. 340], noting that the blue one differs from the other two, but says no reproductions have been reported. Griscom, however, shows not one but two different reproductions of this piece (p. 19), neither of which is identified as to their makers. At least one of them, however, is an L.G. Wright product, shown in Measell and Roettels (p. 98, 133) in amber, milk white, deep lavender, green, and light blue. See Griscom for a fuller discussion of the differences between the original and the two reproductions. We feel confident the one shown here is an old original.

Known to us in opaque white and deep amber. Maximum length 4"; length from tip of nose to end of shell opening 3 5/8"; height 2 3/4"; shell opening 1 3/4 x 1 1/2"; basal leaf 3 1/4" by 2 3/4". Originals are very scarce; reproductions becoming somewhat hard to find.

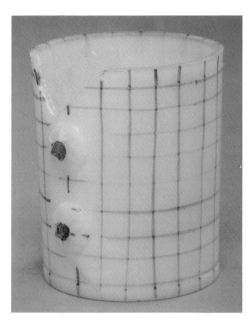

366 -CUFF TOOTH-PICK HOLDER

Although usually regarded as a toothpick holder, this piece may have been intended for cuff links on the gentleman's dresser as it simulates a man's sleeve cuff with two buttons in relief. At the top and bottom, about 3/8" from the edges, is a stitching design and above the buttons is a "V" notch, 7/8" long and 1 1/4" wide.

Maker unknown. Known to us only in white. Height 2 5/8" with a 2 1/8" diameter. Scarce.

367 - BEARDED OLD MAN GRAPE CARRIER TOOTHPICK

Some collectors call this figure a "Santa Claus," but he is clearly an aged worker burdened by a large grape basket on his back and pausing to rest. Great care was given to moulding the features of his face, notably his flattened nose, broad mustaches, and a long thick beard. The basket weave consists of three layered horizontal strips and single vertical ones. The peasant's sleeves are rolled up and the short pleated skirt reveal his hairy legs. His hands rest on his knees, one of which is braced against a rock pile. A splendid and evocative conversation piece.

Maker unknown. Probably French. Known to us only in white. Height 4 3/8"; base diameter 2 1/4". Rare.

369 - TWO FIGURES WITH BARREL TOOTHPICK HOLDER

Deftly simulated in glass, a large wooden barrel with double metal staves near the top and bottom form this receptacle for matches or toothpicks. Two young lads — vineyard workers we assume — grip the barrel on each side. Each appears to be steadying and supporting the weight of the barrel by bracing it with one leg underneath, but in fact the barrel rests on a round pedestal base. It is a tiered affair, with a ring of beads at the bottom surmounted by elongated ovals. The glass is of good quality and highly opalescent.

Embossed "S V" inside the bottom. See H-1 (p. 58, No. 328) where Heacock calls this piece "Two Women," with which we disagree.

Known to us in white and blue. Height 4 1/8"; top diameter 1 3/4"; bottom diameter 2 3/8". Scarce.

368 - OLD MAN WITH BASKET MATCHHOLDER

Somewhat similar to the "Bearded Grape Carrier," this bearded figure is also kneeling on one knee and carrying a huge woven basket strapped to his back. He wears a peaked cap, knee high boots, and holds a long walking stick. At his side he has a cask tied to a rope from his waist. The surface of the base is stippled and edged with a string of beads. This piece, too, is thought provoking.

Illustrated as a "Porte Allumette" in PC (P. 110, No. 1588) and in color (p. 328, No. 1799), designated simply "Sujet" (i.e. "figure"). Our example is signed "Portieux" across the outside of the base.

Known to us in white, blue, caramel; possibly made in green also. Height 4"; top opening 2" by 2 1/8"; base diameter 2 1/2". Scarce.

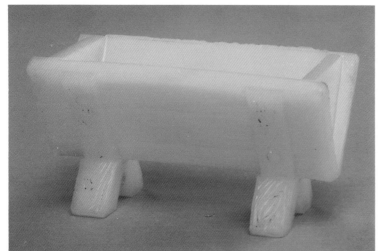

370 - FEEDING TROUGH

Often called "the manger" by some collectors, this representational piece, perhaps a lay-flat toothpick holder, is formed as three heavy planks placed on a sawhorse and held fast by two nails.

Maker unknown. Kamm (K-1, p. 27) conjectures Bryce Brothers as a possibility.

Known to us only in white. Length 3"; width 1 7/8"; height 1 1/2". Scarce

372 - FROG MATCHHOLDER

Squatting on a square grassy mound, this frog appears to be vocalizing for a role in a Wagnerian opera, or more likely preparing to catch the next fly that comes his way! Instead, the frog will gobble up toothpicks, of course, or matches, as the rough ground surface is suitable as a match strike. A beautifully proportioned three-dimensional figure.

Maker unknown, but we believe not recent. Known to us only in white. Height 4 3/4"; base 2 7/8" square. Scarce.

371 - MONKEY BY HAT TOOTHPICK HOLDER

Seated alongside a large top hat, this rather morose looking monkey on a bandstand box is dressed in a full-length smock with a pinked collar and a meticulous pattern of sequins on the back. Its long tail extends down the box, loops around a center knob, and comes to a curl at the end. The top surface of the box is closely ribbed, perhaps serving as a match strike. The glass has a brilliant luster, and the mould work is precious throughout, with extraordinary care given to each detail. The head is solid and the rest of the body hollow. Why so many pieces as fine as this one were not signed is indeed infuriating.

Illustrated by Heacock (H-1, p. 60, No. 1322), who ascribes it to Belmont Glass of Bellaire, Ohio, circa 1890 (?), his attribution. being based on Wheeling area museums. He expresses some reservation, however, because one of these pieces was reported to him in "emerald green," a color which he says did not become popular until 1900, long after Belmont closed. To our knowledge, it has not been reproduced.

We know it only in opaque, both white and black. Length 3"; width 1 3/4"; height to top of head 3 5/8". Rare in white; very rare in black.

373 - FROG WITH TULIP TOOTHPICK

This charming toothpick holder is modeled as a plump little frog alongside what appears to be a tulip blossom. They are set on a round base with vertical ribbing all around. The glass is quite opalescent.

Attributed to Co-Operative Flint Glass Co., by Heacock (H-2, p. 85) who reprints a circa 1911 catalog page, noting that this toothpick had been previously unlisted. Named simply "Frog Toothpick," the catalog states it is shipped 18 dozen in a barrel, total weight 170 pounds. Where are they all now!

Known to us only in white. Height 3 1/2". Rare.

374 - JOLLY MOOR WITH BASKETS MATCHHOLDER

With bald head and crossed legs, this figure may appear at first glance to be a Buddha, but his resplendent collared cloak, puffy pantaloons, and long pig tail running half way down his back are not at all in keeping with the meditative sixth-century BC religious leader. More comical than serious, his moon face, plump cheeks, and broad grin suggest a swarthy Moroccan or a character out of the Arabian Nights. The stippled elongated oval below the figure serve as a match strike. The glass has an extraordinary brilliance quite dazzling in the way it catches the light.

Marked with the unidentified initials "S V," it is most likely European. We know it only in dark blue. Length 4 1/2", width 2 7/8", height 4 1/4". Rare.

375 - INDIAN CHIEF MATCHHOLDER

Representations of the American Indian are frequent in milk glass pieces, often as portraits embossed or painted on plates and tomahawks, as well as figural containers for toothpicks or matches. Among the more elusive of the latter is the example shown here, together with one of the recent reproductions of which there are several. As you can readily see, the copy is "fatter" overall and lacks much of the excellent mould work which defines the features of the original. Contrast the fine straight nose with the copy's broad flat one. Compare the well formed and distinct eyes with the copy's distorted eyes, one of which sags. In the copy, the high cheekbones of the original look more like malevolent outgrowths. And in general, the Indian's noble and perfectly proportioned face is transformed into a pudgy caricature. What remains of the paint helps to highlight the fine features of the original.

Maker unknown, previously shown without attribution in Lindsey (plate 12) and in Marsh (plate 18) who incorrectly attributes this piece as well as the Challinor Indian Head Cigar Holder (plate 19) to Greentown. See also Griscom who states "Believed to have been made by McKee, in milk glass only" (p. 23). We have found no documentation to support that claim, however. Reproductions in many colors, both opaque and transparent, were made by St. Clair and Summit; the white and red slag version shown here is marked "Joe St. Clair" in script.

We have found the original only in opaque white. The original measures 2 3/4" high, 2" in diameter; the reproduction slightly larger. The original is rare; reproductions are generally available.

376 - THE HUNTER MATCHHOLDER

This engaging piece has been variously called "The Sleeping Boy" and "Rip Van Winkle," although it is in fact a depiction of a hunter, evidenced by the hunting rifle that lies on the mound of grass in front of him. The figure is elegantly dressed in frock coat, cuffed sleeves, and high walking boots. A stylish quilted pouch, hanging from a shoulder strap, lies on the grass behind him. His curled and powdered wig bespeak his courtliness, and the little rabbit peering out from the hollow stump as well as a pheasant on the other side seem more curious than fearful of the satirically named "hunter."

Marked "PORTIEUX," and shown in PC (p.110, No. 1589), it is a Porte-Allumette, although claimed as well by collectors of toothpicks, and is designated "Chasseur." See also "Three Conversation Pieces: Portieux's 'Main,' 'Chasseur,' and 'Gamin,'" (GCD, Feb/Mar 1996, pp. 58-64).

Known to us in opaque white, blue, and green, as well as vaseline, but possibly made in amber and clear frosted. It is 3 1/2" high, and the ovoid base measures 5" long by 2 1/2" at the widest end. Somewhat hard to find.

377 - COLUMBUS HANGING MATCHHOLDER

A handsome representation of a young Columbus. With hair blown back, the figure is given an appropriately adventuresome aspect. Sporting a mustache and typical Renaissance head wear and large collared coat, he is indeed a gentleman of distinction. The glass is of excellent quality, very suitable for a wall ornament made possible by a hole in the back.

Maker unknown, but early. It carries an indistinct patent date which appears to be of the 1870s, possibly 1876.

Known only in white with satin finish. 4" high and 3" across at the shoulders. As it escapes mention in Lindsey, we think it must be rare.

378 - MANTEL CLOCK MATCHHOLDER

Candy containers and other glass novelties such as this matchholder formed as clocks seem to have been fairly popular, and there appears to have been no prescript as to where the hour and minute hands should be placed. This example, with traditional Roman numerals, is set at 10 minutes after 10 o'clock. It cannot be mistaken for a toothpick holder, as the horizontal ribbing on the sides is designed to serve as a match strike. The same purpose may also be intended by the heavily stippled surface of the base at both ends. An attractive checkerboard pattern is embossed on the back.

Maker unknown, but most likely English. Known to us only in black. It measures 3 3/4" long; 3 1/8" high. Scarce.

379 - LIZARD AND FROGS TOOTHPICK AND SALT SET

An appealing item whose two separate oval elements are fashioned so they nest together. The toothpick upper portion has a smooth surface embossed with leaves and branches. It is dominated by a large three-dimensional lizard, exquisitely detailed, with little frogs moulded on each side. The underside has a small lip which fits down into the matching saltcellar embossed with three frogs. Since each piece is independent of the other and could easily go its separate way, it is not often one finds both parts of this beautiful set together.

Maker unknown. Known to us only in white. Toothpick 2" high; saltcellar 1" high. Rare.

380 - BUTTERFLY HANGING MATCHHOLDERS

We follow Warman (Plate 20) in naming these three butterflies *Alpha*, *Beta*, and *Gamma*, and include them because Warman's photo is not very good. Because each butterfly has it own distinctive features, we have amused ourselves by trying to see whether we could actually classify them according to their proper orders among Lepidoptera by reference to paintings from the American Museum of Natural History (reprinted in the *Encyclopædia Britannica*, 1942 ed.).

Alpha comes close to "Vanessa io," the peacock butterfly common in Europe and Asia.

Beta looks like "Catocala ilia," known as the ilia underwing, found generally throughout the U.S. and most of Canada.

Gamma is a dead ringer for "Actias luna," the luna moth considered to be the most beautiful North American insect. Likewise, we think it is the most pleasing of the three.

The wing surface of *Alpha* serves as the match strike; *Beta* has the striker under the base; *Gamma* has a glass divider forming two compartments and a striker surface only on the right side (a pity for left handed people).

We do not know the makers, but Eagle Glass might be a possibility for at least one of them.

Known to us only in white, with *Beta* most often found painted; *Gamma* rarely; and *Alpha* hardly ever. *Alpha*: width 4 1/8"; height 3 1/2". *Beta*: width 4 3/8", height 2 1/4". *Gamma*: width 3 3/4", height 3 3/8". All are scarce.

Vases

381 - THREE FIGURES WITH SATYR VASE

This is another of the fanciful, somewhat erotic French creations. Below the vertically ribbed upper half are three figures, nude but for loin cloths. They seem to be young ladies, or possibly children, holding on to the curving horns of the impressive Satyr heads that appear between them. A long strand emerging from each corner of the head of the "creature" swings up to become the drapery on each of the human figures. Note the curling ram-like "hair" on the human heads. The base is formed as a series of vertical convex ovals with intricate intersecting frames. We regret that such provocative, perhaps symbolically significant pieces such as this in the Portieux catalog are all simply named "sujets" (i.e. figurals) rather than given a descriptive name more helpful than the one we have had to invent for this item.

It is illustrated in color in PC (p. 331, No. 7838). Known to us only in white. Height 9" and 4 1/4" across the flaring scalloped top. Scarce.

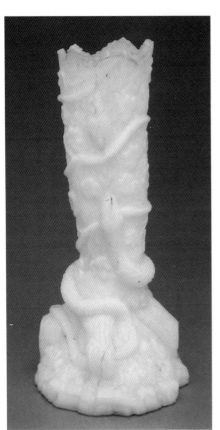

382 - SNAKE AND TREE TRUNK VASE

A rather sinister, intricate piece, formed as a tree trunk entangled in a twisting, curling vine, its large roots cut off close to the trunk proper. In and out among the roots and vines and up the rough trunk crawls a slender snake, eyes fixed intently on an unsuspecting bird sitting on a vine tendril. A piece of astonishing tension.

Another of the enigmatic milk glass items embossed "S V," this one marked inside the deeply concave underside of the base.

Known to us only in white. It is 7" high and 3 1/8" wide across the base. Scarce.

385 - KING'S HEAD VASE

An elegant, cylindrical vase with fluted top and footed base. Three rows of beads running down the sides of the cylinder form three panels, two of which have a central raised circle from which sixteen keeled and pointed rays extend. The third panel bears the profile of a man with pointed beard, mustache, and what appears to be a band or crown with stars on it. The stem sweeps upward from a six paneled base. The entire piece exhibits a fiery brilliance. One wonders whether the figure may represent Louis XIV, dubbed the "Sun King" of France.

Maker unknown. Known to us only in white. It is 6" tall with a top diameter of 3" and a base diameter of 2 1/4". The height of the cylinder is 4 3/4". Rare.

383 - GRANT MEMORIAL VASE

The center of this beautifully designed, fiery opal vase bears a bust with a banner below carrying the words "Gn. Grant." The figure does not much resemble portraits of Grant, suggesting it may have been a generic design for use with other famous names as well. Above the wreath-framed bust is a federal eagle with outspread wings and an American shield. The top of the vase is flared with wide stripes and a scalloped edge. The reverse side is much the same, but without the bust. Apparently issued as a memorial piece.

Maker unknown, and not shown in Lindsey or Marsh. Known to us only in white. Height 4 7/8"; top opening 4 1/8"; base diameter 2 5/8". Scarce.

384 - FRANKLIN D. ROOSEVELT STATUETTE VASE

Although it lacks any inscription, there is little doubt that this piece represents Franklin Delano Roosevelt. It is a hollow "Head Vase," made perhaps during our mid-century when such vases, especially in ceramics, became very popular. The glass is of good quality with a high sheen and the features are true to life.

Maker unknown. Known to us only in white. Height 7 3/4"; width at base 4 1/2". The oval opening in the hat measures 2 3/4". Very scarce.

386 - LEAF AND SWIRL ("Indien") VASE

The design symmetry and classic shape of this vase make it a model of elegant simplicity. As one may readily see from other examples in this book, such restraint is not exactly a hallmark of this French company whose designers tended to favor exotic and wonderfully ornate creations. Each section of the four-part mould of this blown vase is identical, together forming four large leaves overlaid on a gracefully swirling background. A row of smaller upright leaves circles the neck of the vase which flares sharply and is fluted at the top. Around the base a simple ring of petals completes the design.

Made by Vallerysthal originally and also by Portieux, it is found in several catalogs. Shown in SW (p. 2, top row right), whose Vallerysthal catalog illustrations appear to come from a German version, as this vase is grouped among *blumenvases* (flower vases). In VCC, it is shown decorated as No. 4596, p. 313. Undecorated, it is shown in PC, p. 102, as No. 1493, called "Indien" which may indicate the inspiration for the design. And shown once again in two different decorations in PC, No. 7866, p. 332.

Known to us in white and pale green. Height 8"; other sizes are also listed in the PC catalog. Scarce.

387 - CASTLE FLOWER HOLDER

This delightful little vase is not an entire castle exactly, but one of the subordinate towers, a turret. Moulded as brick work with a multi-notched ridged top edge and similarly ridged base, it is quite imposing for such a relatively small piece, especially because of the glass itself, extremely opalescent and of the very best quality.

Made by Molineaux, Webb, Manchester, England, pattern and shape No. 29780/1, registered July 14, 1885. See Lattimore, plate X, and Thompson (T-1, p. 45).

We know it only in white opaline as shown. Height 3 1/4" ; width 3 1/8". Very rare.

388 - SWEDISH FLAG BEARERS VASES

These perfectly cylindrical vases flaring out only slightly near the bottom are tall enough for gladioli. Of moderate weight, the plain white milk glass vases are hand painted with figures of a girl and a boy in native costume, she dressed in blue and he in green. They stand on a snow covered ground and support the flag of Sweden on tall wooden poles. The colors of the flag, a yellow cross on a blue field, are those of the national coat-of-arms. They are hand blown, the undersides being deeply concave with large, unpolished pontil scars. As a pair, they are quite impressive.

Marked in script on the underside "Lappland" (the Swedish spelling) and "JOHANSFORS / SWEDEN."

We know them only in white. Height 12 1/2", base diameter 4 1/4". Availability unknown, probably scarce as a pair.

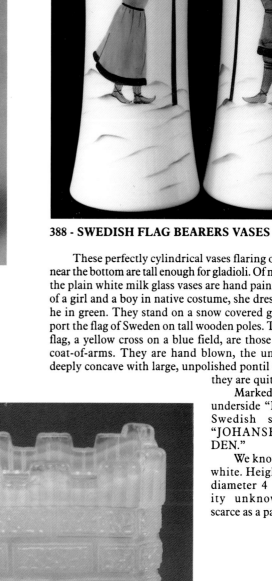

389 - ELEPHANT FLOWER BOWL

A massive open back elephant whose trunk curls down between its legs and almost reaches to its feet. The rough textured skin has the look of leather.

Made by Fenton (No. 1618) in 1929-1930. Illustrated in Heacock (H-F1, p. 110) from a 1929 catalog, where it apparently first appeared, and on page 77 in teal blue. Heacock pictures it again in ebony and jade green (H-F2, pp. 28-29). James (p. 15) and G-S (p. 61) also list other colors and finishes: in black with both a satin and a glossy finish, in transparent crystal, green, amethyst, and rose. Length 9"; height 6". All the references cited above stress the rarity of this piece.

391 - NEPTUNE FLOWER POT

A companion to the Mermaid Jardiniere in the preceding illustration, this heavy, octagonal flower pot has the same face of father Neptune embossed on three sides along the top margin. Long reed-like growths emerge from his mouth, ending in round leaves that form the irregular, deeply scalloped rim at the top. And like the Jardiniere, a mass of elongated droplets simulating a waterfall cover the sides.

Embossed "Portieux" inside the base, it is called "Cache-pot sujets" in PC (p. 99, No. 1444) and also shown with painted decoration (p. 328, No. 7193).

Known to us in white and caramel. Height 6"; width at top 6 7/8"; width at bottom 3 3/4". Very scarce.

390 - MERMAID JARDINIERE

One of the superb Portieux fantasies, this massive rectangular jardiniere features tantalizingly sexy mermaids reclining on large lily pads at each corner. With arms folded behind their heads, long tresses, and shapely fish scaled legs ending in wide fins, they are everything we imagine a mythological siren should be. From the mouth of father Neptune, whose face commands the center of the long axis, seven stems emerge, each ending in large leaves, one of which joins a stem rising from behind a mermaid to form the undulating top margin. A simi-

lar effect is created on the short sides. All the remaining surface is covered with long droplets, apparently simulating ripples of waterfall. The pebbled underside is raised by four thick conical feet, and the bottom edge is defined by a pattern of twenty-two elliptical loops each traversed by a cord passing through the middle. The overall configuration of the jardiniere is remarkable. The sides slope slightly inward from top to bottom, and the inner surface of the mermaid corners are not simply squared but angled gracefully.

Illustrated in PC (p. 99, No. 1443) under the heading of "Articles de Fantaisie" and in color (p. 328, No. 7194). It is marked "Portieux" inside at the bottom.

Known to us in white and blue. A foot long, and 6 1/2" wide, it has a maximum median height of 5". Rare, especially in blue.

392 - FLOWER TROUGH CENTERPIECE

For this four-part flower trough centerpiece whose purpose is purely functional, the simplicity of the vertical ribbed pattern is ideal. Consisting of two long rectangular and two half circles, they can be arranged in various ways to suit the occasion and the space available. A simple circle, for example, can be created and the long troughs may be set elsewhere on the table or omitted altogether. For a large buf-

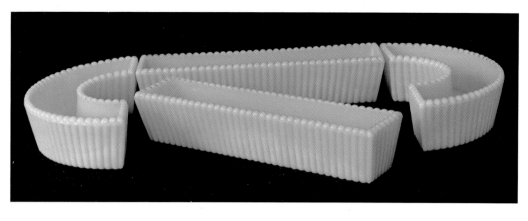

fet table, one might place the long troughs together, either side by side or end to end. A very versatile table grouping.

Each piece is marked Portieux. Illustrated as numbers 1275-1278 in PC, p. 90, with other table accessories, they are called "Chemin" (runners) for the table and were made in two sizes.

Known to us in white and blue opaque only. Each element in the example illustrated is 2 1/4" wide and 2" high; the arch is 7 1/2" across, and the rectangular trough is 9" long. Somewhat hard to find.

393 - MONKEY HOLDING VASE

Just what the monkey is hugging so tightly between its arms and legs is difficult to make out. The lower half of the vase itself is ribbed, but the portion above has a series of overlapping fans or shells, then a plain surface which ends in a broadly fluted top. If we were to relate what we see to vegetation, it could possibly represent the bark and leaves of a tropical plant. The monkey, squatting slightly and with downcast head, looks to be very intent upon his duty to keep the vase upright!

Maker unknown. Known to us only in white. Height 9 1/8". Rare.

394 - STORK VASE

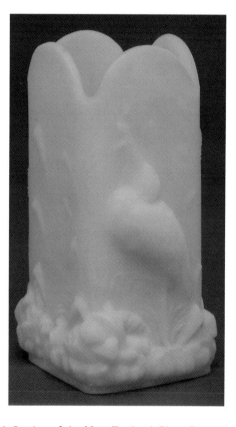

Perfectly square with arches shaping the top of each of its four sides, this vase has a large stork in high relief on the front panel. It stands with one leg upraised and the other set on a lush ground of foliage, with tall marsh reeds and cattails rising high on all four sides. The stork has a slithering eel or grass snake caught in its bill. All of the embossing is superb, and the fine detail of the anatomical features and feathering can be appreciated only with a magnifying lens. There is a small circle, about 1/2" in diameter moulded *inside* the base, but it is a mould mark with no identification significance.

Designed by Joseph Locke, of the New England Glass Company, it was made about 1884, a few years after the factory's move from Cambridge, Massachusetts, to Toledo, Ohio, and its name change to Libbey Glass Company. (See Fauster, p. 227.)

While the vase is well known in Locke's famous "Amberina" glass as a rare example of pressed glass in the field of hand blown Art Glass, it is also something of an anomaly as "art glass" in the field of press-moulded milk glass. Fauster, cited above, reports finding Locke's design for this vase in his "Amberina Sketch Book," and says the Stork vase stands out as "the only pressed piece" illustrated among the other sketches for hand blown glass.

Known to us in clear, satin etched, Amberina, and in milk glass with satin finish as shown here. Height 4 1/2", and 2 1/4" square. Very rare.

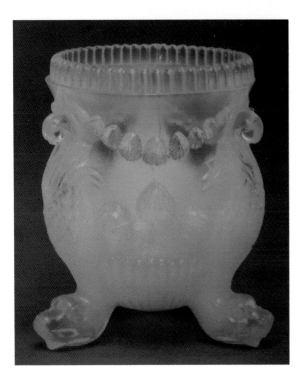

395 - DOLPHIN AND SHELL FLOWER HOLDER

The scaly bodies of three fanciful creatures — commonly referred to as dolphins — are placed equidistant around the sides of this lovely vase, their heads serving as three feet. The top edge and lower portion of the vase are ribbed. An unbroken chain of sea shells is draped from tail-end to tail-end, with a large single shell flanked by two small snails embossed in each of the intervening spaces. The craftsmanship of the three-part mould is excellent.

Although the actual maker is unknown, it is a French product, attested in part by a square paper label printed "FRANCE 165" which was found on one example. The motif of dolphins and shell is more familiar to collectors in the form of a covered butter dish made in two sizes by Portieux and Vallerysthal. They were produced at least as early as 1894, illustrated as No. 5499 (p. 186) in a Portieux catalog of that date. The butter dish design was reproduced extensively, beginning in the 1950s, by Westmoreland in a slightly larger sized "candy dish." We have also seen a very similar dolphin covered dish, with roses instead of shells, illustrated in a publication, housed in the Corning Museum, of the pressed-glass collection in a Mining and Industrial Museum in Germany [1986], where it is identified as a sugar bowl, attributed to Meisenthal, and dated circa 1920s.

We know this vase in dense white milk glass, in a milky white opal, and in purple marble. Height 3 3/8", diameter 2 1/4". Very scarce.

396 - CRAYFISH ("Ecrevisses") VASE

The sides of this large vase, with broadly fluted top, feature three splendidly detailed crayfish whose claws are clutching at a cluster of overlapping leaves above their heads. A series of twelve grooved "feet" rounded at the edges decorates the base.

Illustrated in PC (p. 102, No. 1482) and in color (p. 331, No. 7841). Known to us in white and caramel. Height 8 1/4"; top diameter 4 1/2"; base diameter 3 1/4". Rare.

397 - THREE DUCKS VASE

Three winsome ducks in the wild are moulded around this vase, their necks and heads straining upward toward the broad and deeply fluted opening. Tall leaves and corn-like reeds fill the upper portion of the stem. The base is ridged and scalloped.

Illustrated in PC ("Canards" No. 1481, p. 102, and with painted decoration as No. 7840, p. 331). Known to us only in white, but no doubt made in other colors, both plain and decorated. Height 8"; diameter of base 3". Scarce.

398 - CHINESE ("Chinois") VASE

A very artful creation, this austere tall vase, simulating bamboo, is held by a seated Chinese figure. His robe and characteristic pig-tail, crossed bare legs, and slippers suggest he may be a monk.

Shown in PC (p. 103, No. 1495) and in color (p.332, No. 7854). Known to us in white, blue and green. Height 8". Rare.

400 - THE HUNT ("Trophee") VASE

Embellished by a broad fluted rim at the top, rising from multiple crosswise wavy lines, and a braided pannier at the bottom, the central portion of this vase is a lively celebration of a successful hunt. The elaborate design depicts the heads of cats or more likely beavers, on two of its sides, as they appear to be swimming down a cascading waterfall. On another side is the head of a hound dog holding in its mouth a rabbit by the hind legs. And on the opposite side is another dog, possibly a water spaniel, with two large fish dangling from its mouth. Additional realistic touches include huge flowers around the rabbit to indicate land, and spears of sea grass around the fish to suggest a water milieu.

Shown in PC (p. 102, No. 1485) and in color (p. 331, No. 7844). Known to us in white, green, and caramel. Height 9" with base diameter 3 1/2". Rare.

399 - DRAGON FANTASY VASE

This intriguing coiled dragon appears to be devouring a large fluted vase grasped in its open mouth by sharp teeth. The mythical aspects of the creature, replete with discrete scales, is enhanced by the fanciful small wings or fins fanning out from its body. The vase itself is deeply grooved with a series of dots just above the broad upper jaw. A very curious domed structure is inserted incongruously into the mass of coils, perhaps to suggest a castle under siege?

Maker unknown. It is quite in keeping, however, with many similar pieces listed in the 1933 Portieux catalog as "Articles de Fantaisie."

Known to us only in blue. Height 9 1/2". Rare.

401 - ORIENTAL LAUGHING-CRYING VASE

Made of good quality, glossy milk glass, this curious footed vase has faces, somewhat coarsely moulded, on each side, one broadly smiling, the other scowling. The eyes are oriental, the nose crudely formed, the neck stubby, and the area around the open mouths has block-like impressions as if to simulate cracked lips! The "ears," if they can be so called, are shaped as six connected loops running the entire side of the vase. Five bands circle the base which is deeply concave on the underside. An exceedingly bizarre creation!

Maker unknown. Almost certainly a modern piece and most likely of Asian origin.

Known to us only in white, although we have seen a smaller version in clear crystal. Height 6"; top 3 3/4" diameter; base 3 1/2" diameter. Not readily available.

165

W. J. PATTERSON.
VASE.
DESIGN. No. 13.525.
Patented Jan. 16, 1883.

Garfield-Lincoln Vase

Lincoln and Garfield vase patented by William J. Patterson on Jan. 16, 1888. The patent drawing is reprinted from G. Peterson, *Glass Patents and Patterns*, p. 76.

402 - LINCOLN AND GARFIELD VASE

The names Lincoln and Garfield are embossed below the heads of these two presidents, obviously linked together as victims of assassins' bullets. The faces are very well moulded and the likeness is especially good. As noted elsewhere, traditional classical laurel wreaths are used to grace the heads of both presidents. The top of the vase is slightly flared and carries a faint design of plumes and beads. On each side, a star atop flat pleated drapery separates the two presidents, a feature in keeping with the funereal motif that occasioned this piece.

The patent date Jan. 16, 1888 appears on the underside. The patent was granted to William J. Patterson of Beaver, Pennsylvania, who stated "The vase may be made of metal, porcelain, glass, plaster of Paris, earthenware, or any other material from which vases are usually made." It is not known to which glass factory he assigned the patent, and the same vase may exist in one or another of the other materials mentioned. The patent design drawing is reprinted in A. G. Peterson, *Glass Patents and Patterns*, p. 76.

Known to us only in white. Height 8 1/2"; 3 1/4" diameter at the base. Rare.

403 - SWAN VASE

Three open-neck swans standing amid bulrushes are moulded around the sides of this Sowerby vase which resembles a similar "closed-neck" swan pattern made by Challinor, Taylor and another version ("open neck") made by Westmoreland. The pattern of this English vase appears to be the prototype for the American versions, predating by about twelve years Challinor's "Flying Swan" (whose earliest catalog references are circa 1891), while Westmoreland's swan pieces are much more recent. The main distinguishing feature of the English pattern, which is found in several other pieces besides this vase, is the half-moon platforms serving as supports for the swans' legs. For a fuller account of these similar patterns, see the entry under "Special Feature Articles" in this book.

The English vase carries the Sowerby peacock logo and registry mark for Aug. 14, 1879.

Shown here in Sowerby's "Giallo" (a creamy lemon opaque yellow), it is also found in "Patent Ivory," turquoise, and other colors. Height 3 3/4". Very rare in yellow, scarce to rare in other colors.

404 - LADY'S HEAD VASE

Identical heads of an idealized lady, perhaps a prototypical Greek goddess, are moulded on each side of this splendid vase. The features are formed in the classical style of antiquity, perfectly serene and expressionless. Long tresses frame the face, and a mass of foliage rises up and around the head. Her prim beaded, pleated and scalloped collar is quite Victorian, thus evading perhaps any prude's censure that it is a nude Aphrodite.

Made by Atterbury, it is illustrated in the company's 1881 catalog (see F-574A). Known to us only in white. Height 5 1/2" and 3" in diameter at the base. Possibly rare.

406 - PEACOCK VASE

This enchanting blown vase may as well be called Twelve Exotic Birds. The pattern around the sides of the vase is repeated three times, each section consisting of a spread-wing pelican near the top, a long-tailed pheasant just below, and then a baby peacock facing its mother who dominates the scene, giving the vase its name. The ribbed portion at the top is both practical and aesthetically appropriate, as it narrows and provides a collar for the body of the vase. The design features may hint at a possible Phoenix & Consolidated Art Glass origin, but the opaline glass of this vase is much lighter in weight than many of the similar Phoenix vases.

In a letter dated Oct. 18, 1995, Charles Gillinder, President of Gillinder Brothers, Inc., of Port Jervis, New York, stated: "The ten-inch high blue opal peacock vase was made by Gillinder. My wife and I have this piece in a green opal, and I must say it is one of my favorites. I cannot, however, determine an exact date of manufacture. We now currently believe the ten-inch was originally made by Gillinder & Sons. After it closed, the mold was moved here to Port Jervis. I have to think that some glass was made from the mold while it was here. Unfortunately, the mold was destroyed in the 50s."

Known to us only in blue and green opal, but possibly made in milk white as well. Height 10 1/4"; base diameter 3 1/2"; maximum width about 6 1/4". Scarce.

Reissue note: Mr. Charles Gillinder's letter, cited above, adds the following information concerning reissues. "In 1948 we made a larger version of the ten-inch size, and hope to offer this 15-inch size in 1996." The larger size version was advertised for sale in 1997, made in "opalescent white milk glass" and priced at $49.95. The original mould of this vase is said to date "from the late teens or early 1920s" (GCD, X:4, Dec/Jan 1997, inside back cover).

Beginning in 1995, Gillinder Brothers produced a smaller Peacock vase, only 6 1/4" high, from a mould also believed to be a Gillinder & Sons original. This version has the baby and mother peacock only, as the upper portion bearing all of the other birds was cut off, thus leaving a top opening of 6 1/4", as wide as the height of the vase. Initially offered in transparent pink, blue, and green pastels at $59.95, it was advertised again in 1997 in dark blue at $44.95.

405 - FIDDLE AND BANJO MINIATURE VASES

These little vases are charming examples of decorative pieces, practically useless but so appealing. Nicely detailed, they are surprisingly heavy. An identical pair of blown vases in a larger size (about 9" high) were also produced by the same company.

Made by Imperial in the early 1950s and impressed with its trademark. Designated "1950/87 and 1950/88," by Garrison, p. 124.

We know these pieces only in white. They measure 3 1/2" high. Somewhat hard to find.

Famous Pieces in Rare Colors

407 -BOAR'S HEAD COVERED DISH

Although illustrated many times in the standard milk glass literature, this piece merits inclusion if for no other reason that it has come to be regarded as the *sine qua non* of any serious collector of animal covered dishes. Moreover, this is the first time it has been shown in blue, making it doubly worthy of a place in our book. One member of the NMGCS reported that she acquired a blue Boar's Head from a person who said, "Great grandmother bought it in St. Paul, Minnesota, as a premium filled with head cheese" (see O.N., IX:4, Sept. 1994, p. 8). The features of the animal's head — its ears, tusk, snout — are extremely well moulded, as are the leaves surrounding it, serving as a bed of garnish. With the proper glass eyes affixed, this piece never fails to elicit admiration. The base has a simple but elegant pattern of vertical ribs and is marked on the underside: PATENTED / MAY 29 - 1888.

Made by Atterbury. The base for this dish was also issued with a different cover (see "Fan and Circles" Ribbed Covered Dish No. 161 in this book).

Known in white and blue. It measures 9 3/8" long, and about 6 1/4" high. Rare in white; extremely rare in blue.

408 - ROOSTER ON WIDE RIB BASE COVERED DISH

The well known 5 1/2" Westmoreland rooster on its hallmark wide rib base is rare in this uncommon and attractive purple color.

409 - BABY IN HAT MATCH HOLDER

Although previously shown in Lee (L-VG, p. 32, plate 175), Newbound (N-170) and Ferson (F-534), where you will find this piece fully described, we include this example because of the infant's most unusual, possibly unique, mixed coloration of opaque black glass for the upper half of the body and milk white lower half. The match striker is on the underside of the child. Maker unknown. Usually found as an all white baby lid, glossy or satinized, on a black hat base. The hat is 2 3/4" high, 4 1/4" wide and 4 3/4" long. Overall height is about 4 1/2". Extremely rare.

410 - SWAN MINIATURE LAMP

A choice piece in any color, this much admired swan lamp is shown here in an unusual color combination. Although Smith (S-1, p. 206) mentions the existence of one like this — with white body and blue base, neck, and head — it is not illustrated. Now here it is, complete with its original proper shade for you to enjoy.

Also known in all white, blue, pink, and green milk glass. Height 7 3/4". Extremely rare.

411 - ALLIGATOR COVERED DISH

Previously shown only in Ferson and only in milk white (F-91), this remarkable piece in a heavenly blue opaque glass cannot fail to delight every collector of animal covered dishes. Like so many other pieces that fill the pages of this book, most collectors must content themselves with the opportunity just to gaze in envy as the likelihood of actually having such rarities in one's own collection is sadly very slim.

This Vallerysthal "trinket box" is illustrated among "Boites & Coffrets" in VCC (No. 3910, p. 310) and in SW, p. 8. Length 12". Extremely rare in any color.

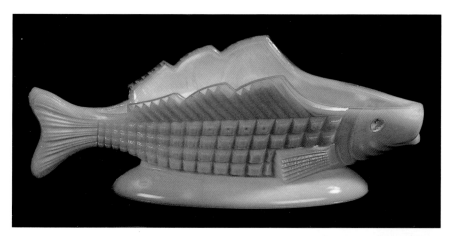

412 - WAFFLE FISH PICKLE

A striking piece, much sought after by collectors, this is another of Challinor, Taylor's dramatic creations. When found without glass eyes affixed, one can see a small, fairly flat eye moulded in the glass itself, so we may assume it was offered for sale either way. Shown in Challinor's circa 1891 catalog and previously pictured only in white in B-204b; M 308b; Lucas, p. 108, and others. Length 9 1/4". Scarce in white, rare in blue, and very rare in green.

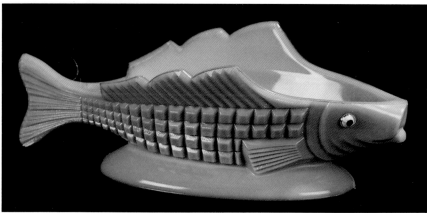

413 - LARGE ROOSTER COVERED DISH

This beautiful rooster on a basket weave base with his thick pebbled comb and sweeping tail is well known to collectors as part of the Challinor, Taylor "Farm Yard Assortment." The rooster was faithfully reproduced by Westmoreland on a diamond basket weave base.

Shown here in blue and green, it is also found in clear crystal and in opaque white. Those in clear and white are sometimes found with painted decoration (see M-325b; F-25). Length 7 1/8". All the Challinor Roosters are hard to find. Rare with fired on colors, very rare in blue, and extremely rare in green.

414 - WALKING FISH COVERED DISH

A good-looking, full-figured fish justly admired by collectors. The simulated scales are very realistic, and with dorsal fin upraised, the creature appears to be "walking," as it were, on its extended lower fins. Previously shown in white and correctly attributed in M-289. Length overall 8 3/4". Very scarce in white, rare in blue.

415 - DUCK ON WAVY BASE

The Duck on Wavy Base, another denizen of Challinor's "Farm Yard," is no doubt the most familiar of the duck covered dishes largely because of the many reproductions of it, notably by the Westmoreland Glass Company whose mould was used by Summit (for Rosso) after its closing. Taiwan imports, very inferior copies having deeply sunken backs, are found in cobalt blue, purple slag, and possibly other colors.

The history of what became of the original Challinor mould has been told many times and needs no retelling here (for a concise summary, see O.N., XIII:1, Dec. 1997, p. 13). Also, see Grizel (*Welcome Home*, p. 56 and p. 77) for an extensive list of the colors made by Westmoreland and others.

For collectors who are still unclear as to how the originals differ either from the later reissues (Duncan Miller/Tiffin) or from the reproductions made by Westmoreland or later copies thereof, a few distinguishing features are listed in the chart below.

Feature	Challinor/ U.S. Glass	Tiffin	Westmoreland Glass & Others
COVERS			
Underside of the rim	stippled	stippled	Westmoreland smooth; some repros are faintly stippled
Underside of the tail	smooth, with stippled edge	stippled and rectangular mould patch repair line	smooth all over
Shape of the tail	rounded arch (depth 1 3/8")	rounded arch (depth 1 3/8")	slightly pointed and narrower (depth 1")
BOTTOMS			
Wavy lines under the flanged edge	extend flush to the nearly vertical sides of the base	extend flush to the nearly vertical sides of the base	shorter and do not extend to reach the sharply sloping sides of the base

The Challinor duck is found in clear crystal, often with remnants of paint, and in opaque white, white with fired on colors, blue, and the distinctive "Challinor green" shown here. Incidentally, we have found that when the original glass eyes are still intact in a Challinor duck, they will be green with black pupils.

Base across the top measures 8" by 6"; height to top of head about 5".

Westmoreland ducks and those made later from the Westmoreland mould, as well as other copies of the "Westmoreland type" as described above are generally available. Tiffin ducks are somewhat hard to find. Challinor ducks in opaque white and crystal are hard to find; white with fired on decoration very scarce; rare in blue, and extremely rare in green.

416 - BLOCK SWAN

This superb creation is best known to collectors in opaque white. Its abstract design is dramatically rendered by deeply pressed grooves and blocks, an achievement in geometric artistry matched only by another of Challinor's products, the Waffle Fish Pickle Dish, and by Atterbury's celebrated Duck.

Once arbitrarily attributed to Sandwich, as so much else was in the absence of information available to earlier students and collectors, it is of course a documented Challinor, Taylor product. The swan appears to have been made available on either a flanged base or the traditional basket weave base, both of which are shown here. We might add that it also occurs in clear crystal, sometimes with discrete frosting, which is quite spectacular in the right light with the design on the underside of the base visible through the glass. Previously shown in white (B-186; M-277b; N-133) and in blue on a basket weave base (F-9).

Scarce in white, rare in blue, and extremely rare as pictured in opaque black or green.

Special Feature Articles

Atterbury Duck Reproductions

Before discussing the reproductions of the Atterbury Duck, justly popular for more than a century, we should offer some remarks about the originals themselves because they are still not fully understood.

The Originals

It would appear that the earliest ducks were embossed PAT^D PENDING on the underside of the base. Innes (p. 404) as well as the Fersons (p. 20, No. 46) report that some were also embossed with "patent applications" though none so marked has come to our attention. Thus far, we know the patent pending ducks only in all amethyst and in all white. *A distinctive feature of these ducks is that the tail is completely solid and smooth on the underside.*

Better known and more generally found are the ducks that carry the actual patent date PAT^D MARCH 15-1887 on the *underside* of the base. The Fersons state that such Ducks occur in white, white with blue head, white with amethyst head, all blue and presumably all amethyst both light and dark. *The underside of the tail on these ducks is not solid but grooved, rather like a large thumb-print indentation, surrounded by a perfectly flat surface.*

Although the thumb-print tail feature is invariable for all dated ducks we have seen, we have received reports of some patent pending ducks also having thumb-print instead of the expected solid tails. These may be explained as later day "marriages" perhaps, but it is equally possible that the newly reconfigured tops with thumb-print tails were placed on existing patent pending bases left over during an *overlapping* period of Atterbury production while the factory was introducing its new bases marked with the March 1887 patent date.

The L. G. Wright Reproductions

The best known reproductions were sold by the L.G. Wright Co. and probably made for them by Fenton. In a letter from Frank Fenton, quoted in O.N. (X:1, 1994, p. 9), he stated "The duck that Fenton produced never had an 'F' mark in it. The duck was made from a mould owned by Mr. L.G. Wright of the Wright Glass Company and was produced before we started to mark anything with an 'F' [around 1982]." Measell and Roettels state that the Wright mould was made by Weishar's Island Mould and Machine Co. in 1941. This should serve to correct Grist's statements (p. 32) concerning the reproduction ducks.

The Wright ducks were made at least in the 1970s and some in the late 1980s as well. Because some of the Wright Ducks were made in the original colors it is important to be able to distinguish them, *especially the tops*, since marriages of Wright tops with original bases occur. The Wright Ducks are easily recognized if both top and bottom are in place, as the underside of the base is not marked in any way with patent information. The tops are also readily discernible by the configuration of the underside of the tail. Whereas the thumb-print indentation of the Atterbury duck is edged by a *smooth flat surface*, the Wright reproduction has a narrow, *evenly rounded edge* around the indentation.

Original Wright colors included at least white, all amethyst, white with amethyst head. Other colors include amethyst with white head, blue with white head, purple slag and blue slag and several occur with a satin as well as a glossy surface (we know these in white and blue slag).

Anomalies or Marriages (?)

A vexing problem remains for the collector concerning several anomalies; namely, ducks that lack any patent markings but whose tails are like those of the Atterbury originals — a thumb-print with a flat rather than rounded edge around it. We are aware of these in several colors. One is green with a white head, which Fenton displayed as made in the 1950s (although a veteran collector insists she owned one long before this). An identical duck is known in blue with a white head, and another in light purple slag for which no attribution has yet been found. A most curious previously unmentioned color variation, which we have not seen, was reported to us just as this book is going to press. It is described as white with an amethyst head and amethyst streak running lengthwise down the center of the back! This duck is presumed to have come from the collection of Jacob Rosenthal, famed inventor of Greentown's chocolate glass, who later worked at Fenton until 1933.

If the statement by Frank Fenton quoted above is correct, these ducks were either not made by Fenton or were made from a different mould than were the Wright ducks. But see also O.N. XI:1, 1995, p. 10, informing us that the green duck with white head was made by Fenton for L.G. Wright "using the excellent Wright mould." If so, then the Wright mould was altered after that duck was poured!

To add one more puzzle to these reproduction ducks, Innes states the Atterbury Ducks were "reproduced several times, most recently from an old mould... [and] even a patent mark or number is no longer absolute proof of early origin" (pp. 404-406). He states the Ducks were made in "opaque, amethyst, turquoise blue, and green [!]," but also shows pictures of white ducks with blue heads and a white duck with amethyst head. Despite Innes' recognized authority in Pittsburgh glass, we believe the Fersons are definitive here.

Fig. 1. Atterbury, white, patent dated.

Fig. 2. Atterbury, amethyst, patent pending.

Fig. 3. L. G. Wright reproduction, slag.

Atterbury's 8" Hen and the Fenton Versions

I - Atterbury

The 7" Atterbury and 7 1/4" Challinor, Taylor hens with glass eyes are well known to collectors of animal covered dishes. Many are unaware, however, that Atterbury produced a larger hen, both wider and a full inch longer. The differences between them are not merely in their size. The tail of the 8" hen, for example, is broader, sharply angled backward, and the surface inside the divided tail, in all those we have seen, has coarse ridges running the entire length. The eggs are polished and more prominent; of the two anterior eggs, the first is much smaller than the second. The rim of the covers in both sizes are alike, smooth and slightly rounded. The double banded top margin of the base protrudes very slightly from the woven surface below.

These large Atterbury hens are known to us in white, white with a cased blue or amber head, and a beautiful translucent blue. Length of base 8", width 6 1/2". Length of top 7 1/8", width 6". Height of top to tip of tail 4 3/4"; height to top of head 4 1/2". Height of base 2 1/2". These hens are hard to find in white and are scarce to rare in translucent blue or in white with cased heads.

II - Fenton

Note: The fullest and most accurate account of the Fenton large hens is by Ferill J. Rice, "Fenton's Hens on the Nest," in *The Daze*, Feb. 1991, p. 7. We are indebted to that excellent article for some of the information that follows.

Fenton Type A - Early

The prototype for the large hen made by Fenton is almost certainly the Atterbury 8" hen, as they both share many of the same features — a broad, slanted tail; large head; coarsely grooved area between the tail; and the first of the two eggs up front much smaller than the second. The most striking difference, however, is that the Fenton hens do not have eye sockets for glass eyes; instead, the eyes are moulded directly in the glass, perfectly round and bulging. The feathering lacks the fine detail of the Atterbury hens. Fenton first introduced this large hen, which we designate "Type A," in 1953 (Fenton's #5182). It has a basket weave base much like Atterbury's. To our knowledge, none of these are signed.

These early hens are known to us in white, lavender, pale opaque green, white with a green or amethyst cased head, and light transparent amethyst with a white head. Length of base 8", width 6 1/2", height 2 1/2". Length of top 7 1/4", width 5 3/4", height to top of head 4 1/2". Although not old, they already are fairly hard to find.

Fenton Type B - Reissues

In 1968, Fenton reissued the same hen cover but on a much different base. The top edge of this base has twenty scallops and slants outward. It is marked on the underside "Fenton" (in script) enclosed in an ellipse.

Hens with this base are illustrated in Heacock (F-3, No. 226), Fenton's #5182MB large hen on nest made from 1971-73 in blue and white marble, and on pp. 117, 119 in carnival, made in 1971.

Length of base 8", width 6 1/2", height 2 1/2". Length of top 7 1/4", width 5 3/4", height to top of head 4 1/2". These are known to us in white, blue slag, and carnival, but see Rice, cited above, for a full account of the extensive array of colors, as well as the dates when first introduced, and when discontinued.

Fenton Type C - "Chickenserver"

Fenton also used the same hen cover for its Hen on a large egg server tray, first introduced in 1953 (Fenton's #5188). "When the piece was made, Mr. William (Bill) Fenton declared that Chicken Salad should be served in the dish or basket and the piece was from then on known as the 'Chickenserver'" (see Rice, cited above). The hen is placed at the center of a massive flared base expanded by 2 1/2" to create an egg service with depressions that accommodate a dozen eggs. A handsome fern spray is faintly embossed between each egg depression. The hen cover fits snugly in a low rising scalloped "nest" with a wide basket weave pattern that looks like tile or brick work. This design is also found on the base of Fenton's 5 1/4" Chick covered dish (#5185) first introduced in 1953 and discontinued in 1956, making these quite scarce today. They were sometimes offered as individual servers to make up a complete breakfast set.

Maximum length of base approximately 12 1/2", width 11". Length of area upon which top sits 8", width 5 3/8"

Heacock (F-2, No. 515, p. 61) illustrates it in white with a cased green head (issued in 1953-4), and states it was made in all white milk glass in 1955-56. G-S (p. 66) illustrate it, however, in a transparent green top with a white head as # 5188 and consider it rare. They mention it also in amethyst. We have seen the base with an amethyst top with white head and an opaque light lavender upper breast.

In Fenton's "Spring 1997" catalog, issued in the fall of 1996, the egg server is offered as "Hen Egg Plate" (# 5188 TJ) in what appears to be white and/or pearl with colored decoration for $112 in an edition limited to 950 pieces.

Maximum length of base approximately 12 1/2", width 11". Length of area upon which top sits 8", width 5 3/8". Most of the Fenton hens are hard to find, and some colors are quite scarce.

Fig. 1. Atterbury Hen

Fig. 2. Fenton Hen
(circa 1953)

Fig. 3. Fenton's "Chickenserver"

Fig. 4. Fenton's matching Chick

Notes on Portieux's Chimeres Design

The Portieux designers apparently favored "Chimeres" as evidenced by the astonishing variety of pieces we find in this pattern. See, for example, the Candlestick in this pattern, item number 66 in this book.

The following items are all shown in the 1933 Portieux catalog:

Covered Sugar (p. 64, No. 941, also in color. p. 324, No. 6662). On this piece, the bird's "tail" has fewer coils and the wing is much shorter. The cover lacks the bird motif and is adorned with elaborate linear swirls and long leaves.

Cake Stand (p. 119, No. 1666). Smooth above but elaborately embossed on the underside with seven birds beautifully designed. It is 6 1/4" high, 10" in diameter across the top, and 5 1/4" diameter at the base. A variant short stem appears as No. 1667, and both tall and short versions with completely flat border are shown as No. 1667 and 1668.

Butter (p. 67, No. 997, also in color on p. 327, No. 6713).

Three Tier Pastry Centerpiece (p. 117, No. 1652), with three ascending flat shelves topped by a long trumpet-shaped apical ornament projecting from the top shelf. It is over two feet tall! A superb piece of glass which we have yet to see.

Two Tier Pastry Centerpiece (p.117, No. 1649), similar to the preceding but with only two layers of pastry shelves. It is also a most impressive piece being about 18" tall.

Double Salt with Central Handle (p. 36, No. 575).

Double Salt without Central Handle (p. 37, No. 598), lacking a handle but joined by a transverse bar.

Mustard with Cover (p. 33, No. 483).

Compote with Cover and Matching Plate (p. 46, No. 711).

Compotes, Open (p. 53, No. 780) tall stem and (No. 781) short stem.

Epergnes (p. 56, No. 822), essentially the compotes

with trumpets emerging from the center, shown in two sizes.

Basket (p. 85, No. 1198).

Novelty (p. 88, No. 1253), a peculiar turnip-like object

Handled Candlestick (p.133, No. 1884), with flat base, loop finger holder, and a short top that flares out petal-like.

Lamp Font (p. 138, No. 1963), shown as an attachment ("Lampe Belge") for a matching stick.

We have examined pieces of this exotic pattern in slightly varying shades of opaque blue as well as white. The design on the underside of the cake plate suggests clear and transparent colors. They are generally unmarked, but we have seen a sugar embossed "Portieux" and "France" on the bottom and also bearing a round "P. V. France" paper label.

Pieces in this pattern range from uncommon to very rare.

Bulldog Doorstop

Steeped in controversy which has yet to be resolved to everyone's satisfaction, this realistic 7 pound bulldog is certainly well known to collectors. Still, it is just too impressive not to find a place in this book. Its large pugnacious head, thick neck, upright ears, and widely spread front legs all exemplify an *"I won't budge"* assurance. The same intransigent attitude among some collectors seems to permeate the conflicting reports on this piece! Without attempting to settle the dispute, we will merely summarize what we have found and leave our readers to draw their own conclusions.

That it is the original creation (numbered "78"} of the Westmoreland Specialty Co., is well attested and undisputed. But rumor has it that the mould was loaned to Tiffin Glass who made the doorstop in white and in black with a satin finish. The source of this assertion stems from Fred Bickenheuser who pictures a bull dog, in opaque black, that indeed appears to be identical to Westmoreland's, and states "This TIFFIN BULLDOG showed up in the production records of Tiffin glass in 1926" (see *Tiffin Glassmasters*, Bk II, p. 159). It may very well be that Tiffin did produce a "bulldog," but there is no way of knowing whether the dog pictured by Bickenheuser is actually a documented Tiffin product. We do know that Tiffin made small bulldogs (about 2 1/2" high) and *it is possible that these are the ones referred to in the "production records."* Alas, the small bulldogs, too, were made by a number of different companies and they are not always easy to sort out.

Charles West Wilson probably knows this piece better than anyone. Although he does not mention Tiffin directly, he does say "it is highly unlikely that he [George West] would have considered such an unbusinesslike arrangement as the loan of a mould" (pp. 308-09). The dog, says Wilson, was made by Westmoreland as early as August 1915 and he cites a press release of Jan. 1916 indicating it was made in black and white. He further notes that between 1925 and 1927 it was made in amber, adding the generalized statement that "others will be found in various Westmoreland colors," including a "Westmoreland green."

Garmon and Spencer, repeating the notion of the supposed back and forth loan of the mould, also list a variety of colors, including one in black with white head, but without citing specific sources of their information (see G-S, p. 199).

The bulldog mould was used in the early 1990s by Summit Art Glass to produce the doorstop in cobalt, often dark enough to be almost mistaken for black, as well as cobalt with iridescent finish. Grizel, *Westmoreland Glass: Our Children's Heirlooms* (p. 33) reports the bulldog was also made in white, black, and chocolate glass, all easily recognized as new by the huge yellow glass eyes and red leather collar. On the authority of John Schnupp, Westmoreland's Production Manager, Grizel insists in capital letters — "Westmoreland NEVER LOANED their moulds to anyone at any time, so if Tiffin included these dogs in their production records, Westmoreland most likely made the doorstop for them."

Base measures 6" by 4"; overall height 7 1/8" but it can vary slightly owing to the weight of the head which may tend to sag while annealing. Rare in any color.

Fig. 1. Left to right: Summit (cobalt iridescent) / Westmoreland (white and black). The small bulldog in vaseline is a reissue.

Comparison of the McKee and Westmoreland Lion Covered Dishes

The original McKee Lion is an extraordinary representation of the King of Beasts, with its outsized head and rather small body. So far as we know it has been found only in white, and on a split ribbed base.

Although the Westmoreland Lion is remarkably similar, we do not believe that it was pressed from an original McKee mould as there are obvious differences. Nonetheless, the resemblance is strong enough not to discount the possibility that Westmoreland, with its extensive mould making facilities, may have made a casting from an original McKee piece. One strong indication of that is in the straw or grass marks which are virtually identical on the surface of the two covers and next to impossible to replicate except from a casting.

The Westmoreland Company itself appears not to have advertised the Lion, nor have we found it illustrated in any of their catalogs to which we have access.

Our first knowledge of the existence of the Westmoreland Lion came in seeing an advertisement by the P. & J. Lamp Co. in 1955. It was subsequently advertised in 1983 by AA Importing (reprinted in *The Glass Collector*, Spring-Summer 1983, p. 48). Easily recognized as a Westmoreland product by its distinctive wide ribbed base, the Lion was listed at $2.00.

When the Westmoreland Company went out of business in 1985, the Lion mould was apparently acquired by Helen & Phil Rosso, Wholesale Glass Dealers, Inc. of Port Vue, Pennsylvania. They listed it for sale, in cobalt only, for $8.50 in a May/June 1987 advertising brochure. We believe Summit Art Glass Co. was commissioned to make them.

In October 1994, the Rossos again offered the lion, this time available in milk white as well as in red and white slag. In August 1996, they advertised it in green and white slag, made by the Mosser Glass Co., and in April 1997 it was offered in vaseline.

The obvious difference between the two Lions, of course, is in the patterns of the bases, McKee's split rib as opposed to Westmoreland's wide ribbed base. Fortunately, the possibility of a "marriage" is no threat, because the tops are not interchangeable on the two bases. The McKee lion is too large to fit the original Westmoreland base, although it will fit, but just barely, on the Rosso base. The Rosso base is readily identified anyway because it has the newer Westmoreland logo pressed both inside and outside the base.

Even if the tops are separated from their proper bases, one can recognize Westmoreland copies, as the head droops somewhat so that the distance between the paws and the chin is only 3/8" whereas in the McKee original the distance is 5/8". The McKee lion also has finely delineated hair compared to the relatively little hair detail of the Westmoreland/Rosso lions.

As noted, the bases of the Rosso lions are marked with the newer logo devised when David Grossman acquired the company in 1981 — three short vertical bars circled by the word "Westmoreland." The Westmoreland lions advertised in 1955, therefore, could not carry that mark, and all the ones we have seen carry no mark at all. Moreover, the early Westmoreland milk glass lions are lighter in weight than the more recent Rosso reissues. The original issues by Westmoreland must have been made in very limited quantities because they are almost rare today.

See further, O.N., V:1, Dec. 1989 (picture page) and O.N., X:2, March 1995, p.6,9,10.

Fig. 1. Left to right: Original Westmoreland / Original McKee.

Fig. 2. Left to right: Summit (Russo) / Original Westmoreland.

Elephant with Raised Trunk Covered Dishes

Although this sturdy footed, alert elephant with raised trunk is well known to collectors, many are not aware of the different varieties and sizes that were made. The main features of the elephant, though minimal, are very good in detailing the eyes, tail, deep creases in the front of the head, a fine upraised trunk extending forward, and legs offset so as to create a sense of motion. The head is especially impressive, with large frontal lobes and ears set back, and the massive body has a prominently defined backbone.

Two vastly different sizes are known. The common form is about 8" in length, 3" wide, and 4 1/2" high, but there is also a gigantic version fully 13" long.

The 8" Elephants

The 8" elephant is found with at least four different covers, all of which are interchangeable on the same base, however. They are as follows:

1. **Plain Back**: This is the elephant described above, with a smooth back except for the raised vertebrae.
2. **Flower Holder Back**: This elephant differs only in having large round holes in its back, presumably for inserting the stems of flowers.
3. **Raised Circle Back**: In this variant a different mould would have been required because the back has a raised round concave area moulded at the center.
4. **Ashtray Back**: In this variant the raised concave area is not round but elliptical, occupying most of the lid. This "ashtray" area is 3" long and 2 1/4" wide with what appear to be cigarette rests in front and behind. James (p.54) suggests it could also be meant for a sponge and pencils.

The 13" Elephant

The 13" size is known to occur with a plain or a flower holder back. We have not found any with backs of the type 3 or type 4 variations found in the 8" elephants.

The Makers

There is general agreement that these elephants were first made by the Co-Operative Flint Glass Co. Weatherman, *Colored Glassware*, p. 50, illustrates the flower holder and the raised circle back variants from a trade catalogue of the depression period. James (p. 54) illustrates the ashtray back and dates it circa 1920-1930s. Toohey (pp. 11, 17, 43) shows both sizes, dates the 13" size from 1927 and gives several additional references. She also notes that the Elephant was produced again in the 1980s probably by the Indiana Glass Co. and sold as a Tiara Exclusive. See Garmon and Spencer (pp. 32-45 and p. 145) for additional illustrations and attributions to makers of the Co-Op elephant at various periods.

Millard (No. 315) called it a British piece and gave the length as 9". It is possible such an Elephant exists, but we have not been able to find evidence to support this.

Colors and Decorations

Known to us in opaque, both white as well as black. We have not seen all of the variants in white. It is also known in many transparent colors including amber, light blue, light pink, clear crystal, and green. The recent Tiara elephants are known to occur in three frosted colors but not to our knowledge in opaque colors. They are apparently produced from the original mould, but considerable wear or the frosting process has reduced the sharp details.

Toohey illustrates the 13" size in black satin, but it also occurs in glossy black and several transparent colors.

A version of the elephant is found with incredibly ornate decoration combining both paint and the application of eight gem stones of various sizes and colors placed on the head and around the body. This embellishment may not have been done at the factory but by a jobber or distributor. The example shown here has an old worn paper label inside the tray which is difficult to read except for the words "GLASS OF GLASS" and enough of the letters to spell out Indianapolis. It identifies a well-known decorator of blanks which were purchased from various glass factories. Unfortunately, the metallic paint flakes easily, but the colored stones in this example are all intact.

All of these elephants are rather scarce, and in some colors even rare, as are any of those in the 13" size.

Reproduction Notes

In a 1991 A.A. Importing Company catalog (#56) several elephants are illustrated. At least one of them we believe to be a foreign import. We have seen this in opaque black and in a dark transparent blue, but presume collectors will find it in other colors. This import differs from the original in several ways, and because collectors have frequently been confused, we offer a fairly detailed description of it.

Most noticeable is the much less forward projecting trunk. In the import, the straight line distance from the tip of the trunk to the opening of the base is 1 1/4" whereas in the original it is 1 3/4". This is accentuated by the reduction in the head lobes so that there is a nearly even slope from the back to the base of the trunk. Behind the frontal lobes in the original elephant is a transverse groove which lies in front of a single raised ridge. In the reproduction there are three raised ridges. This type is illustrated in the above catalog on pg. 57 as No. PG6668 and advertised in black for $8.50. The elephant illustrated on p. 56 as No. PG6656 in cobalt blue, however, is clearly similar to the original with the swollen head lobes and forward directed trunk. This latter elephant is also illustrated on p. 20 (No. PG 6613, in pink) and p. 19 (No. PG 16058 in red). It seems likely that the original mould, or a direct copy of it, was being used on these latter elephants. In any event two very distinct reproduction types of the 8" size exist.

Fig. 1. Left to right: Reproduction / Original Co-Operative Flint Glass.

Fig. 2. Left to right: Large (13") and small (8") Plain Back versions.

Fig. 3. Raised Circle Back version.

Fig. 4. "Glass of Class" decoration.

Challinor's "Flying Swan" Four Piece Table Set

It seems that only the most dedicated experts can sort out the many different Swan patterns and assign them to their makers. The so-called "Flying Swan" design of the table set shown here was for a time attributed to the Westmoreland Specialty Glass Company. But later researchers have concluded that it originated with Challinor, Taylor, based in part on the statement by Kamm (K-2, p. 68) that she saw the pattern illustrated in an undated Challinor catalog. In addition, the characteristics of the marbled glass in these pieces are so unmistakably the same as in other products definitely known to be Challinor's "mosaic" as to make the attribution a virtual certainty.

On these grounds, Heacock was led to agree with both Ferson and Lucas in ascribing the pattern to Challinor, although thus far no positive documentation has come to light. (See the comprehensive discussion by Heacock in HCG-1, pp. 45-47). Judging from their rarity, the Flying Swan table pieces may have been produced for only a short period and perhaps in no great numbers. They probably were discontinued when the factory became part of the U.S. Glass Company, for they do not appear in the latter's 1891 catalog.

Having pretty much accepted the Challinor attribution, Heacock then raised the further question whether Challinor was in fact the *originator* of the pattern. A swan vase made by Sowerby, illustrated as No. 403 in this book, bears a close resemblance to the Challinor Flying Swan design. Although it may be impossible to know with certainty which came first, such evidence as we have points to Sowerby's version predating Challinor's. Sowerby registered the design in 1879. It was not until 1886 that Challinor received a patent for its "Variegated Glassware" (see Ferson, p. 128). So at least as far as pieces made in mosaic are concerned, it seems plausible to assume Challinor's products are later than the English ones.

One can easily distinguish between the Challinor and Sowerby look-alike swans in three ways. (1) The neck of the Challinor swan is "closed" — that is to say, the space between neck and body is filled with a thin film of glass, whereas in the Sowerby swan the space is open. (2) The Challinor swan has no legs showing below the puffed breast; Sowerby's swan has legs that rest upon a half-circle platform, an additional feature missing in Challinor's design. (3) The Challinor design has embossed ferns on the sides, whereas the Sowerby design includes cattails.

Robert Lucas reports that some of the Challinor Flying Swan pieces have a swan intaglio design instead of a plain surface on the undersides, indicating two different bottom plates were used interchangeably.

Another American manufacturer, the Westmoreland Glass Company, produced three swan items which reveal an admixture of the Sowerby and Challinor versions. In two of these Westmoreland pieces — a vase and a toothpick holder — elements of both predecessors are curiously mingled. Like Challinor's swan, Westmoreland's lacks legs and the supporting platform, but like Sowerby's, the necks are open and the sides have cattails. The third item, a covered candy dish, is clearly a copy of Challinor's covered butter dish, but with a few differences. The Westmoreland swans' necks are open rather than closed; the swan finials are slightly different in size and configuration; and the upper rim of the base is slightly stippled, whereas Challinor's is smooth and rounded. In brief, we believe Westmoreland relied primarily on the Sowerby prototype for its swan vase and toothpick holder, but copied Challinor's swan butter dish for its candy dish.

Finding the Flying Swan complete table set is very difficult. They have been found in clear crystal, opaque white, and in a number of "variegated" colors. These include marbled yellow-amber (butterscotch) in both light and dark brown shades; marbled purple (rarest of the colors, according to Lucas); and the extraordinary "butterscotch blue marble," as Lucas describes it (p. 131), illustrated by Ferson in a creamer and sugar (F-376, 379) and seen in the butter dish pictured here.

Fig. 1. Flying Swan creamer, covered sugar, covered butter, spooner.

"Hen and Rabbit" and "Three Rabbits" Salt Shakers

These attractive, flat-bottomed egg-shaped salts embossed with either "three rabbits" or a "hen and rabbit" are well known to many collectors. What is less well known is that at least three different versions were produced, although they are all of identical size and are fitted with cone-shaped metal closures.

Type 1 (*Three Rabbits*) On one side, two upright rabbits embossed in profile and facing away from each other. On the opposite side, a single sitting rabbit facing right (as you view it).

Type 2 (*Hen and Rabbit*) On one side, a running rabbit with one ear held up and away from the body, and the head not tilted upward. On the opposite side a fat hen with a chick in front of her, one on her back, and two others behind her.

Type 3 (*Hen and Rabbit*) On one side, a hen very similar to that of Type 2, but without a well-defined comb, a tail that extends higher — almost as high as the head — and greater detail to the body feathering. On the opposite side, a running rabbit but unlike Type 2, this one has ears flat against its back, head tilted upward.

Lechner attributes all of these salts to the Eagle Glass and Manufacturing Company (1894-1937), illustrating the Hen and Rabbit on p. 78 (which looks like Type 3), and the three Rabbits salt on p. 79.

Peterson shows the three Rabbits salt (P-2, p. 36 "J") and pictures both sides of a Hen and Rabbit (p. 163 "E") which also appears to be Type 3. Another salt shown by Peterson is simply called "Hen" (p. 30 'R'). Apparently this one does not have a rabbit on the opposite side; if so, it is unfamiliar to us. Peterson calls it rare.

Millard pictures the Rabbits salt with an incorrect flat metal screw top (M- 171-b), and may be mistaken in stating that there is only one rabbit on each side. Nearby he shows a Hen salt (M-171-d) which he says has "a hen on each side." We assume this may be the same rare salt as Peterson's "Hen," mentioned above, and which we have never encountered.

Fersons illustrate the three Rabbits (F-447), noting that an embossed "A" on the bottom has suggested to some collectors the maker is Adams Co. or, according to others, Atterbury. We discount either one of these attributions. Fersons also illustrate the Hen and Rabbits salt (F-456B) without discussion. We have found Type 3 shakers with "A" and "Pat. apld for" marked on the bottom. The Type 2 shaker that we have examined lacks any markings.

Newbound (N-284) shows the Hen and Rabbits, stating the design patent was to "M.T. Thomas early 1900" but we have not been able to trace that source. Newbound describes it as having the "head of a hen on one side and rabbit head on the other," which appears to be incorrect because the entire body of a hen is visible even in the small photograph she shows of it. We are familiar with other novelties (an Easter egg and an open basket) embossed with just the head of a hen or the head of rabbit, or both, but there is no such salt to our knowledge.

Known to us only in white, usually with paint or gilt coloring. Height 3 1/4" (including the metal closure), base diameter 1 5/8" and maximum width 2 1/4". All are scarce, the Hen and Rabbit versions a bit more so than the three Rabbits.

Fig. 1. Left to right: Type 1, Type 2, and Type 3.

McKee and L. G. Wright Animal Covered Dishes

Nine of the L. G. Wright Company's 5" so-called "Candy Boxes" are obvious copies of original McKee animal covered dishes. The origin of three other non-McKee animal covered dishes made by L. G. Wright — namely, a Dog, a Turtle, and a Cow — remains a mystery.

Collectors have puzzled over whether the animal covers made by Wright were pressed directly from the original moulds. The question has been answered by Measell and Roettels in *The L.G. Wright Glass Company*: "... the overwhelming majority of Wright's production actually came from new moulds" (p.6), and that includes the reproductions of the McKee animals.

Fortunately, the bottoms of the McKee and Wright covered dishes are wholly dissimilar and pose no problem for the collector. Instead of the McKee hallmark split rib type, the Wright bases have a basket weave pattern and a scalloped upper edge. Therefore, only the tops, when not signed with the McKee name in script, can be confusing, especially when made in opaque white, or if one is not familiar with the colors used by McKee. One must always be on guard, however, for the possibility of forgeries, as such deception has actually been found recently of a fake McKee signature impressed on a Westmoreland camel covered dish. (see O.N., XII:2, March 1998, p. 7)

The features of the animal covers noted below will help distinguish the old originals from the Wright reproductions. We also offer some comparisons to similar animal covered dishes made by other manufacturers, such as Kemple, Westmoreland, Greentown, and St. Clair.

In addition to the information contained in the book by Measell and Roettels, cited above, a comprehensive review of these and other L. G. Wright reproductions is given by Anne Cook, "L. G. Wright: Covered Animal Dishes" (GCD, October/November 1991, pp. 30-38).

Comparisons of McKee and L.G. Wright Animal Covered Dishes

Animal/Feature	McKee	L. G. Wright
OWL		
Circle around the eyes	finely grooved	smooth
Inner ear	deeply concave, hollow	shallow and nearly completely filled in
Feathers on back of head	small, not in rows, and at least 6 or 7 rows present	large, even, in 5 distinct rows
Feather tufts around eyes	end dorsally in irregular points	end dorsally in a straight line
Inside top area where feather tufts arise	deeply indented as a hole	not differentiated from surrounding area
FROG		
Area of top lateral of rocks	narrow (6 mm.)	broad (11 mm.)
Depression inside top front	45 degree angle from main depression	smooth all the way around, not angled
Foliage between legs	each frond finely branched	lacks branchlets
CAT		
Ears	stick almost straight up	protrude at about a 40 degree angle
Front legs	narrow, well defined, minimum width of legs 8-9 mm.	project as an undifferentiated triangle

Fig. 1. Wright / McKee Owl

Fig. 2. Wright / McKee Cat

Animal/Feature	McKee	L.G. Wright
Substrate area around cat's body	fine, even striae extending to the edge	rough crisscrossing elevated lines
Hair on back	fine and detailed	rough with lumpy areas, poorly defined
Eyes	fully rounded	less rounded

Note: Westmoreland's similar cat differs from both of these in having a perfectly smooth surface (substrate) around the cat's body. Its tail and ears are like the L.G. Wright cat, although the eyes are a bit more rounded. The hair detail is better on the Westmoreland cat than on the Wright one. Newer reproductions of the Westmoreland cat appear to have a much more swollen right side of the head, i.e., the area to your left as you look at the animal. It almost appears as though the mould "slipped," although some earlier Westmoreland cats may also show this feature.

The Kemple cat closely resembles the Westmoreland version, but the eyes bulge a bit more, the entire body is quite a bit thinner overall, and the fur is not nearly as distinct as it is on Westmoreland's cat, especially the older original issues.

Animal/Feature	McKee	L.G. Wright
ROOSTER		
Rooster's body	wide, maximum width 2 3/8", sides slope out	narrower, maximum width 2 1/4", sides slope down
Breast feathers	finely detailed, with central shafts and less individual barbs	coarse, unevenly spaced, and distinct

Note: Although the crisp details overall are muted, the rooster is nonetheless one of Wright's successful copies of the McKee originals.

Animal/Feature	McKee	L.G. Wright
HORSE OR PONY		
Inside body cavity	slopes down sharply at right angle to the adjacent surface	slopes gradually from adjacent surface

Animal/Feature	McKee	L.G. Wright
Hair inside ear	fine, evenly spaced, individually distinct	coarse, unevenly spaced, less distinct
Head	erect, facing straight ahead, and nose well away from the body	somewhat bowed, turned slightly to the left, and nose closer to the body

Note: Except for the posture and features of the head, this too is not a bad copy.

(Kemple) The Kemple horse is easily recognized, as are all the other Kemple animal dishes, by the smooth and very wide (3/8") rim on the underside of the cover.

(Summit) The Summit horse has a reticulated undersurface and a narrow margin which is also reticulated. In addition, the fine hair along the back and base of the tail of the original is barely evident in the Summit horse.

(St. Clair) The St. Clair horse ("Reclining Colt") is quite a good copy. Look for it mainly in chocolate glass, as well as blue opaque and purple carnival glass.

Animal/Feature	McKee	L.G. Wright
SWAN		
Inner body cavity	formed by a sharp drop at right angle to adjacent surface	formed by gradually sloping down from the adjacent surface
Animal/Feature	McKee	L.G. Wright

Fig. 3. Wright / McKee Swan

Animal/Feature	McKee	L.G. Wright
Large wing feathers	each has central shaft and fine barbs evenly spaced	lack distinct central shaft and fine barbs
Bill	3/4" long from tip to cere	5/8" long from tip to cere
Neck	evenly "pebbled"	crude, rough, and irregular

HEN

Animal/Feature	McKee	L.G. Wright
Comb	has large, round, ball-like side rows in contrast to median row	has small side rows not in contrast to median row
Long wing feathers	have discrete central shaft and neatly defined lateral barbs	have irregular central shaft and poorly defined barbs
Wattle	large, rounded, and conspicuous; hemispherical	small, not hemispherical, extending from bill at sharp angle
Breast area above front chick	has a traverse impressed loop	no break or loop

Note: The L.G. Wright hen is a good reproduction, but not nearly as finely detailed as the original.

Animal/Feature	McKee	L.G. Wright

LAMB

Animal/Feature	McKee	L.G. Wright
Substrate area around body	has irregular floral type mounds	has elongated curving lines

Animal/Feature	McKee	L.G. Wright
Ear	relatively long and slender; length 1/2"; width 3/8"	relatively short and broad; length and width subequal 7/16"
Underside rim	slightly crazed	completely smooth
Tail (viewed from behind)	inserted into body in a sharp "V" narrowed into a "V"	blending into body imperceptibly, not

Note: The Kemple Lamb, which of course is on a split rib base, can readily be distinguished from Wright's version as follows: the ribs on the underside of the base do not meet at the center; the margin on the underside of the cover is wide (3/8"), and completely smooth, not crazed. In other respects, the Kemple Lamb is more like the original McKee; namely, the shape and size of the ears, the floral mounds on the substrate, and the tail inserted into the body in a sharp "V".

Animal/Feature	McKee	L.G. Wright

TURKEY

Animal/Feature	McKee	L.G. Wright
Underside of the top	lacks a sharp rim within 1/4" margin	has a sharp rim within 1/4" margin
Conical area within the fantail	composed of rays radiating up and out from a central "stem"	composed of overlapping scales looking like a pine cone
Shoulder feathers	small, irregular, and overlapping	long semi-horizontal stripes with cross bands running through each stripe
Front wattle	strongly produced, noticeable bifid at tip, and composed of an overlapping series of loops	not bifid, consisting only of simple concave horizontal half lines

Note: Compared to other Wright reproductions, the turkey is not one of their better efforts.

The turkey believed to be reproduced by Summit (and probably others) has a front wattle that is almost linear, is non-bifid at the end, and has only small irregular lumps on the surface. The conical area of the tail just below the fantail is a mass of irregular semi-transverse globs. The wing shoulder is similar to that of the McKee turkey and there is no ridge on the inner margin of the underside of the top. The split rib base lines on the underside meet at the center.

The Boyd turkey usually has a "B in diamond" embossed inside the base. The ribs on the bottom meet at the center. Its features are much like the Summit reproduction discussed above.

Fig. 4. Wright / McKee Turkey

Squirrel Covered Dishes

Unlike some of Vallerysthal's more intricate covered dishes, this one (seen in the middle of the photo) is especially noteworthy because of its clean simple lines. The top and base together form a large acorn with smooth convex stripes running the length of its surface, eleven on the cover and seventeen on the base. A mass of very sharp pointed diamonds forms the husk, connected by a bent twig to a flat, nine-lobed oak leaf on which the acorn rests. A bushy tailed squirrel, with large, broad ears, almost rabbit-like, serves as the finial. Between its front legs, the squirrel grasps a tiny acorn. The body hair and the fur on the tail are well defined. Many painted examples are found with the upper part of the body a dark rusty red.

Illustrated as a sugar in VCC (p. 304, No. 3768). It is sometimes signed "Vallerysthal" inside the base.

We know it in white and blue. Height overall is 5" to the tip of the ears. The cover itself measures 6" long and 3 1/8" wide at its largest part. Scarce.

Notes on the Squirrel Covered Dishes

A Unique Variant

We have encountered a close variant of this dish, a single unmarked example in opaque blue, which fits perfectly on the signed base and appears to us to be an original Vallerysthal product. Discounting the fact that the ears are smaller, as that may be the result of damage repaired, there are only a few minor modifications in the details of the squirrel's fur and the acorn in its paws. The main difference is seen in the size and shape of the depression formed on the underside of the cover. In the signed example, the cavity, slightly narrowed at the waist, runs the entire length of the squirrel figure above it, whereas in the variant, the depression is hour-glass shaped and extends only as far as the front legs.

L. G. Wright Reproduction

It is especially important to identify the Vallerysthal squirrel accurately as it has been confused with quite a different one of more recent vintage. Seen here (on the left) and also shown in blue milk glass in Ferson (F-15), this L. G. Wright squirrel was incorrectly attributed to Vallerysthal by the Fersons, one of the very few errors in that excellent book. Unfortunately, the error is repeated by Newbound who shows it in white (N-135, right). Although the overall "squirrel-on-acorn" design is similar, the differences are easy to see. The squirrel's paws, poorly delineated, merely touch rather than grasp the nondescript acorn that lies in front of them. Most striking of all are the extremely short ears that protrude only slightly above the head. In fact, were it not for the large curling tail, one might mistake the animal for a stoat, mink, or marten. The body hair is faint, and in contrast to the sharp diamond points on the acorn husk of the French original, these are blunt. No doubt this is an attractive piece and well worth collecting, but it lacks the symmetry and fine detail of the original.

Measell and Roettels believe the mould for the Wright squirrel was probably made by Weishar's Island Mould and Machine Co., of Wheeling, West Virginia. The L.G. Wright Co. records indicate it was produced in opaque blue and white in the early 1950s. Measell and Roettels state that it was discontinued after 1962. It was reissued, however, in the early 1990s but only in cobalt and clear crystal.

It measures 6 1/2" high to the top of the tail. The cover alone is 7" long with a maximum width of 4 1/8". Hard to find in opaque colors.

Import Reproductions

To add to the confusion, collectors are faced with yet other reproductions, one of which is shown here

Another reproduction is also found, very similar to the pointed ear version just described, but in a much better quality of glass quite unlike the typical Asian imports. Maker unknown. We know this in white and in a light aqua blue. Availability unknown.

Vallerysthal's Ribbed Covered Butter Dish Series

Of the many Vallerysthal tableware pieces, this group consisting of six round butter dishes and a similar oval one is surely among the most attractive.

The Six Round Butter Dishes

The round ones all have the same base accommodating interchangeable covers, each embossed with different figures. The design of the base consists of eighteen vertical, slightly convex ribs or panels which run the entire height of the base and abut a flat nar-

Fig. 1. Left to right: L.G.Wright / Vallerysthal / Reproduction (Taiwan ?)

(on the right). It is clearly much more like the Vallerysthal squirrel in size and features than the L.G. Wright one. The most immediate difference may be seen in the squirrel's upright ears which measure 3/8" wide in the reproduction compared with 1/4" in the original. The slightly turned head of the original is straight ahead in the copy, and the long, slender front legs hold an unnaturally elongated acorn. The diamond husks are less sharp, and the oak leaf rounded rather than tapering at the ends.

This reproduction is illustrated in Newbound (N-135, left) who states it was offered by the "AA Importing Company in the early 1980's" (p. 66). Almost certainly a Taiwan import, we know it only in blue, and it is not hard to find.

row rim, about 1/4" wide, circling the top edge. The design is continued on the underside with eighteen convex ribs tapering to a central circle. Each base is 2 1/8" high, 4 3/8" diameter at the top and 3 3/8" diameter at the bottom. With the cover in place, the total height is 2 3/4".

The covers have narrow rims projecting downward from the top so they slip neatly inside the edge of the bases to hold them secure. The side of each top continues the eighteen rib or panel motif, aligning with those of the base. The flat tops are embossed in high relief with six different subjects as follows [Note: the numbers are those assigned to each piece in the Vallerysthal 1908 color catalog pages, reprinted in this book]:

191

Pig (*No. 3895*): A large fat pig shown in side view standing on a mass of grassy vegetation beside a barn. The tail has a fine curl.

Fish (*No. 3896*): A "C" shaped fish with excellent scale and fin definition. It swims and swirls on a surface that seems almost to undulate with its movement.

Goose (*No. 3897*): A waddling folkloric long-necked goose with large webbed feet beside a nearby reed-filled watering hole.

Beehives (*No. 3898*): A pair of old fashioned basket or grass woven beehives placed side by side in front of a large picket fence. Bees are swarming about the entrance to each hive below which we see a profuse array of flowers and leaves.

Cow (*No. 3899*): Viewed from the side, a full-figure cow with short sharp horns fills the cover, obviously the most appropriate subject for a butter dish. It appears to be walking on some muddy ground, perhaps on a fallen log with lush grass behind and a fence or gate in the distance.

Lion (*No. 3900*): A huge lion's head, its features well delineated, though not appearing at all ferocious, virtually fills the entire surface of this cover.

Found unmarked as well as signed "Vallerysthal" inside the base or lightly etched "Made in France." Probably all of these butter dishes were made both in white and blue, and all are extremely rare, the lion perhaps the rarest of them.

Fig. 2. Fish

Fig. 3. Goose

Fig. 4. Beehives

Fig. 1. Pig

Fig. 5. Cow

The Cow Oval Butter Dish

The related but much larger elliptical member of this set has the same rib or panel design as described above, but with twenty-four instead of eighteen panels, the ones on the underside converging to a center that is oval rather than round

The only animal we have seen on the cover of this oval butter dish is a full bodied cow (No. 3804 in the Vallerysthal 1908 color catalog, p. 307) standing in high grass and in a field defined by a fence, or gate, in the background. Unlike the round pieces, the figure on the cover is framed by a circle of beads at the outer edge. As with the round pieces the cover has a lip that slides inside the top of the base.

We should note that in examining two examples, we find some variation, suggesting different or slightly reworked molds, perhaps. A specimen in white milk glass has the figure of the cow deeply hollowed out on the underside of the lid. The cover itself is not marked, but the name "Vallerysthal" is faintly evident on the inside bottom of the base. Another example, this one in blue milk glass, does not have any depression on the underside of the lid, and both the cover and the base are clearly embossed "Vallerysthal." In addition, the glass is much heavier and the horizontal rim around the top of the base is wider and thicker.

The base measures 7" long and 4 1/4" wide at the top, tapering to 5 1/2" long and 3" wide at the bottom. Known in white and blue, it is very rare.

Fig. 6. Lion

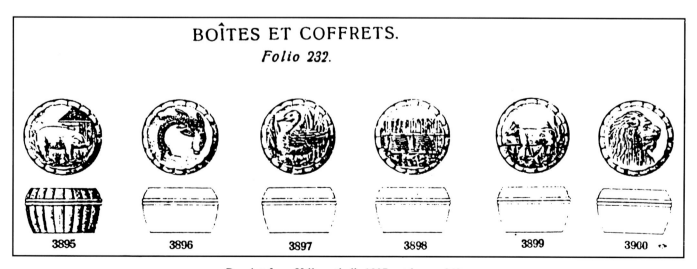

BOÎTES ET COFFRETS.
Folio 232.

| 3895 | 3896 | 3897 | 3898 | 3899 | 3900 |

Reprint from Vallerysthal's 1907 catalog, p. 240.

Fig. 7. Oval Butter (Cow), white.

Fig. 8. Oval Butter (Cow), blue.

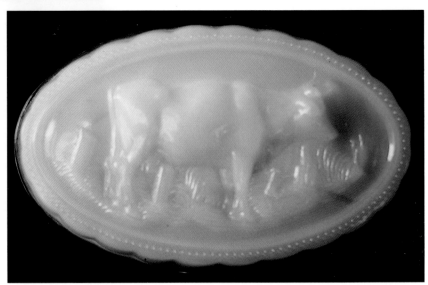

Snail on Strawberry Covered Dishes

Although illustrated in previous publications, noted below, many collectors are unaware that this Snail on Strawberry design has two variants. Newbound (N-122) states that Vallerysthal made it in a 5 1/2" and also "a somewhat larger size" (p. 61). To our knowledge, Vallerysthal made only one size. The slightly larger one is a variant made by its affiliate, Portieux. In some of the French catalogs the same piece is shown several times to illustrate different color combinations. Of the signed "Portieux" and "Vallerysthal" examples we have examined, some very minute details are difficult to describe, but the most easily seen differences are the following:

Feature	Portieux	Vallerysthal
THE COVERS		
Snail's body	straight ahead	curves to the right
Strawberry seeds on surface	slightly elevated	very elevated
Bottom leaf on the left side	lies almost flat	sharply elevated
Upper leaf on the left side	large and distinct	partial and indistinct
THE BASES		
Largest leaf (forming part of the multi-leaf foot)	angled and joined by a ridge to the middle triangular leaf	curled and not connected to the middle triangular leaf

The Portieux piece is illustrated in PC (plate 65, No. 963) and in color (plate 325, No. 6671). The Vallerysthal version is illustrated in VC (1907), p. 234, No. 3764; and in SW (p. 4, top right). It also appears to be the version shown in Millard (M-204, left) and in Newbound (N-122), although the reference given by Newbound to a 1933 catalog is not Vallerysthal's but Portieux's.

Known to us in opaque white and blue and in clear crystal.

Signed examples establish the slight difference in size: Portieux's version is 5 1/2" high; Vallerysthal's is 5 1/8" high. Both, however, measure about the same across the bottom, a maximum length of 4 1/2".

Portieux version hard to find; the Vallerysthal one is very scarce.

Fig. 1. Left to right: Portieux / Vallerysthal

The "Dog Plates"

Although these three plates have not been overlooked in previous publications, they have never been shown together and some collectors still are uncertain about their origins. Besides, we simply like them well enough to justify a place in this book.

(A) Three Dogs Plate

The relative scarcity of this plate may be judged by its absence from BMW — "the big three" — Belknap, Millard, and Warman. It is shown by Newbound (N-269) who echoes Ferson (F-397) in suggesting this plate was probably made by Westmoreland Specialty Co. for the reason that its open loop border is identical to that company's well-known Three Kittens Plate.

We would offer the additional corroborating evidence that the border is also the same the one used by Westmoreland for its Woof Woof plate. Moreover, an examination of the undersides of both the kittens and dogs plates reveals an identical mould configuration forming a "collar" that follows all around the contours of the animal figures. These features, together with the similar characteristics of the glass itself, make it virtually certain this plate was created by Westmoreland, perhaps as a companion piece for its Three Kittens Plate.

We know it only in white, the dogs occasionally found painted and with floral decorations or souvenir place names on the face of the plate.

To our knowledge the Three Dogs plate occurs only in a 6" size. The Kittens plates, however, were made in three sizes — 6", 7", and 8" — the smallest being hardest to find.

Unlike the readily available Three Kittens Plates which continued in production, on and off, from about 1901 or earlier (see Wilson, p. 209), the Three Dogs Plate may have been discontinued not long after it was first introduced near or at the turn of the century, and is quite scarce today.

Fig. 1. Three Dogs Plate (Westmoreland)

(B) Dog and Cats "He's All Right' Plate

In many ways the most intriguing, this "dog" plate departs from the other two in having a single dog's head — a burly bulldog only its owner could love! — flanked on each side by adorable kittens whose dainty bows tied around their necks complement the large one at the bottom of the plate. The contrast of these feminine touches surrounding the brawny bulldog is most amusing, and no doubt explains in part the slogan "He's All Right" to assure us the kittens' acerbic companion is not as mean as he may look.

Documented in an advertisement by Gillinder & Sons of Philadelphia, in the January 1903 issue of the *Crockery and Glass Journal*, the plate is shown as "No. 46 Decorated" (see William Heacock, *Old Pattern Glass According to Heacock*, Antique Publications, Marietta, Ohio, 1981, p. 201).

We know it only in white. Diameter 6 1/4". Scarce.

Fig. 2. Dog and Cats "He's All Right" Plate (Gillinder)

(C) Three Puppies Plate

This is a charming plate. Huddled together, the three puppies seem intent upon a squirrel at the bottom of the plate, though the squirrel appears oblivious to their presence as it sits upright nibbling on a nut. This plate, as well as the previous one, is shown in Belknap (B-20c and d), and it also appears in Newbound (N-278), but without attribution.

Again, the plate's border is a most likely clue to its origin, for as Belknap states "the unique open leaf border" is found only on the Three Puppies and the

"He's All Right" plates. A Gillinder attribution would not be amiss.

We know it only in white. Diameter 7 1/4". Scarce.

Fig. 3. Three Puppies Plate (Gillinder?)

Cat on Wide Rib Base (Old and New)

We include these two examples of the popular Cat on Wide Rib Base covered dish to show an original and a recent reproduction. In addition, both specimens are unusual, the old one because it still has a remnant of the red mustard label affixed to the side, and the new one because of the striking color combination of red head on white body. Collectors look for such labels on any of these old covered dishes that were used as containers to package condiments because they are evidence attesting to their age, as well as adding to their appeal and to their value.

Made by the Westmoreland Specialty Company at the turn of the century, the cat was reissued in the 1950s, perhaps initially at the request of and exclusively for Forslund, a major furniture and gift store in Grand Rapids, Michigan, and then a regular item in the company's catalogs continuing up to the time of its closing (see O.N., X:2, March 1995, p. 5). The post-1985 reproductions are pressed from the Westmoreland moulds acquired by Phil Rosso, a wholesale glass distributor in Port Vue, Pennsylvania, and carry the new Westmoreland logo in the cover and the base.

The originals were made in white, blue, and combinations of blue and white; later issues were made in a variety of colors both opaque and transparent, as well as marbled.

It measures 5 1/2" across the top of the base.

The old one, as shown, is hard to find; otherwise generally available. Westmoreland's companion Dog, incidentally, was never reproduced, the mould apparently not having survived beyond the early years, and it is becoming quite scarce.

Fig. 1. Original Westmoreland Specialty Company.

Fig. 2. Recent reissue (marked with newer Westmoreland logo).

Shaw's Night Lamp and Revolving Clock

This extraordinary combination lamp and clock invention was the brain child of Charles H. Shaw, of Brooklyn, New York, patented on April 6, 1886 (No. 339,220). In the patent application for his "Night-Clock," as he called it, Shaw states, "The object of my improvement is to produce a simple, cheap, and neat clock, which will be convenient and effective for indicating time in a dark room."

It consists of a milk glass globe, marked with numerals from one to twelve. This is placed on a revolving metal disk or platform that makes a complete rotation once every twelve hours. The platform rests on a handled octagonal brass base which looks like an oil lamp font, but actually contains the keywind clock mechanism. The arbor or hour shaft is vertical so that it can propel the rotating disk. A stationary upright arrow, affixed to the side of the base, extends upward reaching the series of numbers on the globe to mark the moving hours. A small kerosene lamp is a separate unit that goes inside the milk glass shade to illuminate it.

The use of an oil lamp appears to be a later refinement, however, because in Shaw's patent papers he specifies a "candle or candlestick" to illuminate the globe, as one can see in his patent sketch. An additional refinement, missing in the example shown here, was the placement of a movable paper arrow indicator at the top of the globe to serve as a "dosage reminder" or other program timer — time to feed the baby or milk the cow, perhaps.

The entire piece measures 6 3/4" high, and 4 3/4" across the base. And if you are wondering "Does it work?" — indeed, it does!

As to the maker, Shaw assigned his patent to one John P. Adams, also of Brooklyn. Adams may have owned or been affiliated in some way with the actual maker of the lamp, identified by the markings on the underside of the base which read: "The Standard Novelty Co. PAT APR 6 1886." The clock was distributed by the "sole agents" W. C. VOSBURGH MFG. CO., of New York and Chicago.

The clock mechanism is marked "ANSONIA CLOCK CO." This well-known firm was founded in 1850 in Ansonia, Connecticut. But the clockworks for Shaw's device were made at its second factory built in Brooklyn, New York, in 1875. Five years later, it burned down and a new Brooklyn plant was built to replace it in 1881. Not long after, in 1883, the Ansonia factory was shut down and all operations moved to Brooklyn. The company prospered for many years, with numerous international awards and prizes, and sales offices in New York, Chicago,

London, Bombay, Yokohama, and Shanghai. It ceased operations in 1929. For a full account, see John A. Shuman III, "Clockmaking As An Art: Ansonia Clock Company," *The Antique Trader Weekly*, Sept. 28, 1994.

An interesting variant, identical except for the use of a Burmese instead of a milk glass globe, is described in an article by John Sewell, "A Rare Illuminated Clock," GCD, IX.1, June/July 1995, p. 79.

Shaw's "Night-Clock" was featured on the cover of the *Spinning Wheel* for June 1955. The editors of the magazine state, " In 1887 the *Scientific American* endorsed the clock with the comment: 'A simple, practical and useful device which embodies a day, night,

and medicine clock and which also provides a soft and sufficient night light.'"

They go on to say, "When found today in any condition permitting restoration (which has one mandatory condition, the milk glass globe must be intact) these clocks have antiquarian value in spite of the fact they are only seventy years old [as of this writing, 112 years old]. And that value, for a perfect specimen, will surprise anyone excepting an experienced clock collector " (p. 4). The same value may be presumed by the "experienced" milk glass collector for a rare milk glass globe on an equally rare antique clock.

Shaw's patent application and drawing (April 6, 1886).

Fig. 1. The Shaw Lamp assembled.

Fig. 2. The Shaw Lamp component parts.

Patent Ivory Queen's Ware "Two Handled Bowl"

To our knowledge, not enough attention has been paid to the obvious similarities between the floral design of Sowerby's two handled bowl, shown here, and Challinor, Taylor's "No. 313 Opal Ware," a pattern well known to collectors. Lucas refers to the latter as "Tree of Life" (p. 74) while others call it "Daisy" (see B-110b; M-81-b; F-165). Actually, the discrepancy in the names given to this pattern may be owing to

the fact that Challinor actually made three similar but different versions which can be quite confusing. Although Millard pictures Challinor's Daisy pattern bowl alongside this two-handled Sowerby bowl, he does not remark upon their similarity in design nor does he attribute either to its makers.

Let's try to sort out the Challinor variants. Some, like the bowl shown in Belknap (B-110b) and Ferson (F-165), have four panels, all of which have only the Daisy pattern. Others, like the sugar bowls shown in Belknap (B-101) have panels consisting only of a "Tree of Life" pattern which resembles somewhat the Sandwich and famed Portland designs. A third variation is a "hybrid" pattern as seen in Belknap (B-106c) consisting of six panels — three adjacent panels of "Daisy" and three of "Tree of Life."

The basic element common to all of these Challinor's patterns and the Sowerby one is a mass of floral blossoms and leaves amid intertwining branches virtually covering the entire outer surface. Depending upon the size of the piece, the pattern may be repeated four or more times in adjacent framed panels. The Sowerby bowl has eight panels with two *different* floral designs that alternate in pairs around the bowl. One pattern has large daisies and leaves much like those in the Challinor "Daisy" version, the other pattern has smaller flowers and leaves more like the Challinor "Tree of Life" design.

Thus, it is Challinor's hybrid pattern that is virtually the same as the English one. They also share other similar features. For example, on the inside bottom of the bowls, both have an embossed cluster of flowers and leaves surrounded above by a narrow band containing chevron-like narrow leaves and flower blossoms. A series of fine ribs runs vertically around the sides. Unlike the hybrid type, however, Challinor's all-Daisy pattern bowl lacks all of the interior embossing, except for a huge flower cluster in the bottom of the bowl.

A major distinguishing feature between the Sowerby design and the Challinor hybrid version may be seen in the inner surface of the bowls just above the vertical ribs. In that area, the Sowerby bowl has a mass of flowers and leaves, lightly embossed, whereas the same surface is perfectly plain in the Challinor pieces. In addition, the underside of the Sowerby bowl has a large single embossed daisy, another feature absent in any of the Challinor products I have seen. And none of Challinor's pieces, of course, is formed with the distinctive comb or stave-line handles.

The question "Which company was the originator of this look-alike floral pattern?" may not be difficult to answer.

The Sowerby bowl carries the peacock trademark and lozenge for June 6, 1879 as the date of registry for its design (No. 335972) noted by Jenny Thompson (T-1, p. 32) as "New bowl (sometimes found decorated to simulate carved ivory)." It is shown in the 1882 *Sowerby Pattern Book IX* (p. 8, No. 1407).

The earliest production dates for Challinor's No. 313 Opal Ware, however, are 1885-1893, according to Lucas (p. 73), suggesting therefore that the Sowerby design predates and most likely is the prototype for Challinor's "hybrid" pattern. Indeed, the English origin of the American copy is almost implicit in Ruth Webb Lee's description of it: "The detail is so fine and the glass has such a clear bell tone when tapped that one of the most prominent collectors in our country confided in me some years ago that in his opinion it was too good to be American and was probably English" (L-V, p. 254). We might add that Challinor's manner of painting the small floral designs on some of their pieces also appears to be in direct imitation of a technique also originated by Sowerby.

This large two-handled Sowerby bowl, an example of which is in the Victoria & Albert Museum, is truly impressive. Designated by Sowerby as "Patent Ivory Queen's Ware," the glass is a creamy light custard color

Fig. 2. Interior view.

and of good weight. The embossing both on the outer and inner surfaces is crisp and exquisitely detailed.

It measures 7 5/8" across the top, 3 1/4" deep, and about 5" high to the top of the handle. At least scarce, possibly rare.

Atterbury's Compotes on Tripod Pedestals

Among Atterbury's many elegant tableware designs, one of the most outstanding is the ribbed tripod pedestal. This intricate creation was used as the stem to support a number of different bowls. For example, it served as the pedestal for a smooth, round lacy edged bowl having an "Entwined Fish" or a "Chick and Eggs" cover, as illustrated in F-362.

But bowls with other designs were also affixed to this same tripod stem. One of these is very well known to collectors because it was reproduced by Westmoreland. The bowl is designed with ribbed sides and four equidistant clusters of an open work pattern around the edge. It is fitted with a matching ribbed cover having a three ring finial. The Atterbury original is shown in *Fig. 1* (right) alongside Westmoreland's reproduction (left). According to Charles West Wilson, Westmoreland began reproducing this piece in the mid 1930s as its No. 3 Footed Comport and Cover

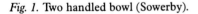

Fig. 1. Two handled bowl (Sowerby).

(p. 231). In subsequent years (from the 1940s through the 1960s), Westmoreland also issued other items on this tripod stem as part of its very extensive "Doric Line." Speaking of Westmoreland's reproduction of the ribbed compote, Wilson remarks: "A piece like this is a remarkable achievement in glass. The only problem in owning it is having to endure the gnawing thought that out there, somewhere, is the real thing!"

Fig. 1. Westmoreland (left) / Atterbury (right)

Because the reproduction is so good, collectors have had some difficulty distinguishing between it and the original. Even Belknap, for example, seems to have been unaware of its Atterbury origins. The piece he illustrates as "Tall Ribbed Compote: No. 3 Covered Compote" (B-119) is actually the Atterbury original, as Mr. Wilson also recognized, but Belknap assumed it was an early Westmoreland product, stating: "If my memory is correct, I noticed this piece for the first time about 1925. I have not been able to find out whether or not Westmoreland was producing it during that period." Obviously, it wasn't, and he had an Atterbury piece without realizing it.

It may be difficult to distinguish Westmoreland's earlier 1930s issues from the later ones, but I suspect a difference may be seen in the treatment of the open work on the bowl. The early pieces, we believe, copy the original Atterbury design more closely by having the open work turned up, whereas in the later issues it is spread out almost horizontally as seen in *Fig. 1*. This may be evidenced in the example shown by Millard (M-119), where the base is unquestionably the Westmoreland reproduction, but the open work of the bowl is upturned like the Atterbury originals, rather than flared out. The example illustrated in Newbound (N-97) appears to be Atterbury, not Westmoreland. If so, the value she assigns to it ($35-40) seems to us more appropriate for the reproduction than the original.

As for the tripod base itself, one difference between the original and the reproduction is readily observed in *Fig. 2* where one can see a vertical central support inside the tripod of the original (left), and its absence in the reproduction (right). But there are many other differences as well. *All of the originals we have examined have a thin wafer connecting the stem and the bowl, whereas the reproductions have wider bands directly attaching the top to stem, thus adding slightly to the overall height.* Notice also the well-defined ribbing around the top of the tripod in the original, a feature missing in the completely smooth surface of the reproduction. Just as distinctive is the difference in the edges of the bowls. Atterbury's rib design is continuous to the outer rim, whereas Westmoreland's ribs end abruptly, butting up against a broad band circling the top. This same difference is observed in the covers as well, as may be seen in *Fig. 3* (Atterbury on the left; Westmoreland, right).

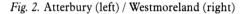

Fig. 2. Atterbury (left) / Westmoreland (right)

Fig. 3. Atterbury (left) / Westmoreland (right)

We conclude by illustrating three other variant tops for the tripod base. The compote in *Fig. 4* is shown without a lid but it accommodates the same ribbed cover as seen in *Fig. 1*. The bowl differs only in the design of the open work border which consists of twenty evenly spaced beaded loops. In *Fig. 5*, the tripod stem supports an open compote in Atterbury's Wicket Border pattern, with the ovals greatly elongated. Finally, a 9 1/2" Wicket Border plate was used to create the salver shown in *Fig 6.*

Fig. 5. Atterbury, Wicket Border Open Compote

Fig. 4. Atterbury, Beaded Loop edge

Fig. 6. Atterbury, Wicket Border Cake Salver

202

Crucifix Candlesticks

Although some collectors put a low priority on acquiring religious objects, they tend to think otherwise when an object of that type is established to be rare.

The problem with crucifix candlesticks is the opposite. They appear frequently at most antique shows and flea markets, but at such wildly differing prices that a collector is at a loss to know which are common and which are rare. Equally puzzling is trying to determine when they were made and what companies to attribute them to. This is not surprising as they were made over a very long period and by many different companies.

The fact is, however, that crucifix candlesticks are among the most intriguing categories for the discriminating collector precisely because of their variety and the challenge of attributing them to their makers, to say nothing of the beautiful quality of much of the glass used in their production.

Aside from Barlow and Kaiser's treatment of the Boston and Sandwich products, the most helpful general survey of crucifix candlesticks is Heacock's article "Religious Figures in Glass" which appeared in the first issue of the *Glass Collector's Digest* (June/July 1987, pp. 81-91). Heacock worked with old catalogs and was able to establish with reasonable precision the age and manufacturer of many of the candlesticks. Keep in mind, however, as Heacock himself cautions us, that he was working with catalog illustrations, **not** with actual specimens. Therefore, his work needs to be studied with candlesticks in hand.

We present here an introduction to some of the variety that exists and a guide to help you know what to look for when trying to evaluate a given crucifix.

The collector should pay attention to the following variations:

- Look at the base to see if it is hexagonal, octagonal, or round.
- Examine the socket to see if it is flared out or more petal shaped; whether it too is hexagonal or octagonal, or rounded with various types of striations.
- Examine the stem and cross bar — is the stem straight or flared out at the base?
- How are the feet of the Christ figure placed?
- Are the details of the figure well defined or vague?
- Is there an angled "INRA" embossed above the head? [For those who may not know, these are the Latin initials are for "Iesus Nazarenus, Rex Iudaeorum" — Jesus of Nazareth, King of the Jews.]
- Is the back of the cross flat, concave, or convex, and does it have any design on it?

Using these criteria, you will soon find many subtle differences within a group of crucifixes that otherwise appear to be bewilderingly alike.

Type A - Crucifixes with Twelve-Sided Bases

These candlesticks are the top of the line. They are unusually tall (13") and have a small cross embossed on each panel of the hexagonal socket which flares out at the top into a distinct petal. Below the socket is a wafer which attaches the socket to the cross below. The detail is excellent and the sticks often are made of flint glass. The cross bar measures 4 1/4" long. *Fig. 1* is an excellent example.

Made by the Boston and Sandwich Glass Company. The separate wafer is diagnostic. Many other crucifix candlesticks have a wafer-like area below the socket, but only the Sandwich ones have the wafer separate.

The Sandwich company made these beautiful sticks not only in milk white but in a variety of transparent colors as well, many of which are very rare. At least scarce in milk glass. Beware of reproductions.

There are several other examples which also have the small cross embossed on each panel of the socket; among them is Hobb's "No. 2 Calvary Candlesticks" shown in an undated (circa 1880) catalog (see Bredehoft, *Hobbs, Brockunier & Co. Glass*, p. 135). At least one true variant exists in flint glass which has a much narrower circular wafer and a narrower additional step between the twelve-sided base and the curving, concave panels that sweep upward from the base to the stem of the cross. This variant also differs in having a deep concavity just below the feet of the figure (also present on the back of the stick). It is also 13" tall but the cross bar is 4 1/2" long.

Fig. 1. Type A

Fig. 2. Type B

Type B - Hexagonal Base Crucifixes with Hexagonal Flared Sockets

Sticks of this type were made by a number of companies and there is still much work needed before we can be reasonably sure of many attributions.

One of these, shown in *Fig. 2,* is 11 1/2" tall with cross arms 4 1/4" across. It has what appears to be a wafer connecting the socket to the stem, but close examination will show that it is made from a single mold. Below the "wafer" there is a swollen area at the top of the stem. The quality of the glass is excellent.

Maker unknown, but considered by some collectors to be a product of the New England Glass Company. It is scarce.

A similar but much smaller stick (9 3/4" high and 3 1/4" across the horizontal bar), shown in *Fig. 3,* also has a pseudo-wafer. The top of the socket edges are more acutely curved outward than in the preceding stick. The feet of the figure rest on a slanting rectangular slab. The area below the "wafer" is not produced.

Fig. 3. Type B

In the article cited above, Heacock illustrates this crucifix and assigns it to McKee & Co. He states that the head is bent to the left, but his illustration, typical of many old catalogs, probably has the image in reverse.

This candlestick has apparently been reproduced, as seen in *Fig. 4* (right), for while the earlier examples show great detail in the figure, others are smooth and lack definition — the legs, for example, are pebbled in the original but smooth in the reproduction.

The stick in *Fig. 4* (left) is very similar to the one shown in *Fig. 3*, but has two pseudo-wafers between the socket and the stem. In this version, the feet rest on a slanting rounded slab rather than a rectangular one. The back is very different from the "McKee Stick" of *Fig. 3* in that this one has a flat rather than concave cross and there is an elongate arrow-like raised strip beginning at the base of the cross and tapering to an elongate point near the middle. It measures 9 1/2" tall with a 3 1/2" cross bar. The maker is unknown and we believe it is scarce.

Fig. 4. Type B

Still another hexagonal base stick, shown in *Fig. 5*, is relatively crudely made. The Christ figure lacks much of the fine definition found in those previously discussed. The stem of the cross near the bottom flares out rather than being straight. The "INRI" embossing is lacking, and in general all the details are muted. It is 9" high and the short cross bar measures only 2 1/4".

Heacock assigns it to the Co-Operative Flint Glass Co., circa 1893. We would tend to date it later. This crucifix is usually available.

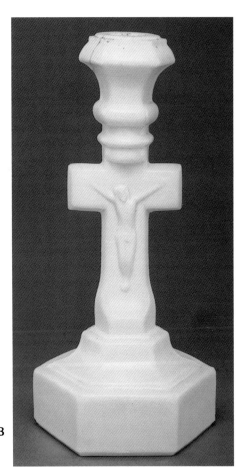

Fig. 5. Type B

Type C - Hexagonal Base Crucifixes with Octagonal Non-Flared, Striated Sockets

Fig. 6 is a handsome 9 1/2" stick with very short horizontal bar, only 2 3/4" across. It is readily recognizable by the gradual way the stem widens from the cross arms down to the base. The octagonal socket is surmounted by a round top with a low hexagonal inner protrusion to receive the candle. The glass is of good quality; the figure detail only fair. Maker unknown. Usually available.

Fig. 6. Type C

Fig. 7 is an 8 1/2" tall variant of the stick shown in *Fig.* 6. It differs chiefly in that the widening stem of the cross does not continue in an even sweep to the base but is parallel sided on the bottom third. The concave panels below the stem are also shorter. It lacks the "INRI" embossing above the head.

Made by the Cambridge Glass Company. See N-70 (right), and probably also Archer (plate 7, No. 3). This, too, is usually available.

A variant exists, differing primarily in having the concave basal panels much larger. The detail is poor, the figure being almost smooth with the arms fading laterally so that the hands are undifferentiated and the "INRI" area is represented only by a lump without lettering. Except for the difference in the concave panels, one might think this stick was merely the worn mold of the one shown in *Fig.* 8.

Fig. 7. Type C

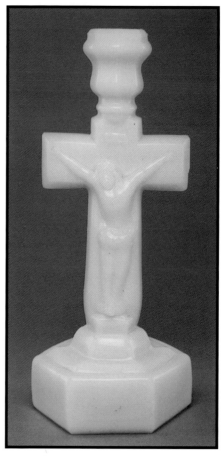

Fig. 8. Type D

Type D - Hexagonal Based Crucifixes with Octagonal Petal-Like Sockets

Candlesticks of the type shown in *Fig.* 8 have an octagonal socket but the surface curves strongly inward in the center and at the base where it joins a conspicuous "pseudo-wafer." The octagonal opening to receive the candle projects well above the main body of the socket. The stem of the cross is widened on the basal half, then tapers at the base. The back of this stick is convex.

Heacock assigns these to the U.S. Glass Co., based on their 1893 catalog. It is also the crucifix shown in Belknap (B-30) who says it is late. We are very doubtful as both examples we have examined are of heavy flint glass. This, together with the fact that U.S. Glass was a combine of older factories, suggests an early origin. We believe they are scarce.

Type E - Flattened Octagonal Based Crucifixes

The small candlestick shown in *Fig.* 9 is only 7 1/4" tall with the horizontal bar measuring 3 3/8" across. The hexagonal socket is relatively large with a rounded top, lacking the secondary terminal area for the insertion of the candle. Both the front and back surfaces are deeply grooved, simulating wood. The figure detail is excellent. The glass has a somewhat grayish cast.

Heacock believes it is French; Belknap illustrates it (B-30a) and also comments on the gray tint suggesting a French origin. We believe it is the Westmoreland Specialty Company crucifix, No. 54 in a 1912 catalog, in reverse image. Somewhat hard to find.

Fig. 9. Type E

Type G - Round Based Crucifix with Floral Design On The Back

This antique candlestick, shown in *Fig. 11*, has a broad round base of three layers, the one in the middle being broadly convex. The stem bulges at the base, and vertical stripes are deeply pressed around the socket. The back of the cross has a pattern of ivy leaves. It is 8" high with a cross bar 2 3/4" long.

Made by Atterbury and illustrated in its 1881 catalog. They are discussed by Heacock, cited above, and also shown in F-330, 331.

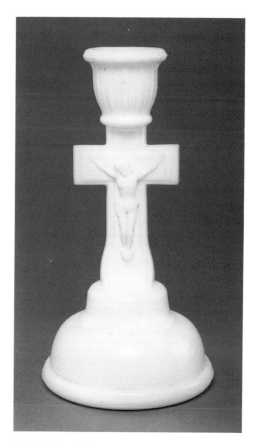

Fig. 11. Type G

Type F - Round Based Crucifixes with Petal Sockets

The candlestick in *Fig. 10* differs greatly from the preceding ones with its round base and large sweeping concave panels rising up the sides. The stem is straight throughout. The hexagonal, petal socket has a plain, round opening to receive the candle. The cross is finely striated both front and back.

Maker unknown. Possibly French. We believe it is scarce.

Fig. 10. Type F

The French Catalog Reprints

On the following pages, we feel fortunate in being able to include reprints of twenty-four color pages from two very rare catalogs issued by the French glasshouses, Vallerysthal and Portieux.

The first of these reprints, consisting of the catalog front cover and fourteen color pages, is of the "Société Anonyme des Verreriers Réunies des Vallérysthal & Portieux. Établissement de Vallérysthal (Lorraine). Collection de Dessins. Articles décorés à froid. 1908." It is reprinted with the kind permission of The Corning Museum of Glass from its magnificent holdings in the Collection of the Juliet K. and Leonard S. Rakow Research Library. This catalog throughout this book is cited as "VCC."

The second catalog, consisting of the front cover and ten color pages, is of the "Société Anonyme des Verreries Réunies de Vallérysthal (Moselle) et Portieux (Voges). Etablisse-ment de Portieux. Collection des

Dessins des Principaux Articles. 1933." It is reprinted through the courtesy of Robert Pinkston and Frank Chiarenza. This catalog throughout this book is cited as "PC."

Reprint of the 1908 Vallerysthal Catalog

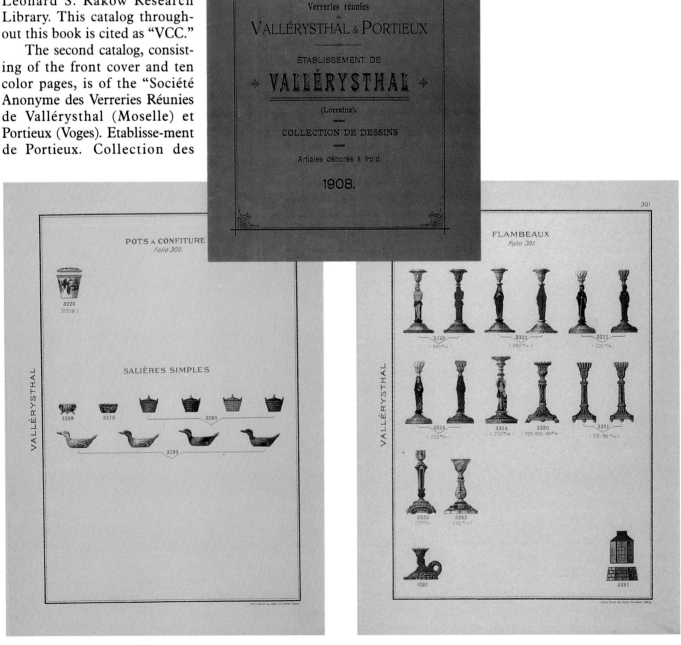

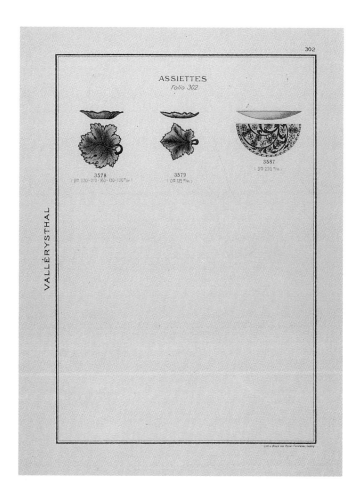

ASSIETTES
Folio 302

3578
3579
3587

VALLÉRYSTHAL

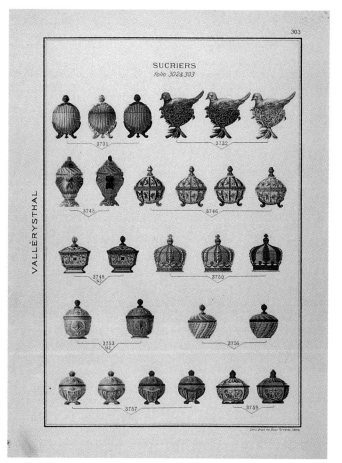

SUCRIERS
Folio 302 & 303

VALLÉRYSTHAL

SUCRIERS
Folio 303

VALLÉRYSTHAL

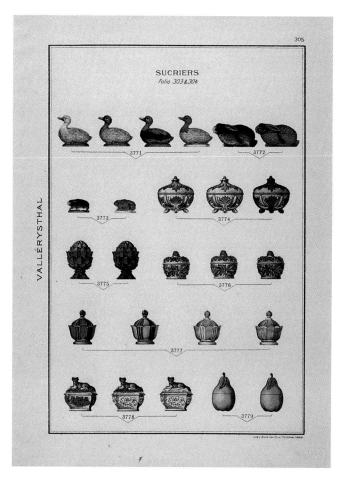

SUCRIERS
Folio 303 & 304

VALLÉRYSTHAL

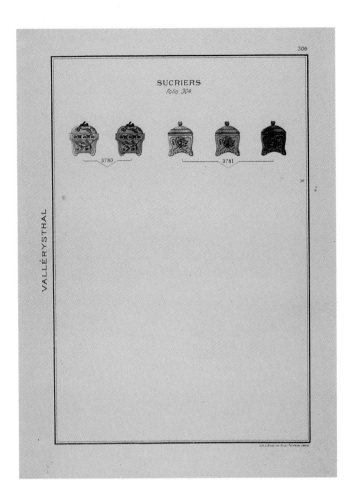

SUCRIERS
Folio 304.

VALLÉRYSTHAL

3780   3781

BEURRIERS
Folio 304 & 305.

VALLÉRYSTHAL

3800   3801
3802
3803
3804
3805

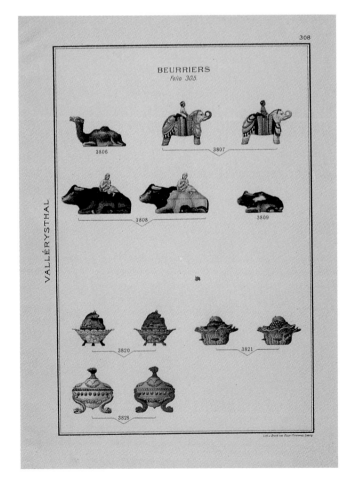

BEURRIERS
Folio 305.

VALLÉRYSTHAL

3806   3807
3808   3809
3820   3821
3828

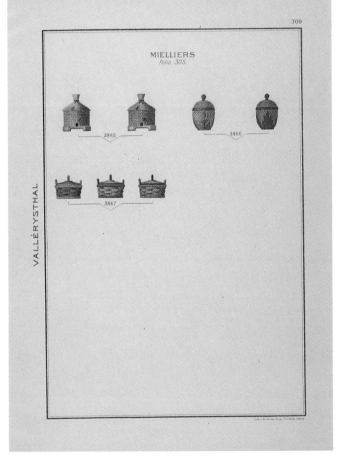

MIELLIERS
Folio 305.

VALLÉRYSTHAL

3865   3866
3867

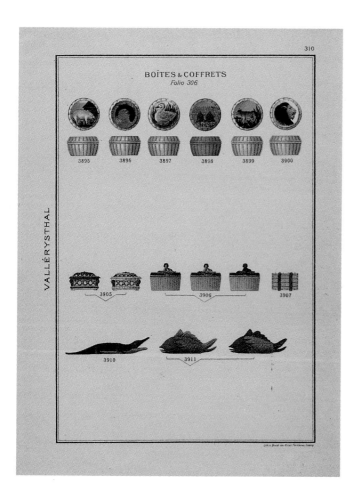

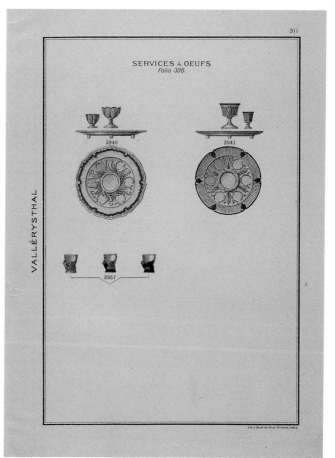

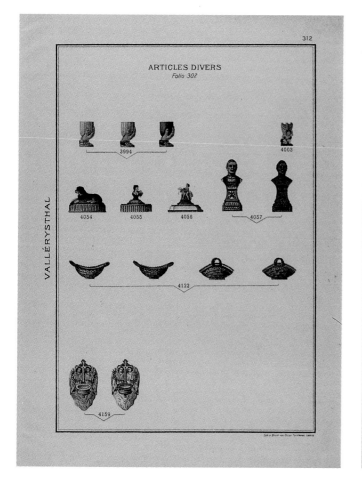

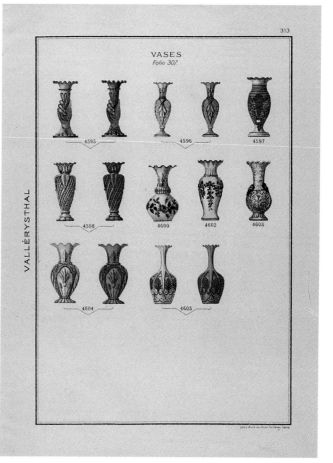

211

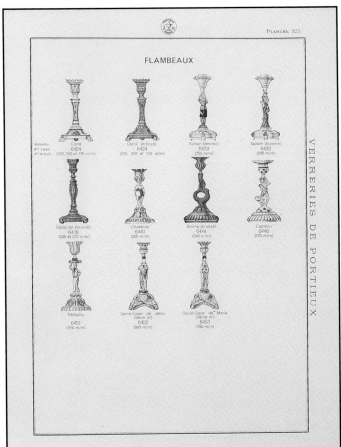

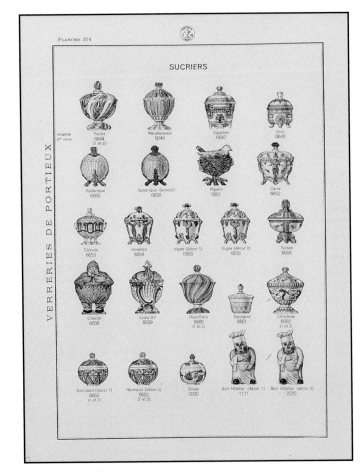

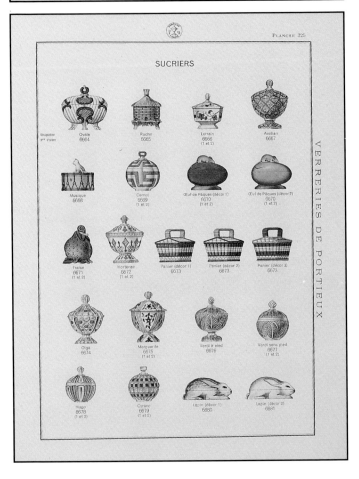

VERRERIES DE PORTIEUX

SUCRIERS

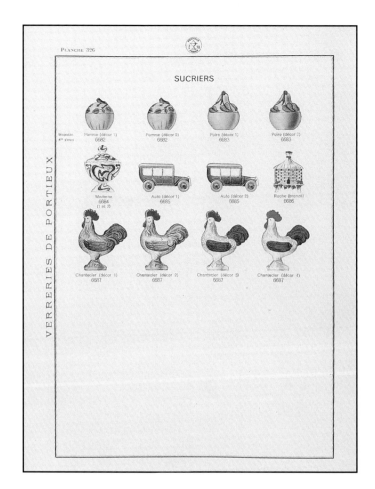

VERRERIES DE PORTIEUX

BEURRIERS

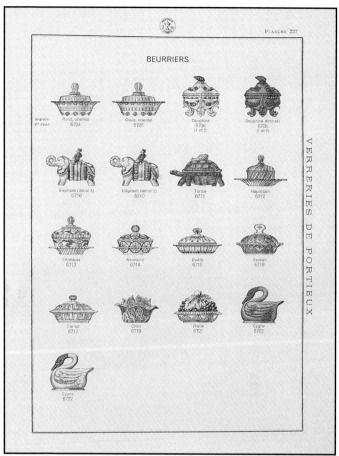

VERRERIES DE PORTIEUX

ARTICLES DIVERS

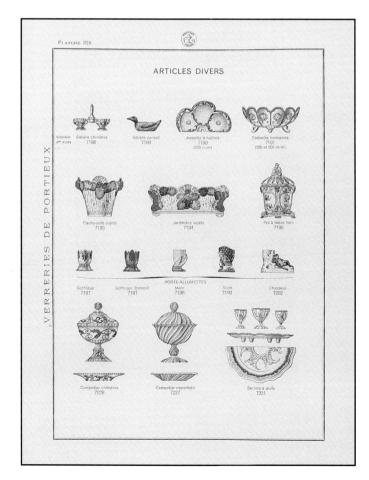

VERRERIES DE PORTIEUX

ARTICLES DIVERS

VASES

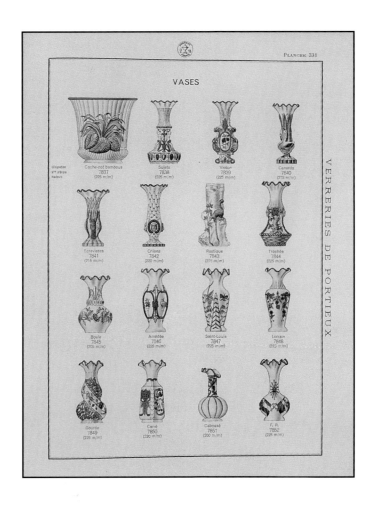

VERRERIES DE PORTIEUX

VERRERIES DE PORTIEUX

VASES

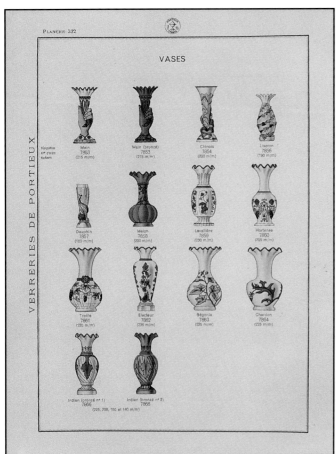

VASES 21
(de 85 à 275 m/m)

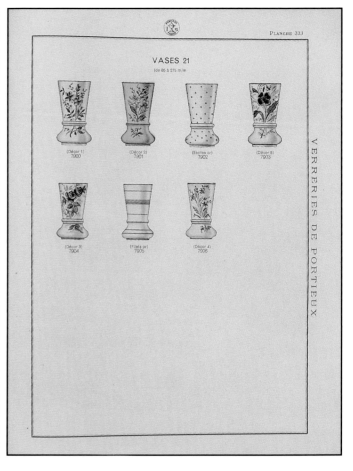

VERRERIES DE PORTIEUX

Checklist of Some Major Manufacturers of Milk Glass

American

Akro Agate, Clarksburg, West Virginia (1914-1951)

Atterbury and Company, Pittsburgh, Pennsylvania (1859-c. 1902)

Bakewell & Ensell; Bakewell, Pears and Company, Pittsburgh, Pennsylvania (c. 1807-1880)

Belmont Glass Company, Bellaire, Ohio (1866-1890)

Boston and Sandwich Glass Co., Sandwich, Massachusetts (1825-1888)

Boyd's Crystal Art Glass Company, Cambridge, Ohio (1978-still operating)

Cambridge Glass Company, Cambridge, Ohio (1901-1957)

Canton Glass Company, Canton, Ohio (1883-c. 1903)

Cape Cod Glass Works, Sandwich, Massachusetts (1858-1869)

Central Glass Company, Wheeling, West Virginia (1863-1939)

Challinor, Taylor & Company, Tarentum, Pennsylvania (1885-1890). The factory burned down shortly after it joined the U.S. Glass Co. in 1891.

Consolidated Lamp and Glass Company, Fostoria, Ohio (1893-1896) and Coraopolis, Pennsylvania (1894-1933)

Co-Operative Flint Glass Company, Beaver Falls, Pennsylvania (1879-1934)

Coudersport Tile and Ornamental Glass Company, Coudersport, Pennsylvania (1900-1904)

Dalzell, Gilmore and Leighton Co., Findlay, Ohio (1888-1901)

Degenhart Crystal Art Glass, Cambridge, Ohio (1947-1978)

Dithridge and Company, Pittsburgh, Pennsylvania (1860?-1903)

Dunbar Flint Glass Corp., Dunbar, West Virginia (1913-1953)

Duncan (George) and Sons, Pittsburgh, Pennsylvania (1874-1892). See also Ripley & Company.

Duncan (George) and Sons, Washington, Pennsylvania (1894-1900)

Duncan and Miller Glass Co. (1900-1955), thereafter Duncan and Miller Division at Tiffin, Ohio plant.

Eagle Glass & Manufacturing Company, Wellsburgh, West Virginia (1894-1913?)

Fenton Art Glass Company, Williamstown, West Virginia (1907-still operating)

Findlay Flint Glass Company, Findlay, Ohio (1888-1891)

Fostoria Glass Company, Fostoria, Ohio (1887 -1891) and Moundsville, West Virginia (1891-1986)

Gillinder & Sons (1861-1891). Reorganized a number of times thereafter, and now operated by fifth generation Gillinder Brothers, Inc., of Port Jervis, New York.

Hazel-Atlas, Washington, Pennsylvania (1902-1956), thereafter operating under different owners.

Hobbs, Brockunier & Company, Wheeling, West Virginia (1845-1891)

Imperial Glass Company, Bellaire, Ohio (1902-1984)

Indiana Glass Company (1907-still operating as affiliate of Lancaster Colony Corp.)

Indiana Tumbler & Goblet Company, Greentown, Indiana (1894-1903)

Jeannette Glass Company, Jeannette, Pennsylvania (1900?-1983)

Kemple Glass Works, East Palestine, Ohio (1945-1956) and Kenova, West Virginia (1957-1970)

Libbey Glass Company, see New England Glass Company.

McKee & Brothers, Pittsburgh (1864-1888) and Jeanette, Pennsylvania (1888-1900) Subsequent names/affiliations to 1952.

Macbeth-Evans, Charleroi, Pennsylvania (1899-1936, when purchased by Corning Glass Company, Corning, New York; still operating in the production of "Corningware")

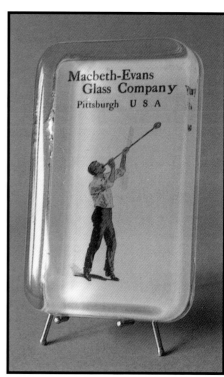

Mosser Glass Company, East Cambridge, Ohio (1964?-still operating)

National Glass Company (1900-1904), a confederation of existing independent companies, including Canton, Central, Dalzell, Indiana Tumbler (Greentown), McKee, Northwood, and others totaling nineteen factories in all.

New England Glass Company, East Cambridge, Massachusetts (1818-1888). Moved to Toledo, Ohio, as W. L. Libbey & Son Company (1888) and now operating as The Libbey Glass Company.

New Martinsville Glass Manufacturing Co. New Martinsville, West Virginia (1900-now operating as Viking Glass Co.)

Ripley & Company, Pittsburgh, Pennsylvania (1866). Name changed to George Duncan & Sons (1874-1892)

Smith (L. E.) Glass Company, Mt. Pleasant, Pennsylvania (1908-still operating)

St. Clair Glass Company, Elwood, Indiana (1941-1971)

Summit Art Glass Company, Ravenna, Ohio (1972-still operating)

Tarentum Glass Company, Tarentum, Pennsylvania (1894-1918)

United States Glass Company, Pittsburgh, Pennsylvania (1891-1963), a confederation of existing independent companies, including Central Glass, Challinor, Taylor, George Duncan, Gillinder, Hobbs Glass, and others totaling eighteen factories in all. Most were closed by the time of the Depression, with only Tiffin and Glasport plants continuing to 1963.

Viking Glass Co., see New Martinsville Glass Manufacturing Co.

Westmoreland Specialty Company, Grapeville, Pennsylvania (1892-1924). Name changed to Westmoreland Glass Company (1924-1985). From

1889 to 1892, operated as The Specialty Glass Company in East Liverpool, Ohio.

L. G. Wright Glass Company, New Martinsville, West Virginia (1936-still operating)

English

Davidson - George Davidson of the Teams Glassworks, Gateshead (founded 1867). Trademark is a demi-lion emerging from a mural crown (used from c. 1880 to 1890).

Derbyshire - John Derbyshire, Regent Road Flint Glass Works, Salford (founded 1873). Trademark is an anchor with the initials JD superimposed (used from 1873 to 1876, the full period of this short-lived company).

Greener - Angus & Greener, Wear Flint Glass Works, Sunderland (founded 1858); Henry Greener (1869-1884); Greener & Company (founded 1885). Two trademarks were used: first, a demi-lion holding a five-point star in its paw (1875-1885); second, a demi-lion holding a battle-ax in both paws (1885-1900).

Sowerby - Sowerby's Ellison Glass Works, Ltd., Gateshead (founded 1847). Trademark is a crested peacock (used from 1875 to about 1930). Sometimes imprinted "Depose" on items intended for export. Sowerby continued in operation until 1972.

GLASS.

SOWERBY, LIMITED.
GATESHEAD.

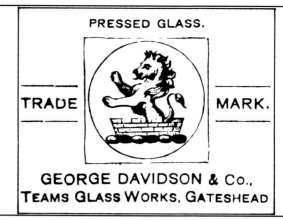

PRESSED GLASS.

TRADE   MARK.

GEORGE DAVIDSON & Co.,
TEAMS GLASS WORKS, GATESHEAD

PRESSED GLASS.

GREENER & CO.,
WEAR FLINT
GLASS WORKS,
MILLFIELD,
SUNDERLAND.

French

The two French companies, Portieux (Vosges) and Vallerysthal (Moselle), whose products figure prominently in the collections of members of the NMGCS, are accordingly well represented in this book. Both companies have their origins in the early 1700s. In 1872 they joined together to form the *Société Anonyme des Verreries Réunies de Vallérysthal et Portieux*. Their extensive production of milk glass flourished from the 1870s well into the mid-1950s. After going their separate ways, Portieux underwent several reorganizations and continued operating until the mid-1980s. Its current status is unknown to us. Vallerysthal, too, struggled to stay afloat, and is still making glass on a very small scale, but very little milk glass, if any at all. For a detailed historical account of these French glass makers, see Rush Pinkston's four part series in O.N. (IV:1 Dec. 1988, pp. 411-413; IV: 2 Mar 1989; IV:3 June 1989, pp. 432-433; and VI: 1 Dec 1990, pp. 619-619-2)

A postscript on the "S V" mark...

The letters "S V" found on a number of pieces illustrated in this book have eluded our best efforts to track down. We can be certain they are not of recent manufacture, however. Many of the covered dishes and novelty items bearing these initials — as we assume they are an abbreviation — have very close counterparts in pieces known to be products of Portieux and Vallerysthal. A few items, such as the Trumpet Vine Covered Dish, we have seen illustrated in a late nineteenth-century catalog of Val St. Lambert, a Belgian company, but we have no way to determine how the "S V" marking might relate to it. Since moulds do change hands from time to time, it is difficult to trace their origins or to determine when a company may have purchased moulds and pressed reissues with the original markings or substituting their own marks. We suspect the similarity between a number of "S V" pieces and known Portieux / Vallerysthal ones is a case of copying designs rather than an exchange of moulds because the differences are more than would be possible by simply reworking the moulds.

Selected Readings

(with abbreviations for references frequently cited)

Archer, Margaret, and Douglas Archer. *Collector's Encyclopedia of Glass Candlesticks.* Paducah, KY: Collector Books, 1983.

Baker, Gary E., et. al. *Wheeling Glass 1829-1939.* Wheeling, WV: Oglebay Institute, 1994.

(B-K) Barlow, Raymond E., and Jean E. Kaiser. *The Glass Industry in Sandwich* [Vols. 1 - 4]. West Chester, PA: Schiffer Publishing Ltd., and Windham, NH.; Barlow-Kaiser Publishing Co., 1983 - 1989.

(B) Belknap, E. McCamley, *Milk Glass.* New York: Crown Publishers, 1949.

Bredehoft, Neila, and Thomas Bredehoft. *Victorian Novelties and Figurals: Geo. Duncan and Sons.* St. Louisville, Ohio: Cherry Hill Publications, 1989.

_____. *Hobbs, Brockunier & Co., Glass.* Paducah, KY: Collector Books, 1997.

Burkholder, John R. and D. Thomas O'Connor. *Kemple Glass 1945-1970.* Marietta, Ohio: The Glass Press, Inc., 1997.

Cottle, Simon. *Sowerby, Gateshead Glass.* Newcastle upon Tyne: Chatsworth Studios, Ltd., 1986.

Dodsworth, Roger. *British Glass between the wars.* Warwickshire, U.K.: Jolly & Barber Ltd., 1987.

Fauster, Carl U. *Libbey Glass Since 1818: Pictorial History and Collector's Guide.* Toledo, Ohio: Len Beach Press, 1979.

(F) Ferson, Regis F. and Mary F. *Yesterday's Milk Glass Today.* Greenburg, PA: Chas. H. Henry Printing Co., 1981.

(G-S) Garmon, Lee and Dick Spencer. *Glass Animals of the Depression Era.* Paducah, KY.: Collector Books, 1993.

Garrison, Myrna and Bob. *Imperial's Vintage Milk Glass.* Arlington, TX.: Self Published, 1992.

(GCD) *Glass Collector's Digest* [articles from 1987 - current]. P.O. Box 553, Marietta, Ohio 45750.

Godden, Geoffrey. *Antique Glass and China: A Guide for the Beginning Collector.* South Brunswick, NJ: A. S. Barnes, 1967.

Griscom, Pauline. *Is It Old? Is It New?* Privately Printed, July 1988 Edition.

Grist, Everett. *Covered Animal Dishes.* Paducah, KY.: Collector Books, 1988.

Grizel, Ruth. *Welcome Home, Westmoreland.* Iowa City, IA: FSJ Pub. Co., 1990.

_____. *Westmoreland Glass: Our Children's Heirlooms.* Iowa City, IA: FSJ Pub. Co., 1993.

(HCG) Heacock, William. *Collecting Glass* [Vols. 1-3, 1984-86]. Marietta, Ohio: Richardson Printing Corp.

(HCC) _____. *The Glass Collector* [Issues 1-6, 1982-83] Marietta, Ohio: Richardson Printing Corp.

(HF1) _____. *Fenton Glass: The First Twenty-Five Years.* Marietta, Ohio: O-Val Advertising Corp., 1978.

(HF2) _____. *Fenton Glass: The Second Twenty-Five Years.* Marietta, Ohio: O-Val Advertising Corp., 1980.

(HF3) _____. *Fenton Glass: The Third Twenty-Five Years.* Marietta, Ohio: O-Val Advertising Corp., 1989.

(H-1) _____. *1000 Toothpick Holders.* Marietta, Ohio: Antique Publications, 1977.

(H-2) _____. *Rare and Unlisted Toothpick Holders.* Marietta, Ohio: Antique Publications, 1984.

(H-3) _____. *Encyclopedia of Victorian Colored Pattern Glass: Bk. 5 : U.S. Glass from A to Z.* Marietta, Ohio: Richardson Printing Corp. 1978.

(H-J) _____, and Patricia Johnson. *5000 Open Salts.* Marietta, Ohio: Richardson Printing Corp., 1982.

Hughes, G. Bernard. *English, Scottish and Irish Table Glass.* New York, NY.: Bramhall House, 1956.

Husfloen, Kyle. *Collector's Guide to American Pressed Glass 1825-1915.* Radnor, PA.: Wallace-Homestead, 1992.

Innes, Lowell. *Pittsburgh Glass 1797-1891: A History and Guide for Collectors.* Boston: Houghton Mifflin Co., 1976.

James, Margaret. *Black Glass.* Paducah, KY: Collector Books, 1981.

(J-PG) Jenks, Bill and Jerry Luna. *Early American Pattern Glass 1850-1910.* Radnor, PA.: Wallace-Homestead, 1990.

(J-PRG) Jenks, Bill, Jerry Luna, and Darryl Reilly. *Identifying Pattern Glass Reproductions.* Radnor, PA.: Wallace-Homestead, 1993.

(K) Kamm, Minnie Watson. *Pattern Glass Pitchers* [8

Volumes]. Grosse Pointe, MI: Kamm Publications, 1939 - 1954.

Kaye, Barbara Joyce. *White Gold: A Primer for Previously Unlisted Milk Glass* [Vols. I (1990) and II (1993)] Self Published.

Kovar, Lorraine. *Westmoreland Glass 1950-1984* (Vol. I). Marietta, Ohio: Antique Publications, 1991.

_____. *Westmoreland Glass 1950-1984* (Vol. II). Marietta, Ohio: Antique Publications, 1995.

_____. *Westmoreland Glass 1888-1940* (Vol. III), Marietta, Ohio: Antique Publications, 1997.

Krause, Gail. *Encyclopedia of Duncan Glass*. Hicksville, NY.: Exposition Press, 1976.

Lattimore, Colin R. *English 19th-Century Press-Moulded Glass*. London: Barrie and Jenkins, Ltd., 1979.

Lechler, Doris Anderson. *Toy Glass*. Marietta, Ohio: Antique Publications, 1989.

Lechner, Mildred and Ralph Lechner. *The World of Salt Shakers*. Paducah, KY:, Collector Books, 1992.

(L-EA) Lee, Ruth Webb. *Early American Pressed Glass* (35th ed.). Wellesley Hills, MA.: Lee Publications, 1960.

(L-VG) _____. *Victorian Glass* (13th ed.). Wellesley Hills, MA.: Lee Publications, 1944.

Lindsey, Bessie M. *American Historical Glass*. Rutland, Vermont: Charles E. Tuttle Co., 1969.

Lucas, Robert I. *Tarentum Glass*. Tarentum, Pa.: Robert Lucas, 1980.

Manley, Cyril. *Decorative Victorian Glass*. New York: Van Nostrand Reinhold Co., 1981.

Marsh, Tracy H. *The American Story Recorded in Glass*. Minneapolis, MN: Tracy Marsh, 1962.

McCain, Mollie Helen. *The Collector's Encyclopedia of Pattern Glass*. Paducah, KY.: Collector Books, 1982.

McKearin, George S. and Helen McKearin. *American Glass*. New York: Crown Publishers, Inc., 1948.

Measell, James. *Greentown Glass: the Indiana Tumbler and Goblet Company*. Grand Rapids, Michigan: Grand Rapids Museum Association, 1979.

Measell, James and Don E. Smith. *Findlay Glass 1886-1902*. Marietta, Ohio: Antique Publications, 1986.

(M-R) Measell, James and W. C. "Red" Roettels. *The L. G. Wright Glass Company*. Marietta, Ohio: Antique Publications, 1997.

Metz, Alice Hulett. *Early American Pattern Glass*. Privately Printed, 1958.

_____. *Much More Early American Pattern Glass*. Privately Printed, 1971.

(M) Millard, S. T. *Opaque Glass* (3rd. ed.). Topeka, Kansas: Central Press, 1965.

Miller, Everett R. and Addie R. Miller. *The New Martinsville Glass Story* [Vols. 1 and 2, 1920-1950]. Marietta, Ohio: Richardson Publishing Co., 1972.

Morris, Barbara. *Victorian Table Glass & Ornaments*. London: Barnes & Jenkins, 1978.

Munsey, Cecil. *The Illustrated Guide to Collecting Bottles*. New York: Hawthorne Books, Inc., 1970.

(N) Newbound, Betty and Bill Newbound. *Collector's Encyclopedia of Milk Glass*. Paducah, KY.: Collector Books, 1995.

Notley, Raymond. *Flint Pressed Glass*. [Shire Album 162] Aylesbury, Bucks, England: Shire Publications Ltd., 1986.

(O.N.) *Opaque News* [the quarterly publication of the National Milk Glass Collectors Society; Vol. 1, No. 1 (1985) to current].

(P-1) Peterson, Arthur G. *Glass Patterns and Patents*. Sanford, Florida: Celery City Printing Co., 1973.

(P-2) _____. *Glass Salt Shakers: 1000 Patterns*. Des Moines, IA: Wallace-Homestead, 1970.

(P-3) _____. *Trademarks on Glass*. De Bary, FL: Dr. Arthur G. Peterson, 1973.

(PC) [Portieux Catalog] *Collection des Dessins des Principaux Articles* (354 pages) date of issue 1933.

Powell, Robert Blake. *Antique Shaving Mugs of the United States*. (c. 1972)

Revi, Albert Christian. *American Pressed Glass and Figure Bottles*. New York: Thomas Nelson, Inc., 1964.

Slack, Raymond. *English Pressed Glass: 1830-1900*. London: Barrie and Jenkins, Ltd., 1987.

(S-1) Smith, Frank R. and Ruth E. Smith. *Miniature Lamps*. New York, NY: Thomas Nelson & Sons, 1969.

(S-2) Smith, Ruth. *Miniature Lamps - II*. Atglen, PA: Schiffer Publishing Ltd., 1982.

Solverson, John E. *Those Fascinating Little Lamps*. Marietta, Ohio: Antique Publications, 1988.

Spillman, Jane Shadel. *American and European Pressed Glass in the Corning Museum of Glass*. Corning, N. Y.: Corning Museum of Glass, 1981.

(SW) *Spinning Wheel Magazine*: Antique Digest - "Glass, Pressed: Vallerysthal Imports to 1914," 1952. Eight pages reprinted in *Opaque News* (X:III June 1995 and X:IV September 1995).

(T-BG) Toohey, Marlena. *A Collector's Guide to Black Glass*. Marietta, Ohio: Antique Publications, 1988.

(T-1) Thompson, Jenny. *Identification of English Pressed Glass: 1842-1908*. Published by Mrs. J. Thompson, Dixon Printing Co., Ltd., Kendal, Cumbria, 1989.

(T-2) _____. *A Supplement to the Identification of English Pressed Glass: 1842-1908*. Published by Mrs. J. Thompson, Dixon Printing Co., Ltd., Kendal, Cumbria, 1993.

Umberger, Art and Jewel. *Collectible Character Bottles*. Tyler, TX.: Corker Book Co., 1969.

_____. *Top Bottles, U. S. A.* Tyler, TX: Corker Book Co., 1970.

(VC) [Vallerysthal Catalogs] referencing various issues dated 1894, 1898, and 1907.

(VCC) [Vallerysthal Color Catalog] *Collection de Dessins*

- *Articles décoré à froid*, dated 1908. Title page and fourteen color pages reprinted in this book with the kind permission of The Juliet K. and Leonard S. Rakow Research Library of the Corning Museum of Glass.

(W) Warman, Edwin G. *Milk Glass Addenda* (3rd ed.). Uniontown, PA: E. G. Warman Publishing Co., 1966.

Watkins, Lura Woodside. *Cambridge Glass 1818 to 1888*. Boston: Little Brown and Co., 1930.

Weatherman, Hazel Marie. *Colored Glassware of the Depression Era 2*. Ozark, MO: Weatherman Glassbooks, 1982.

_____. *Fostoria: Its First Fifty Years*. Springfield, MO: Weatherman Glass Books, 1972.

Welker, John and Elizabeth. *Pressed Glass in America: Encyclopedia of the First Hundred Years 1825 - 1925*. Ivyland, PA: Antique Acres Press, 1985.

Wills, Geoffrey. *English and Irish Glass* ["Victorian Glass, Part 2"] Garden City, NY: Doubleday & Co., 1968.

Wilson, Charles West. *Westmoreland Glass*. Paducah, KY: Collector Books, 1996.

Wilson, Kenneth M. *New England Glass and Glassmaking*. New York: Thomas Y. Crowell Co., 1972.

_____. *American Glass, 1760-1930: The Toledo Museum of Art* (Two Vols.) New York: Hudson Hills Press, 1994.

Value Guide

The values assigned to the items in this book represent our best judgment based on information gained from major dealers, sales records, auction prices realized, and reports from individual collectors.

We cannot stress enough the caution to consider these values only as a guide. Auction sales are often erratic, as everyone knows. Prices vary, sometimes greatly, in different areas of the country. The age, condition, and even the color of an item affects its value. And, of course, *rarity* and *desirability* are prime determinants — the former is just a matter of fact; the latter is a question of each individual collector's preference.

Because many of the items, particularly the covered dishes, appear so rarely in the open market, actual sale prices often exceed greatly the estimates given here. We have signaled those pieces in particular by attaching a plus (+) to the rating, indicating the uncertainty of how high these prized items might sell for. A few marked "NP" simply cannot be priced either because the estimates we received are too divergent to arrive at a consensus or because they occur too seldom in the open market to gauge their value.

Bear these strictures in mind in consulting this value guide, as the authors and the Publisher do not intend to set prices, and do not assume responsibility for any losses that might be incurred from its use.

#	DESCRIPTION	VALUE
1	ALLIGATOR BOTTLE	$1,000+
2	SHAGGY BEAR BOTTLE	$650+
3	MONKEY BOTTLE	$600+
4	BABY HEAD BOTTLE	$300+
5	HAND BOTTLE	
	Large	$125
	Small	$100
6	PIG BOTTLE	$450+
7	WHISKY BOTTLE	$35
8	GRANDFATHER'S CLOCK BOTTLE	$275
9	OUR LADY OF FATIMA BOTTLE	$450+
10	WASHINGTON BUST BOTTLE	$350+
11	COLUMBUS BOTTLE	
	Large	$1,200+
	Small	$900+
12	CZAR BOTTLE	$850+
	CZARINE BOTTLE	$850+
13	LADY BUST BOTTLE	$150

#	DESCRIPTION	VALUE
14	ROMAN WARRIOR PERFUME BOTTLE	$35
15	SPANISH LADY WITH FAN	
	Large	$150
	Small	$125
16	MATADORS AND SPANISH LADIES BOTTLES (each/range)	$175-200
17	ELEPHANT BOTTLE (Small)	$75
18	ELEPHANT BOTTLE (Large)	$1,500+
19	FROG BOTTLE	NP
20	SPANISH PARROTS BOTTLES	
	Large	$125
	Small	$75
21	EAGLE BOTTLE AND CORDIALS SET (complete)	$35
22	THREE BUSTS BOTTLE	$225
23	BOY AND GIRL CLIMBING TREE BOTTLE	$200
24	SOMERS, CT COMMEMORATIVE FLASK	$75
25	CONFEDERATE FLASK	$30
26	PERFUME BOTTLE ("Robinson's")	$185

No.	Item	Price
27	FRANZ JOSEPH COMMEMORATIVE BOTTLE	$275
28	GERMAN IMPERIAL FLASK	$140
29	DIAMOND PATTERN PERFUME BOTTLE	$375
30	ELONGATED LOOP COLOGNE BOTTLE	$175
31	DANCING INDIANS COLOGNE BOTTLE	$300+
32	FAMILY GROUP BOTTLES (complete set with stoppers)	$350
33	SHELL FOOTED RECTANGULAR BOWL (each/range)	$50-150
34	LOOP BASKET WEAVE OVAL BOWL	$150
35	PATENT BLUE PEARLINE COMPOTE (on metal stand)	$140
36	VINE AND GRAPES COMPOTE	$210
37	CHILD PORTRAIT UNDER GLASS EGG BOX	$175
38	PORTRAIT DRESSER BOX	$90
39	HORSESHOE DRESSER BOX	$95
40	"KNEELING CHILD WITH BALL" COVERED BOX	$175
41	SHOE BRUSH DRESSER BOX	$150
42	CLOTHES BRUSH DRESSER BOX	$150
43	HAIR BRUSH DRESSER BOX	$150
44	MUSHROOM HINGED BOX	$175
45	SUEDOIS POWDER BOX	$50
46	LILY COVERED BOX	$65
47	DOG ON DIAMOND BASE COVERED BOX	$350+
48	WOODEN CRATE	$125
49	DRUM POMADE	$500+
50	BALLROOM DANCERS FIGURAL (each)	$55
51	F.D.R. BUST	$1,500+
52	YOUNG VICTORIA STATUETTE	$250
53	ROYAL BUST FIGURAL	$150
54	QUEEN VICTORIA BUST PAPERWEIGHT	$250
55	MAO TSE-TUNG STATUE	NP
56	UNIDENTIFIED STATUETTE	$110
57	NEW ENGLAND GLASS CANDLESTICK (each)	$90
58	NEW ENGLAND GLASS TYPE CANDLESTICK (#1) (each)	$125
59	NEW ENGLAND GLASS TYPE CANDLESTICK (#2) (each)	$125
60	COLONNE ORDINAIRE CANDLESTICK (each)	$60
61	SACRE-CŒUR (MARIA) CANDLESTICK (each)	$150
62	WINGED LADY CANDLESTICK (each)	$150
63	LADY HOLDING URN CANDLESTICK (each)	$165
64	MOUSQUETAIRE, MAN AND WOMAN, CANDLESTICKS (each)	$150
65	SWIRLING CANDLESTICK (each)	$70
66	CHIMERES CANDLESTICK (each)	$55
67	RICHLIEU CANDLESTICK (each)	$55
68	ARTESIAN CANDLESTICK (each)	$70
69	BAMBOUS ORDINAIRE A BOBECHE CANDLESTICK (each)	$80
70	TORTOISE CANDLEHOLDER (each)	$225
71	DOLPHIN CANDLESTICKS (English) (each)	$190
72	BELL-GLASS CANDLEHOLDERS (each)	$230
73	THE DRUNKARD ("POCHARD") CANDLESTICKS (each)	$250
74	POPE LEO XIII CANDLESTICK (each)	$225
75	"MADONNA AND CHILD" CANDLESTICKS (each)	$175
76	CARRE CANDLESTICKS (each)	$50
77	BEADED CIRCLE OR ELLIPSE CANDLESTICK (each)	$75
78	HUNTER CANDLESTICK (each)	$150
79	SIRENE CANDLESTICKS (each)	$325
80	CANDLE HOLDER LANTERNS (each)	
	White	$85
	Pink	$175
81	SCROLL AND CROSS CANDLESTICKS (each)	$100
82	THE GUNNER ("ARTILLEUR") CANDLESTICK (each)	NP
83	ENGLISH CONDIMENT SET	$110
84	ROUND FOOTED CONDIMENT SET	$125
85	EGG-SHAPED CONDIMENT SET	$125
86	CAROUSEL TRIPLE SALT OR CONDIMENT (SV)	$90
87	CAROUSEL TRIPLE SALT OR CONDIMENT (PV)	$75
88	SITTING CAT COVERED SALT	$15
89	RECLINING COW CD (Vallerysthal)	$600+
90	COW ON RECTANGULAR BASE CD	$350+
91	COW COVERED DISH (English)	$1000+
92	STARTLED DOE CD	$1000+
93	DOG ON BIRD PANELED BASE CD	$800+
94	DOG-ON-CUSHION ON WICKER BASKET CD	$350+
95	WOLF-DOG CD	$200
96	SPANIEL DOG CD	$65
97	SETTER DOG CD	$350
98	DUCK ON OVOID BASE	
	Original	$210
	Reproduction	$50
99	DUCK ON MARINE BASE CD	$800+
100	DUCK ON SINGLE STRAND BASKET WEAVE OVAL BASE CD	$125
101	DUCK SAUCE BOAT WITH LADLE	$500+
102	SEA GULL CD	$400+
103	SWIMMING DUCK CD	
	Large	$150
	Small	$75
104	FOX ON LOGS CD	$450+
105	SANDWICH HEN CD	$2,500+
106	VALLERYSTHAL 3 1/2" HEN CD	$75
107	S V LARGE HEN CD	
	White	$90
	Painted	$450+
	Black	$450+
108	QUAIL PIE CD	$3,500+
109	HEN ON FISH SCALE BASE CD	$350+
110	HEN ON A WHEAT BASE CD	$350+
111	TWIN HEN SALTS CD	$275+
112	HENS ON BULGING RIM BASE CD	
	Moulded eye/smooth edge	$175
	Glass eyed/scalloped edge	$225
113	HEN CD (Kanawha)	$90
114	HEN ON FLARED BASE WITH ARCHES CD	$175
115	HEN ON FLARED BASE CD	$175
116	HEN CD (3 5/8" - S V)	$125
117	LARGE HEN ("Polish") CD	$75
	LARGE ROOSTER ("Polish") CD	$75
118	HEN ON PLUMED WARRIOR BASE CD	$155
119	ROOSTER ON OCTAGONAL FLOWERED BASE CD	$450+
120	STANDING ROOSTER CDs (as shown)	
	Westmoreland	$60
	Portieux	$100
	L. E. Smith	$60
	Kanawha	$80
121	VALLERYSTHAL BREAKFAST SET	
	White, unpainted	$425+
	White, painted	$625+
	Colors	$700+
122	MUSTERSCHUTZ BREAKFAST SET	$1,000+
123	NESTING BIRD CD	$225
124	LOVE BIRDS CD	$375+
125	EGG BONBON CD	$350+
126	BIRD EMERGING FROM EGG CD	$300+
127	LION ON OVAL BASE CD	$800+
128	LIZARD ON STRAWBERRY CD	$300+
129	RABBIT WITH EGGS ON ARCHES BASE CD	$190
130	CROUCHING RABBIT CD	$220
131	LOP EARED RABBIT CD	$400+
132	STUBBY RABBIT (Cambridge) CD	$325
133	RABBIT ("Easter") EMERGING FROM SIDE OF VERTICAL EGG CD	NP
134	RABBIT ON AKRO AGATE BASE CD	$75

135	STANDING RABBIT ON FLOWER BASE CD	NP
136	RABBIT ON LACY BASE (Imperial) CD	
	Marbled	$375+
	Other	$200+
137	ANTELOPE JACK RABBIT CD	$500
138	RECLINING RABBIT CD	$275
139	RABBIT ("Easter") EMERGING FROM TOP OF VERTICAL EGG CD	$250
140	RABBITS CUDDLING CD	$500+
141	VALLERYSTHAL SWAN CD	
	Original	$90
	Reproduction	$20
142	CERE SWAN CD	$325
143	FAN-TAIL PIGEON CD	$400
144	MOUSE ON EGG CD	$500+
145	MOUSE ON TOADSTOOLS CD	$450+
146	FROG ON ROCKS CD (Atterbury)	
	White	$3,000+
	White and green	$4,500+
147	SNAIL ON WOODEN BASKET CD	$225
148	RESTING WATER BUFFALO CD	$1,500+
149	WATER BUFFALO WITH RIDER CD	$3,000+
150	DROMEDARY CAMEL CD	$2,000+
151	TURTLE WITH SNAIL CD	$350+
152	FLY ON WALNUT CD	$700+
153	LOBSTER CD	$3,500+
154	RAM CD	$250
155	BABOON ON GALACTIC BASE CD	$1,800+
156	BUTTERFLY CD	NP
157	WOODPECKER CD	$2,500+
158	TWIN DOLPHIN CD	$250
159	FULL FIGURE BOAR ON BASKET (XXX BASE) CD	$150
160	STEER'S HEAD CD	$3,000+
161	"FAN AND CIRCLES" RIBBED CD	$225
162	STRAWBERRY BOWL CD	$175
163	CROOKED HOUSE CD	$225+
164	ALPINE CHALET CD	$200+
165	GINGERBREAD HOUSE CD	$450+
166	TOWN HOUSE CD	$225+
167	BEADED EGG CD	$75
168	PERFUME BOTTLES IN A COVERED BASKET	$45
169	CROWN CD	$210
170	ARTICHOKE CD	$125
171	CROWNED LADIES AND SERPENTS CD	$225
172	TRUMPET VINE CD	$125
173	GRAPES CD	$175
174	GRAPE VINE CD (in filigree bands)	$200+
175	BOAT-SHAPED CD (English)	$145
176	MELON WITH RING FINIAL CD	$150
177	"REMEMBER THE MAINE" CD	$500+
178	THE BATTLESHIP MAINE CD	
	Plain	$70
	Painted	$150
	Beaded cabin roof	NP
179	OLD WOMAN WITH BASKET CD	$1,200+
180	LITTLE GOLFER CD	$300+
181	CHILD WITH LAMB CD	$700+
182	INFANT IN SHELL ON REED BASE CD	$750+
183	GIRL EMERGING FROM SEA SHELL CD	$1,800+
184	BAKER BOY CD	$750+
185	BAKER MAN CD	$850+
186	SAILOR ON BOAT CD	$4,000+
187	BLACK MAN WITH TOP HAT CD	$1,500+
188	MAN IN DERBY HAT CD	$500+
189	ENGLISH POLICEMAN CD	$3,000+
190	SAINT NICHOLAS WITH PACK CD	$400+
191	WINTER SCENE ROUND TRAY	$475
192	BEAR DISH	$125
193	CLOWN ASH TRAY	$95
194	DUCK OPEN RELISH DISH	$200
195	OWL PICKLE DISH	
	Original	$135
	Reproduction	$30
196	BIRD ON CENTERED PEDESTAL DISH	$75
197	PAN-AMERICAN EXPOSITION PLATE	$150+
198	PANSY BORDER WITH LADY PORTRAIT PLATE	$90
199	BLACK BOY CHASING CHICKEN PLATE	$1200+
200	WATERMELON PLATE	$1200+
201	"FOURTH OF JULY CHILDREN" PLATE	$325
202	BRIDGE AND STREAM WINTER PLATE	$125
203	PENNSYLVANIA TURNPIKE PLATE	$95
204	PERFORMING HORSES DISH	$125
205	"PHOENIX GLASS" PLATTER	$60
206	CARD RECEIVER TRAY (Mt. Washington)	$220
207	"FAN AND CIRCLES" VARIANT TRAY	$125
208	OLD WOMAN AND MULE ROUND TRAY	$250
209	FISH-SHAPED TRAY (Swedish)	$45
210	LADY SEATED WITH OPEN APRON - TRAY	$350+
211	THREE KITTENS TRAY	$135
212	PHRENOLOGIST'S HEAD INKWELL	$2,800+
213	BEVELED BLOCK ("Cherub") INKWELL	$150
214	HEMISPHERICAL INKSTAND	$150
215	ORIENTAL INKWELL	$125
216	WORLD GLOBE ADVERTISING INKWELL	$210
217	DOUBLE DOG FACE INKSTAND	$750+
218	INKWELL AND PEN HOLDER TRAY	$125
219	HORSESHOE INKWELL	$125
220	SWALLOW INKWELL	$125
221	MASCOTTE THREE-PART DOMED COVERED JAR	$125
222	OLD KING COLE MUSTARD JAR	$250+
223	NESTING HEN ROUND POMADE	$150
224	PARROT POMADE JAR	$175
225	PAPPY JAR	$2,000+
	MAMMY JAR	$2,500+
226	MONKEY MARMALADE JAR	$210
227	DRUM WITH HAT FINIAL POMADE	$250+
228	"REMEMBER THE MAINE" COVERED JAR	$500+
229	FOX AND FISH COVERED JAR	$1,500+
230	LIGHTHOUSE LAMP	$30
231	FELS POINT GLOBE	$100+
232	CAT AND MICE LAMP	$1,000+
233	CAT LAMP	$350
234	MAMMY LAMP	$1,500+
235	SANTA CLAUS LAMP (electric)	$750+
236	SANTA CLAUS OIL LAMP	$1,200
237	BANANA SPLIT LAMP	$550+
238	HAM AND EGGS ON A PLATTER LAMP	$550+
239	EAGLE MINIATURE LAMP	$450
240	OWL MINIATURE LAMP	$1,800
241	FISH AND SHELLS LAMP	$225
242	LION AND FLOWER BASKET WHALE OIL LAMP	$850+
243	RIPLEY MARRIAGE OR BRIDE'S LAMP	$1,200+
244	SAINT ANTHONY BONBON	$500
245	SAINT NICHOLAS BONBON	$500
246	SAINT CATHERINE BONBON	$500
247	RABBIT HUNTER CANDY CONTAINER	$350+
248	THIMBLE SHOT GLASS	$90
249	STATUE OF LIBERTY (novelty)	$210
250	HAIR RECEIVERS (each/ range)	$50-75
251	VICTORIAN LADY CURTAIN TIEBACK (each)	$275
252	BELLOWS WALL POCKET	$250
253	BEARDED FIGURE WATCH STAND	$1,500+
254	HOLY WATER FONT	
	Vallerysthal	$150
	Pat. Appl. For	$75
255	COIN SORTER (English)	$150
256	NIGHT LIGHT CLOCK	$290
257	PENDANTS AND BROOCHES (each/range)	$75-150+

258	NEWEL POSTS (each)	$255
259	EMBOSSED EASTER EGGS (each/range)	$50-175+
260	GOLF BALL LIQUOR CADDY	$375+
261	STAR AND DOTS HOT PLATE HOLDER	$150
262	ENVELOPE TILE	$125
263	TELEPHONE POLE INSULATOR	$55
264	TAXICAB LIGHT	$90
265	OWL BOOKEND	$450+
266	SEWING "MAKE-DO" PINCUSHIONS	NP
267	OPEN BACK SWAN (Boyd)	$30
268	CARDINAL'S HEAD	$500+
269	WICKER AND FLOWER, HANDLED BASKET	$155
270	FLORAL SCROLL STEIN	$150
271	FIGHTING SWAN CHILDREN'S MUG	$90
272	DEER AND COW CHILDREN"S MUG	$65
273	PUNCH AND JUDY MUG	$150
274	CLASSIC LADY'S HEAD IN MEDALLION SHAVING MUG	$225
275	PITCHER-TYPE SHAVING MUG	$220
276	LION HEAD SHUTTLE SHAVING MUG	$190
277	ANGEL WITH HARP MUG	$200
278	SWAN WHIMSY	$150
279	OPEN BOAT ORNAMENT	
	Without inkwell	$125
	With inkwell	$225
280	NOVELTY MILK GLASS BATTERY LIT LAMPS (each/range)	$35-175+
281	FALSE TEETH (uppers and lowers set)	$125
282	LARGE TOOTH	$60
283	GALLOPING HORSE NOVELTY	NP
284	RED-CLIFF-FENTON "SABLÉ" ARCH BELL	$75
285	HUNTING DOG CARD HOLDER	$95
286	MANATEE FIGURAL ORNAMENT	NP
287	FIRST NATIONAL BANK BUILDING	$180
288	DRUMMER BOY FIGURAL	$225+
289	SPHINX ORNAMENTAL PAPERWEIGHT	$350+
290	LION ON A BRITANNIA SHIELD ORNAMENTAL	$275
291	DOG ORNAMENTAL	$500+
292	ST. BERNARD DOG ORNAMENTAL (Vallerysthal)	$450+
293	"THE ONLY LOVE YOU CAN BUY" FIGURAL	$600+
294	GREYHOUND FIGURINE (Vallerysthal)	$135
295	GIRL WITH LAMB ORNAMENTAL	$290+
296	AMERICAN INDIAN CHIEF FIGURE	$225+
297	POLAR BEAR PAPERWEIGHT	$225+
298	HORSE HEAD PAPERWEIGHT	$125+
299	BEAR PAPERWEIGHT	$125
300	RABBIT EASEL	NP
301	BENJAMIN FRANKLIN PLAQUE	$350+
302	GENERAL ULYSSES S. GRANT PLAQUE	$500+
303	"TEDDY" ROOSEVELT PLAQUE	$140
304	McKINLEY PLAQUE	$250+
305	GEISHA GIRL PLAQUE	$150
306	CUPID ("Cherub") PLAQUE	$250+
307	DUCK OPEN SALT	
	Westmoreland	$35
	Vallerysthal	$85
308	ROOSTER OPEN SALT (each)	$90
309	FIGHTING ROOSTERS DOUBLE OPEN SALT	$150
310	DOG WITH BASKETS DOUBLE OPEN SALT	
	Small	$150
	Large	$175
311	SQUIRREL ON NEST OPEN SALT	$125
312	WALNUT DOUBLE SALT	$135
313	HEN DOUBLE SALT	$125
314	ROOSTER DOUBLE SALT	$130
315	CRADLE SALT	$75
316	SWAN MASTER SALT	
	Salt alone	$75
	Salt in silver chariot frame	$150
317	SQUIRREL ON BRANCH DOUBLE SALT	$125

318	TURTLE OPEN SALT (Hobbs, Brockunier?)	$95
319	TURTLE OPEN SALT DIP (Portieux)	$75
320	OPEN SWAN SALT (Meisenthal)	$75
321	RABBIT	
	Salt	$75
	Toothpick	$90
322	COLUMBUS SALT SHAKER	$1,200+
	ISABELLA SALT SHAKER	$1,200+
323	YOUNG COLUMBUS SALT SHAKER	$1000+
324	MAN WITH HAT	
	Salt	$275+
	Toothpick	$290+
325	GENERAL FITZHUGH LEE (?) SALT SHAKER	$300+
326	CHICK ON PEDESTAL SALT SHAKERS (each)	$500+
327	THRUSH SALT SHAKER	$125+
328	CAT HANDLED CREAMER	$250+
329	LOUIS XV CREAMER	$40
330	HOLLY CREAMER	$135
331	CASQUE (HELMET)	
	Sugar	$125
	Creamer	$90
332	HEART AND SCALE CREAMER	$375+
333	DOLPHIN FOOTED CREAMER	$125
334	PRINCE OF WALES FEATHERS SUGAR BOWL	$110
335	RENAISSANCE COVERED SUGAR	$75
336	IVY LEAF SUGAR	$100
337	DOG AND CAT COVERED SUGAR	$450+
338	HIBISCUS FLOWER COVERED SUGAR	$90
339	CHERRY SQUARE SUGAR	$75
340	ROSE COVERED SUGAR BOWL	$75
341	QUINCE SUGAR BOWL	$150
342	LEMON SUGAR BOWL	$135
343	JEWELED OVAL SUGAR SHAKER	$225
344	PEAR SUGAR BOWL	$135
345	APPLE SUGAR BOWL	$125
346	AVELLAN COVERED SUGAR	$90
347	ROOSTER HEAD FINIAL COVERED SUGAR	$250
348	ROOSTER HEAD FINIAL COVERED BUTTER	$250
349	PLAIN MELON FLAT BUTTER	$175
350	PATENT MELON WARE TUREEN	$200+
351	PLAIN MELON PEDESTAL BUTTER	$125
352	FISH PITCHER (Atterbury, painted)	$350+
353	TREE OF LIFE BUTTER DISH	$175
354	FISH FIGURAL TABLE SET	
	Creamer	$175
	Covered butter	$250
	Sugar	$190
355	MARQUIS AND MARCHIONESS OF LORNE BUTTER DISH	$300+
356	EARL OF BEACONSFIELD	
	Sugar bowl	$195+
	Creamer	$135
357	MELON BUTTER DISH WITH RADISH FINIAL (Vallerysthal)	$250
358	PINWHEEL AND FANS WATER JUG	$155
359	OVAL MEDALLION WATER PITCHER	$135
360	DUTCH MILKMAID CHILDREN'S PITCHER	$75
361	FLORAL BEVERAGE SET (Dunbar Flint Glass)	$70
362	COCOA OR TEA CADDY	$125
363	PEWTER HANDLED SYRUP	$200+
364	EGG SERVICE SET (Vallerysthal)	$225+
365	FROG AND SHELL TP	$150
366	CUFF TP	$110
367	BEARDED GRAPE CARRIER TP	$300
368	OLD MAN WITH BASKET MATCHSAFE	$125
369	TWO FIGURES HOLDING BARREL TP	$135
370	FEEDING TROUGH TP	$65
371	MONKEY BY HAT TP	$175
372	FROG MATCHHOLDER	$200
373	FROG WITH TULIP TP	$110+

374	JOLLY MOOR WITH BASKETS MATCHHOLDER (S V)	$400
375	INDIAN CHIEF MATCHHOLDER	
	Original	$150
	Reproductions	$20
376	THE HUNTER MATCHHOLDER	$125
377	COLUMBUS HANGING MATCHSAFE	$150
378	MANTEL CLOCK MATCHHOLDER	$150
379	LIZARD AND FROGS TP AND SALT SET	$175
380	BUTTERFLY HANGING MATCHHOLDERS	
	Alpha	$125
	Beta	$95
	Gamma	$140
381	THREE FIGURES WITH SATYR VASE	$200
382	SNAKE AND TREE TRUNK VASE	$150
383	GRANT MEMORIAL VASE	$300+
384	FRANKLIN D. ROOSEVELT STATUETTE VASE	$350+
385	KING'S HEAD VASE	$225
386	LEAF AND SWIRL ("INDIEN") VASE	$135
387	CASTLE FLOWER HOLDER	$250+
388	SWEDISH FLAG BEARER VASES (each)	$125
389	ELEPHANT FLOWER BOWL	$500+
390	MERMAID JARDINIERE	$650+
391	NEPTUNE FLOWER POT	$175
392	FLOWER TROUGH CENTERPIECE (set)	$65
393	MONKEY HOLDING VASE	$175+
394	STORK VASE	$275+
395	DOLPHIN AND SHELL FLOWER HOLDER	$150
396	CRAYFISH ("ECREVISSES") VASE	$250
397	THREE DUCKS VASE	$210
398	CHINESE ("CHINOIS") VASE	$225
399	DRAGON FANTASY VASE	$210
400	THE HUNT ("TROPHEE") VASE	$150
401	ORIENTAL LAUGHING-CRYING VASE	$125
402	LINCOLN AND GARFIELD VASE	$275+
403	SWAN VASE (Sowerby)	$175
404	VASE WITH LADY'S HEAD	$175

405	FIDDLE AND BANJO MINIATURE VASES (each)	$20
406	PEACOCK VASE	$250
407	BOAR'S HEAD CD	
	White	$1,800+
	Blue	$5,000+
408	ROOSTER (5") ON WIDE RIB BASE CD	$125
	(dark lavender milk glass)	
409	BABY IN HAT MATCHHOLDER	$500+
410	SWAN MINIATURE LAMP (as shown)	$1,800
411	ALLIGATOR CD	
	White	$2,600+
	Blue	$4,600+
412	WAFFLE FISH PICKLE	
	White	$125
	Blue	$175
	Green	$350+
413	ROOSTER ON BASKET WEAVE BASE CD - CHALLINOR, TAYLOR	
	White	$125
	With fired on paint	$400+
	Blue	$500+
	Green	$1,000+
414	WALKING FISH CD	
	White	$300
	Blue	$750+
415	DUCK ON WAVY BASE CD - Challinor	
	White	$125
	With fired on paint	$275+
	Blue	$500+
	Green	$1,000+
416	BLOCK SWAN CD	
	White	$250+
	Blue	$1,200+
	Green	$2,000+
	Black	$2,000+

Index

(Note: Numerals refer to items numbered consecutively throughout the book.)